COLUMBIA COLLEGE CHICAGO

3 2711 00168 3840

D1786760

FEB 0 2 2010

After the Digital Divide?

Screen Cultures: German Film and the Visual

Series Editors:
Gerd Gemünden *(Dartmouth College)*
Johannes von Moltke *(University of Michigan)*

After the Digital Divide?

German Aesthetic Theory in the Age of New Media

Edited by
Lutz Koepnick and Erin McGlothlin

CAMDEN HOUSE
Rochester, New York

Copyright © 2009 by the Editors and Contributors

All Rights Reserved. Except as permitted under current legislation, no part of this work may be photocopied, stored in a retrieval system, published, performed in public, adapted, broadcast, transmitted, recorded, or reproduced in any form or by any means, without the prior permission of the copyright owner.

First published 2009
by Camden House

Camden House is an imprint of Boydell & Brewer Inc.
668 Mt. Hope Avenue, Rochester, NY 14620, USA
www.camden-house.com
and of Boydell & Brewer Limited
PO Box 9, Woodbridge, Suffolk IP12 3DF, UK
www.boydellandbrewer.com

ISBN-13: 978-1-57113-399-1
ISBN-10: 1-57113-399-2

Library of Congress Cataloging-in-Publication Data

After the digital divide?: German aesthetic theory in the age of new media / edited by Lutz Koepnick and Erin McGlothlin.
   p. cm. — (Screen cultures)
Includes bibliographical references and index.
ISBN-13: 978-1-57113-399-1 (hardcover: alk. paper)
ISBN-10: 1-57113-399-2 (hardcover: alk. paper)
   1. Mass media—Philosophy. 2. Digital media—Philosophy. 3. Mass media—Technological innovations. 4. Mass media and technology. 5. Aesthetics, German. I. Koepnick, Lutz P. (Lutz Peter) II. McGlothlin, Erin Heather. III. Title. IV. Series.

P90.A345 2009
302.2301—dc22

2009020913

A catalogue record for this title is available from the British Library.

This publication is printed on acid-free paper.
Printed in the United States of America.

Contents

List of Illustrations — vii

Acknowledgments — ix

Introduction — 1
Lutz Koepnick and Erin McGlothlin

Part 1: What Is New about New Media?

1: From the Image to the Image File—and Back — 23
Boris Groys

2: Digital Sampling and Analogue Montage — 32
Diedrich Diederichsen

3: Remixability — 43
Lev Manovich

4: New Media Aesthetics — 52
Carsten Strathausen

Part 2: From Aura to Distraction

5: Aura, Virtuality, and the Simulacrum — 69
Sabine Eckmann

6: What Does It Mean to Read Online? On the Possibility of the Archive in Cyberspace — 88
Michel Chaouli

7: Please Hold — 101
Juliet Koss

8: Art, Medium, Progress — 117
Juliane Rebentisch

Part 3: Reworking History

9: Digital Negation and the Fate of Shock after the
   Avant-Garde 131
   Richard Langston

10: Transformations of the Archive 153
    Nora M. Alter

11: The City in the Ages of New Media: From Ruttmann's *Berlin:
    Die Sinfonie der Großstadt* to Hypermedia Berlin 167
    Todd Samuel Presner

12: Fragging Fascism 186
    Margit Grieb

Notes on the Contributors 205

Index 209

Illustrations

5.1	Olafur Eliasson, *Your Black Horizon*, 2005.	79
5.2	Olafur Eliasson, *Your Black Horizon*, 2005.	79
5.3	Michel Majerus, *bring the next line up*, 2000.	83
5.4	Michel Majerus, *if we are dead, so it is*, 2000.	85
7.1	George W. Bush talking on the telephone to the astronauts on the Space Shuttle Discovery; United States Army soldiers stationed in Iraq.	102
7.2	Woman on the telephone at the Femina Tanzpalast, Berlin, 1920s.	106
7.3	Ventriloquist; Telephone; Dummy, ca. 1920s.	107
7.4	Telephone operator in Ida, Illinois, ca. 1910.	109
7.5	Mark Hansen and Ben Rubin, *Listening Post*, 2002.	109
7.6	Chris Jordan, *Cell Phones #2*, 2005.	111
7.7	Pamela M. Lee, Pierre Huygue, Rirkrit Tiravanija, and others.	113
9.1	Scene from *C.S.I.: Crime Scene Investigation*, 2001.	137
9.2	Scene from *Foreigners Out! Schlingensief's Container*, 2002.	145
9.3	Scene from *Smarthouse ® 1+2*, Staatstheater, Stuttgart, 2001.	146
11.1	Screenshot of *HyperCities 2.0*.	176
12.1	Characters from *Return to Castle Wolfenstein* and *BloodRayne*.	191

Acknowledgments

THE IDEA FOR THIS VOLUME originated at the Eighteenth St. Louis Symposium on German Literature and Culture entitled "After the Digital Divide? German Aesthetic Theory in the Age of New Media," which was held in Spring 2006 at Washington University in St. Louis. We would like to thank the conference participants and the contributors to this volume for their engaging reflection on aesthetic theory and the development of new media. We are grateful for the institutional support we received for this project and would like to thank the Department of Germanic Languages and Literatures, the Sam Fox School of Design and Visual Arts, the Mildred Lane Kemper Art Museum, the Department of Art History and Archaeology, the Committee on Comparative Literature, and the College of Arts and Sciences at Washington University, in particular Edward Macias, Provost and Executive Vice Chancellor and then Dean of Arts and Sciences. We also appreciate the generous funds we received from the Pulitzer Foundation for the Arts and the Deutscher Akademischer Austauschdienst (DAAD).

We are indebted to Necia Chronister, Faruk Pasic, Christine McCrory, and Jocelyn Smith for their help with indexing and other editorial tasks during the final phases of this project. Last but not least, we would like to express our gratitude to Jim Walker, Catherine Mayes, Sue Smith, and Jane Best at Camden House for their enthusiasm about and open-minded support of this volume and for their hard work bringing it to press.

Lutz Koepnick / Erin McGlothlin
June 2009

Introduction

Lutz Koepnick and Erin McGlothlin

I.

IN ACADEMIC CIRCLES AS MUCH AS IN industrial research and development environments, the cachet of newness is virtually immune to critical questioning. To break with theoretical paradigms of the past and produce new insights is seen as the true scholar's goal in nearly any branch of the academy. The development of innovative technologies and products is close to the heart of any R&D expert eager to meet the demands of the market and his or her professional calling. And yet few terms seem to produce more unease today than that of "new media," which has been used widely and quite pluralistically since the late 1990s and has superseded that decade's earlier love affair with everything "cyber." Though highly prominent, the term and its potential meanings continue to trigger puzzled responses. Even scholars, critics, and researchers who share a basic understanding of what they mean when speaking about new media often express immediate concern about the term's overt and secret implications, its underlying view of historical lineage, and its privileging of certain media over others.

As the concept of new media came to preoccupy academic writing, cultural criticism, curatorial practice, and industrial research agendas around the turn of the century, it promised some healthy distance from the hyped-up conceptual atmosphere of the 1990s and its frenzied admiration of cyborgs, cyberpunk, cyberspace, cyber capitalism, and cyber studies. The term "new media" acknowledged the fact that, in an era of comprehensive digital capture, storage, and dissemination, nothing about former modes of cultural production and consumption could be taken for granted anymore, neither their aesthetic standards nor their social or political reach, perhaps not even their very right to exist in the future. Just as importantly, however, the concept of new media offered a corrective to how scholars, researchers, and image producers in the final stretch of the twentieth century had promoted advanced technologies as tools to dislodge our need for extended structures of temporality and reliable spatial orientations. Rather than celebrating body-machine hybrids as redemptive liberations from time, matter, geography, and the body, the term new media had the potential to encourage critical reflection about the costs and blessings of ever-increasing mediation and virtualization.

The concept of new media, as it began to appear on critical, curatorial, and industrial radar screens in the late 1990s, at once expressed negativity about the past and envisioned the future as a realm of undefined, fluid, and hence unpredictable processes. The term's dynamic was no doubt pejorative, branding other media that had preceded the rise of new media not merely as old but in fact as outmoded, as unworthy of further attention, as dead.[1] Because of the concept's polemical gesture, reactions to its eminence have often been manifold: at times enthusiastic, at times defensive, at times mixed and undecided. Consider the example of the effect of the rise of discourse on new media on the discipline of film studies.[2] The prominence of new media here—loosely understood as the rise of digital capture, image and sound manipulation, storage, and display—has been seen as having any of four different results: first, radically changing the base of the filmic medium and by extension the circuits of film exhibition, and thus ushering us into the age of post-cinema; second, opening up new possibilities of producing non-indexical images and sounds, but leaving the basic institutional parameters of cinematic pleasure and identification entirely intact; third, simply continuing the formal and aesthetic registers of earlier forms of filmic expression, yet piping these through new channels of communication in order to satisfy the demands of our culture of ubiquitous electronic screens; or fourth, opportunistically advocating formal and institutional transformation while in fact providing nothing other than the same old products and pleasures.

Whether scholars, critics, and filmmakers like it or not, the focus on new media in the relatively young discipline of film studies has caused a frenzied debate about the future viability, not only of the very object of study, but also of the tasks and dimensions of the discipline itself. Scholars who only a decade before had proudly seen themselves at the forefront of curricular reform and innovation now suddenly found themselves either taking up preservationist arguments or calling for a remapping of the very ideas that they had introduced and promoted to respectability. Yesterday's pioneers became the conservatives of the new day. Unease about an undefined present intermixed with nostalgia for the past, the good old days of indexical representation and the darkness of the collective auditorium. Hard-fought disciplinary self-confidence made way for a perplexed view of the possible vanishing of one's institutional legitimacy. Dramatically different generational experiences with formative media caused scholars and instructors to speak in languages no longer understood or shared by their audiences and students. Ever since its rise to fame, the term new media has thus played the role of troublemaker, a concept that asks its users to assume a position on one distinct side of a critical divide or to risk intellectual oblivion by simply ignoring its existence and proliferation.

What is surprising amid all these debates, however, is the fact that no two critics seem to be in agreement about the scope of what they call new media in the first place. The term clearly comes with considerable connotative baggage. Those who speak of "new media" seem to presuppose a firm understanding not only of what constitutes a medium and how media history might affect the relationships between body, mind, and world but also of when old media turned to new media and what might happen to the remnants of the old under the aegis of the new. But even though the term helped to reveal the naive progressivism inherent in many dot.com bubble prospects of comprehensive digitization, its possible implications have often not been carefully examined. Given the speed of innovation in twenty-first-century media cultures, few critics are in fact willing to detail the terms of their understanding in a systematic fashion, rightly fearful that their conceptual work might look helplessly out-of-date by the time the slow medium of book publishing will allow them to reach their readers. So let us ask some of these few outstanding theorists for advice. For no matter how unhappy many might be with the term new media, its polemical gestus, and its inherent fluidity, it looks as if the concept has come to stay and that—rather than lamenting its lack of clarity—our task is to fill it with meaningful and more consensual content.

Lev Manovich's *The Language of New Media* (2001) remains perhaps the most lucid and useful attempt to define new media,[3] in spite of the fact that many critics have developed sophisticated arguments to complicate Manovich's conceptual matrices since the book's publication. For Manovich, the emergence of new media can not be exclusively explained by the rise of digitality, nor does it simply represent an intensification of the logic of mechanical reproduction—of "old media" such as celluloid film and analogue photography—as theorized by Walter Benjamin in the 1930s. Instead, what makes new media new is the way in which they hybridize two distinct, albeit interrelated, technological tributaries: first, the path that led from photography to film to the emergence of the graphical human computer interface in the 1980s, which was dedicated to the development of technological means able to process, exchange, and disseminate information *in* and *across* time; and second, the trajectory that resulted in an ever more comprehensive drive to break down information into discrete numerical data, energized by the ability of computers to encode and store any kind of input according to universal algorithmic or digital formulas. Although neither mechanical time-art nor digitality per se suffices to describe the media revolutions of the past two decades, it is the amalgamation of time-based representation and advanced computing power that, in Manovich's view, sufficiently defines what makes our own mediascapes categorically different from those of the early to mid-twentieth century.

Unlike earlier technical machines and configurations, new media, according to Manovich, combine principles such as numerical representation (each distinct element of data can be encoded in mathematical form); modularity (discrete elements can be articulated in open-ended and variable structures); automation (machines take over some of the principal tasks of recording, processing, modifying, and displaying data); variability (users can use their machines in order to infinitely change the objects produced by other users' machines); and transcoding (code is shared across perceptual or representational modalities; a sound file can be played as an image file, and so on). And yet, even though new media bring into play an unprecedented mix of representational principles, Manovich insists that their language also bears some similarity to the communicative registers of older media, in particular those of film and photography. The historical break associated with new media is not as fundamental as the term suggests. Rather than invalidating the past, new media usher users into an era of open-ended plurality and simultaneity, an era in which both the contents and the structures of older media are mimicked, supplemented, or rewritten according to the technological parameters of the present. In fact, as Manovich does not hesitate to emphasize, by studying the representational strategies of older media products (such as Dziga Vertov's 1929 *Man with a Movie Camera*), we can learn a great deal about the structural possibilities of newer media. The path from old to new is not a teleological one-way street. The past allows us to illuminate the present just as much as the present encourages us to discern the language of past technologies in an ever different light.

William Uricchio and D. N. Rodowick have recently emphasized the existence of a third trajectory toward new media that not only supplements Manovich's dual accent on moving image technology and discrete computation but also amplifies Manovich's critique of teleological historiography and corrects what Uricchio and Rodowick consider a one-sided privileging of cinema—old and new—as the primary switchboard of media development.[4] Accordingly, much of what we encounter as new media today, with its stress on real-time interactivity, its favoring of simultaneity over sequentiality, and its point-to-point modes of access and connectivity, had its historical models in nineteenth-century technologies of image scanning and transmission—a history that energized the development of television and other electronic displays and actually predated the various strains that led to the inauguration of cinema in 1895. Uricchio's and Rodowick's focus on various early machines of image processing and exhibition as a third tributary of new media adds two important dimensions to Manovich's path-breaking perspective. First, to the extent that both scholars situate moving image technologies not as central energizers of new media development but as one among various contributors, Uricchio and Rodowick allow scholars and curators alike to include still-image media such as digital photography into the domain of new media as well. In doing so, Uricchio and Rodowick circumvent a curious reductionism in recent writing on new media art and aesthetics, namely the attempt to see new media work as merely a radical inflection of any form of time-based art. The true challenge, however, would be to think through how new media work changes the parameters of what we consider the role of the temporal and durational in art and cultural production in the first place, including in the arena of film and photography.

Second, as they consider electronic image processing a third path toward new media, Uricchio and Rodowick amplify an important aspect of Manovich's work that Manovich himself, unintentionally as it were, tends to deemphasize because of his privileging of the curious echoes between new-media practice today and the techniques of editing in Soviet montage cinema of the 1920s. Manovich rightly thinks of new media as a discontinuous re-inscription and re-articulation of the old within the new, as a set of technologies and techniques able to actualize certain promises of the past while at the same time changing our very understanding of that past. What Uricchio and Rodowick add to this is the insight that the core of the new in new media defies the very categories according to which we think of history as a succession of old and new. Accordingly, new media are media that are essentially synthetic, integrative, or additive, so much so that they entirely dislodge modernism's dominant insistence on media specificity. What is new about new media is their powerful ability to absorb, incorporate, assimilate, pillage, rework, or simply overwrite the content and formal logic of other media.[5] Their newness lies in nothing more and nothing less than their capacity to erase any clear-cut differentiation between old and new and thus define the present as a hybrid simultaneity of asynchronous practices, meanings, pleasures, and possibilities. New media are new whenever they allow us to remediate the putatively old into uninhibited contemporaneity and thus to charge the present with futurity. Far from making yesterday's technologies and pleasures look helplessly outdated, new media become new to the extent to which they mark the present as an open-ended meeting ground of dissimilar temporalities, heterogeneous logics of representation, and productively inconsistent user practices.

Such theoretical interventions may not entirely alleviate the general unease about the term new media. At the very least, however, they should help soften the polemical edge associated with this concept. Instead of automatically situating the term's user as an unquestionable champion of progressive change and innovation, the combined perspectives of Manovich, Uricchio, and Rodowick call on us to bring past and present into an active conversation and in so doing develop persuasive criteria for deciding what we may label as new in the first place and how this newness alters our relation to the old. Just as important, however, is that by defining new media as technologies enabling complex interactions between past and present modes of representation, storage, and dissemination, the work of all three authors also strongly encourages us to revisit the writing of earlier theorists of film and media for the sake of better understanding the kind of meanings and pleasures circulating in our own contemporary screen culture. For if new media themselves hybridize past and present into volatile configurations, today's writing about these media cannot afford to ignore what earlier generations of critics and theorists had to say about the vicissitudes of media history—that is, about the relationships between technology and art, medium and artistic technique, automation and aesthetic pleasure, technological change and the history of human sensory perception, and, last but not least, the rise of technologies of cultural symbolization and the political, social, and economic dynamic of modern life. Just as—following Rodowick's claims—classical film theory à la Hugo Münsterberg and André Bazin remains of great importance for making sense of the expansive presence of moving images today, so too various earlier attempts for theorizing the links between technology and art might be of essential value for thinking through the future prospects of aesthetic practice and pleasure in contemporary screen culture in general.

After the Digital Divide? is dedicated to this endeavor. Its explicit aim is to recall different intellectual traditions as important tools for the understanding of contemporary screen culture and new media practice, their aesthetic energies as much as their social import. The chapters that follow not only offer various maps of the rapidly changing landscapes of media culture today but also ask how we can employ the legacy of German classical aesthetic and critical theory to come to terms with today's presence of new media and digitality, and also to what extent contemporary screen culture calls on us to reconfigure modernist writing on and critique of the aesthetic of moving and still images. The volume's primary, albeit not exclusive, witness in this endeavor is what might be understood as Germany's first wave of media theory and criticism: the writing of modernist critics such Theodor W. Adorno, Walter Benjamin, and Siegfried Kracauer. As will be argued throughout this volume, the work of these theorists does not merely provide paradigmatic models for how to think about possible relationships between art and mediation, artistic technique and advanced technology, aesthetic form and social relevance—even if we no longer subscribe to their aesthetic preferences or political allegiances. As importantly, their writing also offers a compass for conceptualizing the complex temporal layering of past, present, and future that characterizes our own age of new media, and in doing so asks us to carry out a thorough investigation of forms of scholarship that consider technological and aesthetic developments alike as linear or dialectical progressions from the primitive to the mature, from old to new. One of the principal ambitions of this volume is therefore to question the naive progressivism that informs some of today's writing and thinking about media technologies. Rather than to play out the new against the old, *After the Digital Divide?* urges the reader to think about the past, present, and future of the aesthetic and the technological as structured by critical differences, complex transactions, and meaningful alternatives.

II.

Confronted with the rapid proliferation of mass media such as film, photography, and radio during the 1920s and 1930s, German intellectuals such as Adorno, Benjamin, and Kracauer engaged the whole range of German philosophical traditions in order to account for the redefinition of art and aesthetic experience in modern industrial culture. On the one hand, for these theorists, the breakthrough and popularity of mechanical arts and mass-mediated pleasures posed significant challenges to earlier practices of art, in particular the nineteenth-century legacies of genius aesthetics, idealistic art worship, poetic realism, and bourgeois self-representation. The location of art and the aesthetic, for them, was no longer self-evident. By allowing new types of producers and audiences to participate in the production and consumption of cultural objects, the advent of modern mass media redefined what it might mean to engage in aesthetic activity in the first place. It blurred former boundaries between art and its social context and in so doing necessitated new strategies either to make use of the putative integration of the aesthetic and the political or to actively protect artistic practice against the artwork's increasing loss of autonomy. On the other hand, for modernist critics such as Adorno, Benjamin, and Kracauer, the rise of technologically based time arts since the late nineteenth century could not but redefine the methods, tasks, concepts, and reach of intellectual work and engagement itself. Though Weimar intellectuals took the thought of Kant, Schiller, Hegel, Marx, Nietzsche, or Klages along to the movies to theorize the impact of mechanical reproduction on former notions of the aesthetic, they never tired of emphasizing that the breakthrough of modern media deeply affected the very foundations of theory, philosophy, and aesthetics. Any theory of film or photography had to reckon with the fact that film and photography had changed the very location of theory in society, while any visit to the movie theater or reading of illustrated press materials had the potential to cast new light on the entire legacy of aesthetic concepts.

Consider Siegfried Kracauer's 1927 essay on the mass ornament as one example of this critical practice of simultaneously thinking forward, backward, and sideways in time.[6] The essay famously discusses the curious homologies between Fordist and Taylorist industrial production methods on the one hand and forms of cultural expression and presentation on the other. The synchronized and machine-like dance patterns of contemporary dance troupes such as the Tiller Girls, in Kracauer's eyes, revealed the reconfiguration of subjectivity, individualism, and corporeality in a modern age of industrial assembly lines, efficient rationalization of labor processes, and automated forms of production and symbolic reproduction. Kracauer's Tiller Girls waved farewell to bourgeois notions of individual autonomy and self-expressivity, the classical idea and romantic ideology of the self-production of the sovereign subject and its quasi-entrepreneurial ownership of body and sensuality. According to Kracauer, modern show dance and stadium spectacles considered the human body as nothing other than a non-organic and functional resource for the construction and composition of abstract patterns. They fragmented the body into separate subunits only to then reintegrate them like mere building blocks into the aesthetic unity of the larger post-individualistic gestalt, the collective body of the mass ornament.

Superficial readings of Kracauer's essay often mistake his perspective for a fundamental, if not fundamentalist, critique of modern rationalization and disenchantment. In Kracauer's age of the Tiller Girls, it is argued, humanity becomes robotic and soulless, and hence void not only of any sense of moral or political autonomy but also of the foundations of aesthetic pleasure. The mass ornament, in this understanding, is seen as a foray into a post-humanist and post-historical vacuum, one ruled by the absence of utopian energies and transformative powers, in which the imprints of technology have erased all the meanings and promises formerly embedded in art and cultural practice. But Kracauer is far from coming to such pessimistic or apocalyptic conclusions, not least because the Tiller Girls, for him, embody nothing more than the disembodying logic of modern industrial culture itself and thus provide mimetic representations of what in Taylorist modernity seems to erase the very possibility of mimetic behavior. Contrary to the intellectual elite, who denigrated the mass ornament as a mere tool of distraction, Kracauer insisted on the legitimate character of aesthetic pleasure derived from seeing such dance formations on stage or on film, because they help visualize and render experiential what increasingly eludes visualization and experience in modernity.

> When significant components of reality become invisible in our world, art must make do with what is left, for an aesthetic presentation is all the more real the less it dispenses with the reality outside the aesthetic sphere. No matter how low one gauges the value of the mass ornament, its degree of reality is still higher than that of artistic productions which cultivate outdated noble sentiments in obsolete forms—even if it means nothing more than that.[7]

Instead of scolding the new in the name of the old, Kracauer argues that cultural production and aesthetic pleasure cannot overlook the role of technology, abstraction, and mediation in modern life. By assimilating to the logic of technological fragmentation and distraction alone, contemporary culture can transport art's old promise of mimetic play, redemptive representation, and meaningful community into the future. By becoming fragmented, technological, and distracted, the human body can move through and beyond the era of disenchanting rationalization and thus uphold the legitimacy of aesthetic experience—its higher reason, its distinctive pleasures, its incommensurable wonders.

Written in various drafts during his Paris exile in the mid-1930s, Walter Benjamin's no less famous theory of mechanical reproducibility continues Kracauer's line of argumentation, yet at the same time charges it with more explosive political content.[8] Like Kracauer, Benjamin embraces the transformative powers of industrial culture's newest technologies of representation, mediation, and distribution. Because film and photography—according to Benjamin—no longer require an original in the emphatic sense, they have the ability to brush aside the precarious legacy of bourgeois art and nineteenth-century culture, namely the stratifying rhetoric of genius, uniqueness, and awe, which in Benjamin's eyes had become conceptually untenable and politically dangerous in a time of totalitarian rule. And because the structural logic of film, because of its constitutive technique of cutting and editing, privileges discontinuity over durational extension, rapid interruption over contemplative stillness, shock over awe, it produces viewers and consumers who do not submit to the authority of artistic work but instead seek to assimilate it into the itineraries of their social and political life outside the theatre. The media of industrial culture convert the meditative and absorbed viewer of the nineteenth century into deliberate and active users of cultural materials. They transport culture to the masses rather than inviting select audiences to stand in silent admiration in the face of the original. Although the media of modern industrial culture, in Benjamin's view, thus erase clear-cut distinctions between the political and the aesthetic and supersede the bourgeois idea of radical aesthetic autonomy, film nevertheless recuperates the original notion of the aesthetic from underneath the petrified forms of nineteenth-century art—its stress on the experience and pleasure of sensory perception.

The historical breakthrough of technical arts, for Benjamin, thus did not simply change the role of certain forms of art and aesthetic experience in society, but revolutionized the entire concept of art. For Benjamin, the logic of media innovation and technological change was *irresistible* and *irreversible:* the advent of newer media such as film and photography redefined the location of art and aesthetic experience in society and reconfigured the structural relationships between spectator and work as much as between audience members themselves. In Benjamin's perspective it was just as important, however, that the media of industrial culture transformed the very concepts and categories according to which past and present generations had evaluated the quality of art, discussed its meanings, assessed its political and social investments, and conceptualized art's effects on the beholder's body and senses. At its best, to invoke the old—the legacy of auratic art—under the aegis of post-auratic culture could not but lead to a violation of the formal inventory of technological art; at its worst, it resulted in what Benjamin famously called the aestheticization of politics, that is, fascism, which was understood as an attempt to satisfy the masses with symbolic spectacles of collectivity that obscured the factual fragmentation of society. Any form of art that in the age of its mechanical reproducibility aspired to the auratic was no real art at all. Instead it became ideology, a mechanism masking the orders of the day, a diversion from how media arts promoted distraction as an antidote to the authoritarian effect of the auratic in art.

Though deeply influenced by Benjamin's thought, Adorno's work is of course notorious for not endorsing Benjamin's embrace of the participatory dimension of modern mass media and for instead emphatically trying to uphold notions of aesthetic autonomy. Adorno's view of the role of modern technology in the arts was much bleaker and much more pessimistic than Benjamin's and Kracauer's. Whereas the latter considered mechanical reproduction a liberating and potentially democratic engine of cultural dispersal and distracted forms of reception, Adorno had profound misgivings about the rise of modern mass culture because, for him, it threatened to obliterate the specificity and incommensurability of aesthetic experience. In Adorno's perspective, cultural dispersal and post-auratic distraction were nothing less than industrial capitalism's latest ruse: a strategic weapon to please audiences with scenarios of pseudo-individualization and the ease of vacuous consumption; a marketable tool for promising freedom of choice and individual self-realization while at the same time enforcing utter standardization and conformity; a way of numbing people's minds in order to engineer obedient emotions and attitudes. According to Adorno, Benjamin was right to emphasize the power of media such as film, photography, and radio to bring cultural materials to the masses and produce new forms of cultural appropriation, but he was blind to how technological dispersal could operate as simply another facet of capitalism's logic of fetishism. He furthermore ignored the way in which distraction could lead to a disastrous regression within the registers of aesthetic experience: "Of all fetishistic listeners, the radio ham is perhaps the most complete. It is irrelevant to him what he hears or even how he hears; he is only interested in the fact that he hears and succeeds in inserting himself, with his private equipment, into the public mechanism, without exerting even the slightest influence on it."[9] In Adorno's critical view, mechanical reproducibility and advanced technological mediation, in the realm of music as much as in film, promoted deconcentration as the principal perceptual activity. Yet rather than opening up new horizons of meaning and connectivity, as Benjamin and Kracauer believed, for Adorno, deconcentrated listening or viewing prepared the way for general forgetting, atomistic fragmentation, and a ritualistic reintegration of disconnected elements into some fake unity and manipulative totality.

To be sure, throughout his entire career Adorno often sounded as if he sought to make the technological dimension of modern mass media per se responsible for what he considered the detrimental effects of the popular in the twentieth century. The very possibility of receiving radio broadcasts of symphonic concerts in private homes destroyed the condition of the possibility of attentive listening; the television's small monitor, in its early years, quasi-automatically played into the hands of capitalist reification as it fostered the impression that one could own the world in the form of an image. Adorno's negative view of mass and media culture, most forcefully expressed in the infamous "Culture Industry" chapter of *Dialectic of Enlightenment*,[10] has earned him the reputation of a staunch and highly elitist champion of modernist high art, one defending radical aesthetic autonomy at all costs against the onslaught of mass-mediated distractions. And yet Adorno's embrace of modernist experimentation was more complex than this, for his aim was to show that modernism required the rise of modern mass culture and technological mediation in the first place in order to constitute itself—negatively, as it were—as a site of aesthetic autonomy. Rather than understand modernism and mass culture, aesthetic experience and mere distraction, as being separated by a fundamental divide, Adorno claimed that both owed their existence to the same historical constellation: industrial capitalism. Modernist art emerged as a determined reaction to the reification of aesthetic experience during the second half of the nineteenth century, whereas industrial media culture commodified what serious art no longer dared to say, spuriously fulfilling, as Max Pensky has put it, "under conditions of domination, legitimate human needs for plenty, inclusion, play, and happiness."[11] Neither enigmatic modernism nor the mediated pleasures of industrial culture could thus be understood without reference to the other, one needing the other in order to define its own limits, one borrowing from or negating the other in order to transport the utopias of the past through the present into the future.

As they encountered the rapidly shifting scenes of modern industrial culture and aesthetic mediation, theorists such as Adorno, Benjamin, and Kracauer developed complex critical paradigms simultaneously able to think forward, backward, and sideways in time. Rather than merely hopping on or disparaging the bandwagon of the new, these critics promoted new conceptual frameworks, not only to account for the costs and blessings of the way technology reshaped twentieth-century art, but also to map out the way in which the flux of modern industrial culture changed the present's view of the past itself, including its view of the role of theoretical work and aesthetic speculation. In Max Horkheimer's late Weimar effort to define the tasks of the so-called Frankfurt School, Critical Theory was presented as a form of theoretical practice constitutively aware of its own historical position and involvement and its inability to assume entirely abstract and detached vistas.[12] As the writing of critics such as Kracauer, Benjamin, and Adorno acutely shows, contemporary media culture served Critical Theory as a prime target for probing and sharpening its conceptual armatures. Whether the focus was on film, photography, radio, or other contemporary means of cultural mediation, Kracauer, Benjamin and Adorno sought to theorize the substantial impact of advanced technologies on the making and experience of aesthetic objects—not from a standpoint of historical detachment and non-involvement but from one of self-reflexive engagement and situatedness. To the extent to which Critical Theory, in Horkheimer's view, understood itself as a form of thinking that was part and parcel of the very process it aspired to theorize, the rapid spread of modern mass media proved to be a pivotal test case for critical theorists such as Kracauer, Benjamin, and Adorno, asking them to conceptualize how technological mediation could at once energize and be energized by the work of criticism and cultural theory.

III.

Nearly a century after Weimar theorists sought to account for the future of the aesthetic in a time of mass-mediated diversion, we find ourselves in the midst of a culture of digital technologies whose impact not only permeates all aspects of life but also redefines the status of earlier recording devices such as film, radio, and the photograph. Computerization dramatically shrinks our temporal and spatial horizons; electronic image banks and sound archives expand the present increasingly into the past and future; and mobile telephony, E-mail communication, and video messaging contribute to an unprecedented acceleration of human interaction and a regime of instant and despatialized availability. Once seen as the foremost medium of the twentieth century, film has assumed a curious afterlife in our own century already, its original chemical base and rhetoric of indexicality being replaced by the work of computer graphics and editing, its institutional setting—the dark cinema auditorium—being dispersed into a multiplicity of sites of consumption. Computer-generated imagery (CGI) experts gradually supplant the former role of proficient cinematographers and set-designers; live actors may no longer be needed a few years down the road; digital display devices increasingly take over the classical role of projection and enable viewing pleasures at all times and locations; viewers, if they so desire, can increasingly construct their own movies and viewing angles from various sources and highly disparate viewing stations; and scholars barely manage to ask the question: "What is the future of film and cinema?" without seeing their direction of inquiry sidelined by the arrival of yet another technology of screening still and moving images.

After the Digital Divide? investigates the legacy of German aesthetic and critical theory as seen against this spreading background of digital culture and new media since the 1990s. Instead of simply trying to play out the old against the new, *After the Digital Divide?*—like Adorno, Benjamin, and Kracauer—aspires to think forward, backward, and sideways. True to the spirit of earlier German media theory itself, *After the Digital Divide?* therefore also avoids the suggestion that we need only return to Adorno's, Benjamin's, or Kracauer's writing to find answers to the challenges of twenty-first-century screen and media culture. In fact, various chapters of this volume leave little doubt that the modernist framing of modern media in the work of Weimar and post-Weimar critical theorists is no longer adequate for mapping the complexity of contemporary screen culture and media aesthetics. Kracauer may have been hopeful that modern technology and disenchantment could produce new forms of meaningful collectivity, but how can we, after the Nazi orchestration of mass ornaments, possibly hold on to Kracauer's ambivalent hope, his humanist vision of a technological recalibration of human sensory experience and self-expression? Benjamin's famous opposition of contemplation and distraction, the auratic and the postauratic, may have been helpful for distinguishing emancipatory from politically repressive uses of modern media such as film, but didn't it also misread the long-term trajectory of filmic production and consumption and misjudge the continued viability of the auratic and of aesthetic experience in industrial (and post-industrial) culture? And while Adorno's dialectic of modernism and mass culture may have been effective for thinking through the dynamic of cultural expressions during the age of Fordist and Taylorist industrialism, didn't it also overlook the curious compromises between modernist experimentation and the popular and fail to deliver a viable framework for theorizing the cultural diversification that energized post–Second World War histories?

And yet *After the Digital Divide?* shows that the writing of earlier critical and aesthetic theorists, in spite of such historical and conceptual shortcomings, still has the power to serve as a workable springboard for critical investigations of the aesthetics and politics of new media today. Kracauer's interest in how industrial culture and film change the expressive registers of the human body finds influential echoes in the latest return of phenomenology and its concepts of embodiment to media theory and criticism—recent writing that tries to conceptualize how our interactions with highly mediated environments and ubiquitous electronic interfaces allow us to understand the role of our bodies as the primary medium, a membrane able to mediate different impressions of the real and to situate us in ever-different perceptual positions, a mobile framing device that facilitates somatic points of contact between subjective and objective worlds.[13] Benjamin's focus on the disruptive possibilities of cinematic montage, his reading of film as a technology that "by the dynamite of the tenth of a second" enables viewers to "calmly and adventurously go traveling,"[14] remains of great use for thinking about the role of new media as tools of dispersed and often unpredictable transport and the far-from-solely-illusionistic integration of the actual and the virtual that takes place in new media environments. And Adorno's defense of aesthetic autonomy, however acerbic and snobbish in tone, can still serve as a powerful reminder not only that we cannot talk about art without trying to define the specificity of aesthetic experience but also that we need to encounter artistic technique as something that exceeds the imperatives of the real and hence should not be seen per se as identical with the diverse technologies of distraction and sensory immersion that populate contemporary screen and new media cultures.

It is not difficult to see why the writings of Adorno, Benjamin, Kracauer, and other representatives of early twentieth-century German media criticism and theory are often understood by some critics as prototypically modernist in their address of symptomatic challenges of modern industrial culture yet no longer able to offer systematic maps of postmodern mediascapes. It is equally easy to see why much of their thought nevertheless shows up in today's writing on film and new media culture, often as if no time had passed since the heyday of their conceptual endeavors and our own effort to make sense of the ubiquity of electronically mediated images, sounds, and pleasures in the twenty-first century. *After the Digital Divide?* seeks to stake out a middle ground between these two positions. German Critical Theory, this volume argues and exemplifies, remains of considerable use in various efforts to conceptualize the representational logic, perceptual appeal, and social and political role of new media and screen culture today. At the same time, it offers viable models for thinking through the very flux of any theoretical and critical effort, the rise, vitality, and aging—that is, the historicity—of theory itself. German Critical Theory, in short, provides a panoply of insights for examining and complicating the very notion of "divide" that structures much of contemporary writing on new media culture, art, and aesthetics—the assumption of a fundamental rift between the analogue and the digital and of an incommensurable gap between the modern and the postmodern. Though Adorno's writing on radio or Benjamin's on film may no longer be of help for discussing the mobile trade of mp3 music or the flexible consumption of moving images on cell-phone displays, their thought processes continue to alert us to the fact that the new is never as new as one might think it is because (media) history develops much more messily and not simply according to a model of clean rupture, radical innovation, and traceless displacement.

IV.

After the Digital Divide? brings together the work of theorists and critics who straddle the boundaries of various fields and disciplines. Given the predominance of visual representation and perception in our contemporary mediascapes, it should come as no surprise that considerable attention is dedicated to role of visual materials in today's conceptual encounter with new media aesthetics, be it film, digital or analogue photography, computer gaming, hypertext maps, or installation art. Some contributors, however, also expand and complicate this conceptual horizon by bringing into play the role of music sampling and strategies of reading and literary self-expression in our age of digital dissemination. Though all twelve chapters present sophisticated theoretical interventions, the majority of them unfold their arguments by examining individual films, images, texts, and objects, thus productively combining theoretical reflection and close, focused analysis.

The volume has three parts. Part 1, entitled "What Is New about New Media?" maps out the current topography of new media culture and new media aesthetics and raises important questions about the extent to which it is even possible to transfer older notions of German critical and aesthetic theory to the era of digital culture. One of the central issues in this section is the issue of medium specificity, that is, the question as to whether the very materiality of contemporary media, whether visual, acoustical, or haptic in nature, produces images, texts, objects, and experiences that fundamentally differ from the works and structures of perception discussed by previous generations of media critics and theorists. In the opening chapter of this part, Boris Groys investigates the gulf between traditional images and digital reproductions, drawing our attention to the performative status—the flux and instability—of visual material based on algorithmic code, but also exploring—in continuation of what Benjamin called the exhibition value of reproducible art—some of the fundamental changes in the exhibition and circulation of images today. In chapter 2, Diedrich Diederichsen probes the continued viability of older media-theoretical frameworks, such as the ones proposed by Siegfried Kracauer and Martin Heidegger, for dealing with the ubiquity of sampling in contemporary digital culture, particularly in the arena of popular music. Pointing to a number of stunning limitations of twentieth-century German media theory, Diederichsen seeks to bridge the gap between what he considers the equally one-sided and hence insufficient stress of German media theory on either epistemological inquiry or sociological analysis. Reframing Diederichsen's discussion of sampling, Lev Manovich's contemplation of the role of remixability and modularity in chapter 3 proposes a media ecology that emancipates cultural objects from what Benjamin would have called the burden of the auratic and enables an unprecedented kind of collective diversity and openness. In the last chapter of this first part, Carsten Strathausen finally makes a plea for the continued need for developing a specific aesthetics of new media, a conceptual framework that exceeds merely historical or sociological dimensions. At the same time, however, Strathausen implies that such an aesthetic would have to break with the negativity of Adorno's late aesthetic theory—with Adorno's insistence on radical aesthetic autonomy as much as with his refusal to see more than gloom in whatever future technologies may have to offer the present and our modes of aesthetic experience.

In part 2, the first part's call for reflection on how contemporary screen cultures affect structures of aesthetic representation and perception is turned into practice. The section's title—"From Aura to Distraction"—recalls Benjamin's famous distinction between the spectatorial responses to traditional and mechanically reproduced art forms, the goal of all chapters of this section being to think through the specificity of aesthetic experience in our age of digital manipulation, sampling, and remixability. In the context of a detailed reading of the works of Olafur Eliasson and Michel Majerus, Sabine Eckmann reflects on the renewed role of the auratic as a central element of aesthetic experience today, yet at the same time she seeks to reframe and enrich the concept of aura with the help of notions of the simulacrum and the virtual, notions intimately tied to the rise of contemporary digitality. In chapter 6, Michel Chaouli examines the extent to which today's screen cultures and digital archives have changed our mode of reading and literary appreciation; his essay is driven in both historical and theoretical terms by the question of whether the book—and our act of reading—can survive not only the kind of dispersal caused by hypertext formats but also the peculiar storage and mutability of the written word in the electronic age. With Juliet Koss's argument in chapter 7, the focus initially shifts from digital images and text to that of acoustical culture, only, first, to supplement contemporary discussion of aesthetic perception with the conceptual vocabulary of nineteenth-century empathy theory, and then, second, to return us to a richer notion of visual experience in the digital age, one that considers the entire human sensorium, in particular the haptic dimension. In the final chapter of the second part, Juliane Rebentisch emphasizes that even in an age of ubiquitous new media environments, discussions about aesthetic experience cannot do without a certain emphasis on the autonomy of the aesthetic. In productive argument with Strathausen's chapter 4, Rebentisch returns to the work of Adorno in order to remind us of the need to reinterpret, rather than move beyond, the legacy of classical Frankfurt School thought, so as to take stock of the vicissitudes of aesthetic and visual experience today.

If parts 1 and 2 are mostly dedicated to mapping out different concepts of new media art, screen culture, and aesthetic experience in the age of digitality, part 3—entitled "Reworking History"—turns the reader's attention to the way in which digital images and archives help renegotiate the legacy of the past and create alternate visions of (German) history. Whereas parts 1 and 2 were concerned with probing the viability of older concepts of aesthetic theory for contemporary conversations, the last part of this book focuses on how screen culture today revises our understanding of the past and, precisely in so doing, prepares us for the future. In chapter 9, Richard Langston discusses the work of Christoph Schlingensief and Rene Pollesch as artistic interventions designed to re-vision and recalibrate one central category of the early-twentieth-century avant-garde: the category of shock. To what extent, is his decisive question, does the continued stress on shock in digital culture change our understanding of its role during the pre-digital heyday of modernist and avant-garde aesthetic production, and hence of modernism and the avant-garde in general? Nora Alter, in her contribution, engages with the work of filmmaker Mathias Poledna, who has sought to trace histories of popular sound and image production and to link both across different times and spaces. In conversation with the recent emphasis on sound in film studies, Alter sees Poledna's work as an important intervention that complicates our understanding of the (digital) archive and explores decisive continuities along with critical discontinuities between early moving-image technologies and the importance of computer-generated graphics in contemporary cinema. Todd Presner's chapter 11 presents the web project *Hypermedia Berlin*—a digital and interactive map offering complex slices of the German capital's deep history—and compares it to the presentational logic of Walter Ruttmann's famous 1927 film, *Berlin: Die Sinfonie einer Großstadt*. Like Langston and Alter, Presner reveals both continuities and discontinuities between early twentieth-century modernism and our age of digital culture and stresses the fact that dominant Weimar notions of visuality and spectatorship have been replaced by modes of perception that are attuned to the contiguity of the non-contiguous and the simultaneity of the non-simultaneous. In the last chapter of this third section and of the entire book, Margit Grieb finally explores the curious popularity of Nazi imagery and themes in contemporary computer gaming culture. As Grieb argues, the figure of the Nazi in video gaming has lost much of its historical specificity and instead morphed into a quasi-universal archetype of radical evil; as we consume the darkest chapter of German history as an interactive digital screen presence, we actively participate in a fundamental reshaping and reframing of that past.

V.

Digital culture has largely expanded the presence of both moving images and animating sounds in our daily lives and has thus affected not only the formal shapes of mainstream and art cinemas but also the way in which we perceive, inhabit, and navigate space in general, therefore positioning us in the topographies of the present. Even though German Studies, in particular in its North American variant, has a long history of engaging different German theoretical and philosophical legacies in order to develop critical models of cultural and aesthetic analysis, it is no exaggeration to say that the discipline has been rather slow in addressing the vicissitudes of digital culture and new media aesthetics. After a decade of enthusiastic, albeit at times theoretically unfocused, culturalist criticism, the new millennium has produced scholarship eager to return not only to a more circumscribed notion of aesthetic experience but also to a more stable sense of the aesthetic object, in particular the written and printed text.

An offspring of the interdisciplinary reconstruction of German Studies during the 1980s, German film studies in the United States today has not yet really found a way to compensate for this lacuna. It has reached institutional respectability and identity at precisely the moment when film and cinema themselves are suddenly challenged by newer technologies and cultural practices, and instead of addressing how contemporary screen culture transforms the terms of cinematic representation and spectatorship, German film studies today appears to some extent continuously wedded to explorations of the national, to issues of national identity and specificity in German cinema that seems strangely out of sync with the transnational and technologically hybrid exigencies of moving image production and consumption in the twenty-first century.

In recalling the work of visual and cultural theorists such as Benjamin, Kracauer, and Adorno, and in employing their work for contemporary conversations about the formal, thematic, and social structure of contemporary screen and aesthetic culture, *After the Digital Divide?* contributes to shifting the focus of German Culture Studies today. The thoughts, perspectives, and analyses gathered in this volume offer new arguments to account for the changed position of image and sound production in today's Germany and beyond, to help rethink the domains of film, image, and sound studies, and to examine and reshuffle the theoretical tools for the critical examination of images and sounds in all their different manifestations and places today.

Notes

[1] See, for instance, Wendy Hui Kyong Chun, "Introduction: Did Somebody Say New Media?" in *New Media Old Media: A History and Theory Reader,* ed. Wendy Hui Kyong Chun and Thomas Keenan (New York: Routledge, 2006), 1–4.

[2] For a critical analysis of different responses, see, for instance, Thomas Elsaesser, "Early Film History and Multi-Media: An Archaeology of Possible Futures?" in *New Media Old Media,* 13–25.

³ Lev Manovich, *The Language of New Media* (Cambridge, MA: MIT Press, 2001).

⁴ William Uricchio, "Storage, Simultaneity, and the Technologies of Modernity," in *Allegories of Communication: Intermedial Concerns from Cinema to the Digital,* ed. J. O. Fullerton and J. Fullerton (Eastleigh, U.K.: John Libbey, 2004), 123–38; D. N. Rodowick, *The Virtual Life of Film* (Cambridge, MA: Harvard UP, 2007).

⁵ For more on definitions of new media as tools able to "remediate" the content of older media, see Jay David Bolter and Richard Grusin, *Remediation: Understanding New Media* (Cambridge, MA: MIT Press, 2000).

⁶ Siegfried Kracauer, "The Mass Ornament," in *The Mass Ornament: Weimar Essays,* ed. and trans. Thomas Y. Levin (Cambridge, MA: Harvard UP, 1995), 75–86.

⁷ Kracauer, "The Mass Ornament," 79.

⁸ Walter Benjamin, "The Work of Art in the Age of Mechanical Reproduction," in *Illuminations: Essays and Reflections,* ed. Hannah Arendt, trans. Harry Zohn (New York: Schocken Books, 1969), 217–52.

⁹ Theodor W. Adorno, "On the Fetish-Character in Music and the Regression of Listening," in *The Essential Frankfurt School Reader,* ed. Andrew Arato and Eike Gebhardt (New York: Continuum, 1982), 293.

¹⁰ Max Horkheimer and Theodor W. Adorno, *Dialectic of Enlightenment,* trans. John Cumming (New York: Continuum, 1995), 120–67.

¹¹ Max Pensky, "Minimal Adorno," *New German Critique* 75 (Fall 1998): 190.

¹² Max Horkheimer, "Traditional and Critical Theory," in *Critical Theory: Selected Essays,* trans. Matthew J. O'Connell et al. (New York: Herder & Herder, 1972), 188–243; and "The Present Situation of Social Philosophy and the Tasks of an Institute for Social Research," in *Between Philosophy and Social Science* (Cambridge, MA: MIT Press, 1993), 1–14.

¹³ See, for instance, Vivian Sobchack, *Carnal Thoughts: Embodiment and Moving Image Culture* (Berkeley: U of California P, 2004); Laura U. Marks, *Touch: Sensuous Theory and Multisensory Media* (Minneapolis: U of Minnesota P, 2002); Mark B. N. Hansen, *New Philosophy for New Media* (Cambridge, MA: MIT Press, 2004) and *Bodies in Code: Interfaces with Digital Media* (New York: Routledge, 2006); Caroline A. Jones, ed., *Sensorium: Embodied Experience, Technology, and Contemporary Art* (Cambridge, MA: MIT Press, 2006); Anna Munster, *Materializing New Media: Embodiment in Information Aesthetics* (Hanover, CT: Dartmouth College P, 2006); and Bernadette Wegenstein, *Getting under the Skin: Body and Media Theory* (Cambridge, MA: MIT Press, 2006).

¹⁴ Benjamin, *Illuminations,* 236.

Part 1: What Is New about New Media?

1: From the Image to the Image File—and Back

Boris Groys

IN HIS RECENT BOOK, *PROFANATIONS,* Giorgio Agamben writes, "The image is a being whose essence is to be a *species,* a visibility or an appearance."[1] Agamben's assertion is, of course, true. But at the same time this definition of an image's essence is not sufficient to actually guarantee the visibility of a concrete image. Because an image—I mean here an artificially produced image, for example, an artwork—cannot make itself present or force the viewer to look at it by virtue of its definition alone. An image lacks the vitality, energy, and health to do so. This is especially obvious in the case of an artwork. The artwork initially appears to be weak, ill, helpless, and out of sight; it should be shown to become visible. The curator has to place the image in the museum or, generally, in an exhibition space; he must lead the visitor to it as a nurse or a doctor leads a visitor to a bedridden patient in the hospital. It is no coincidence that the word "curator" is etymologically related to the word "cure." Curating is curing. Curating cures the helplessness of the image, its inability to show itself, its lack of visibility. But at the same time the act of curating makes the weakness of the image even more obvious; it makes the image look even more weak, lifeless, helpless. Thus the question arises: What happens to an image after its digitization? Are digital images stronger or weaker than analogue images?

I suggest that digitized images become both—stronger and weaker. At first glance, digitization allows images to become independent of any curatorial practice. Digital images do not need the closed space of an exhibition to be displayed. Rather, digital images have the ability to originate, multiply, and distribute themselves spontaneously and anonymously throughout the open fields of contemporary means of communication, such as the Internet or cell-phone networks, without any centralized curatorial control. In this respect we can speak of digital images as strong images—images that are able to show themselves according to their own essence, depending on their own vitality and strength alone. Of course, one can always assume that there is a certain hidden curatorial practice or agenda concealed behind any concrete strong image, but such an assumption remains a suspicion that cannot be proved "objectively." One can say that the digital image is a strong image—an image that transgresses the traditional borders of the exhibition space controlled by curatorial power. But then the question arises as to whether the digital image is also a strong image in the sense that it can stabilize its identity throughout all of its appearances. And a strong image can be regarded as truly strong only when it can guarantee its own identity. Otherwise we are once again dealing with a weak image that is dependent on the context of its presentation.

Now it is not so much the digital image as the image file that can be called strong, because one can argue that the image file remains more or less identical throughout the process of its distribution. But the image file is not an image; it is invisible. Only the characters of the film *The Matrix* (1999) are able to see image files, that is, the digital code as such. The relationship between the image file and the image that emerges as an effect of the visualization of this image file—that is, as an effect of its decoding by a computer—can be interpreted as a relationship between original and copy. The digital image is a visible copy of an invisible image file—the invisible data. In this respect the digital image has the same relationship to its digital file as a Byzantine icon has to God—it is a visible copy of something that cannot be seen. Digitization creates the illusion that there is no longer any difference between original and copy and that we are dealing only with copies that multiply and circulate in information networks. But there cannot be any copies without an original. In the case of digitization, the difference between original and copy is obliterated only by the fact that the original data are invisible. But an invisible original remains an original. The digital image functions here like a piece of music whose score is not identical to the piece itself as it is not audible but silent. For the music to resound, it must be performed. The same can be said about the theater and the relationship between a play and its mise-en-scène. One can say that digitization turns the visual arts into the performing arts. To be seen, a digital image should not be merely exhibited but performed. But to perform something means to betray or distort it. Every performance is an interpretation and every interpretation is a betrayal. The situation is especially difficult in the case of the invisible original; if the original is visible, it can be compared to a copy, and in turn the copy can be corrected and the feeling of betrayal is therefore reduced. But if the original is invisible, no such comparison is possible; every visualization remains uncertain. Of course, the situation would change if all visualizations of the same data were identical among themselves—but this is obviously not the case.

Information technology is constantly changing: hardware, software, simply everything. Precisely because of this, the image is also transformed with every act of visualization that uses a different, new technology.

Should one perhaps preserve old technologies so that the image would remain self-identical? As Siegfried Kracauer and Roland Barthes noted, when speaking of photography, old-fashioned technologies shift the perception of a specific image from the image itself to the technical conditions under which it was produced and presented. We are less interested in the subject of old photographs or the individual attitude of the photographer than in the technical aspects of technology that seem to be exotic to us. When we look at old photographs, what we primarily react to is the old-fashioned photographic technology that becomes apparent from a historical distance. However, the artist who took these pictures did not originally intend to produce such an effect, as he had no opportunity to compare his work with the products of later technological developments.

Thus the image itself may possibly be overlooked if it is reproduced using the original technology. And so the decision to transfer this image to new technology and new software and hardware, so that it may look fresh again, becomes understandable; it is not interesting merely in retrospect but rather appears to be a contemporary image in a contemporary context. But according to this line of argumentation, one is caught in the same dilemma from which, as is generally known, contemporary theater is unable to find an way out. Because no one can decide which is better: to reveal the play's epoch or its individuality in its performance. Rather, every performance unavoidably reveals and betrays at the same time one of the two—or even both. In this sense, every act of visualization is a betrayal of the artistic image; one keeps the image intact and makes it obsolete, or one updates it and distorts it.

Today's technology is conceived of in terms of generations; we speak of computer generations and of generations of photographic and video equipment. But where there are generations, there are also generational conflicts and Oedipal struggles. Anyone who attempts to transfer his or her old text or image files onto new software experiences the power of the Oedipus complex over current technology; many things are lost in the process, are destroyed, or become obscure. As soon as technology is thought of in generations, then it plainly and simply ceases to be a medium of identical reproduction, of preserving, stabilizing, and storing. The biological metaphor says it all: not only life (which is notorious in this respect) but also technology, which supposedly opposes nature, has become the medium of non-identity. Of course, one can also use these technical constraints productively; one can play with the technically produced differences of a digital image on all levels. But in this case each presentation of a digitized image becomes a re-creation of this image.

But even if technology could guarantee the visual identity between different visualizations of the same data, they would remain non-identical because of the changing context of their appearances. And here the figure of the curator once again emerges. But now the curator has to cure not the weak visibility of an image but the total invisibility of the digital code. Curating an image is tantamount to performing; it visualizes an image that exists in a mode of invisibility or self-concealment. And at the same time every spectator becomes a curator because he or she also has to perform and situate an image in order to see it.

In this context, Walter Benjamin's "The Work of Art in the Age of Mechanical Reproduction" is relevant.[2] In this essay Benjamin assumes the possibility of a perfect reproduction that no longer allows a material distinction between original and copy. Technology actually developed in the opposite direction; that is, it developed toward the diversification of the conditions under which a copy is produced and, accordingly, the diversification of the resulting visual images. But let us assume that the images are identical under certain stable technological conditions. We know that, for Benjamin, the distinction between original and copy thus becomes a topological one: the original has a specific historical site, and it is through this site that the original is inscribed into history as a unique object. The copy, by contrast, is virtual, placeless, ahistorical; from the very beginning, it manifests itself as potential multiplicity. Reproduction is dislocation, deterritorialization; it transports the work of art into networks of topologically indefinite circulation.

In these terms, the digital original loses its aura in a much more radical way than any traditional original ever can. According to Benjamin, the traditional artwork loses its aura when it is transported from its original place to an exhibition space or when it is copied. But even if a traditional original is moved from one place to another, it remains a part of the same space, the same topography, the same visible world. The digital original (or the digital data, if you will), on the other hand, is moved by its visualization from the space of invisibility and the status of "non-image" to the space of visibility and the status of "image." Accordingly, it undergoes a truly massive loss of aura, because nothing has more aura than the Invisible. The visualization of the Invisible is the most radical form of its profanation. The visualization of digital data is a sacrilege, comparable with the attempt to visualize the invisible god of Judaism or Islam. And this act of radical profanation cannot be compensated for by a set of rules that would enforce visual homogeneity onto the results of this profanation as, for example, in the case of Byzantine icons. As previously argued, modern technology is not capable of establishing such rules.

Benjamin thought that copies—if not originals—are self-identical because they circulate in a homogenous space where they have no specific site or address. But the topological homogeneity of the technological, mass-media space of digital reproducibility is an illusion. The central characteristic of the Internet consists precisely in the fact that, in the net, all symbols, words, and images are assigned an address; that is, they are placed somewhere, territorialized and inscribed into a heterogeneous topology.

Thus, even beyond permanent generational change and corresponding updating, the fate of digital data in the Internet is essentially dependent on the quality of the specific hardware, server, software, browser, and so on being used. The individual files may be distorted, interpreted differently, or even made unreadable. They may also be attacked by computer viruses or accidentally deleted, or they may simply age and perish. In this way files on the Internet become the heroes of their own story, one that is, like any story, primarily one of possible or real loss. Indeed, stories are told constantly about how certain files can no longer be read, how certain Web sites have disappeared, and so on. Additionally, the social space in which digitized images—photographs, videos, and so on—circulate today is an extremely heterogeneous space. One can visualize videos with the aid of a video recorder, but also as a projection, on television, within the context of a video installation, on the monitor of a computer, on a cell phone, and so on. In all of these cases, the same video file looks different even on the surface, not to mention as a result of the very different contexts in which it is shown. One could thus call the effect of digitization on the image a "pharmakon" (using Derrida's term), for it both cures the image and at the same time makes it ill. Digitization, that is, the writing of the image, helps the image become reproducible, to circulate freely and to distribute itself. It is therefore the medicine that cures the image of its inherent immovability. But at the same time the digitized image becomes infected with non-identity; that is, the image is of necessity repeatedly presented as always dissimilar to itself, which means that supplementary curing, that is, curating, becomes unavoidable.

Thus the question arises: how it is possible to reflect on this specific condition of the digital image inside the image itself? The average spectator does not possess a magic pill that would allow him, like the heroes of *The Matrix*, to enter the space of invisibility behind the digital image and confront the digital data directly. Nor does he possess the technique that would allow him to transfer data directly into the brain and to experience it in the mode of pure, non-visualizable suffering, as in another film, *Johnny Mnemonic* (1995). (Pure suffering, as we know, is the most adequate experience of the Invisible.) In this respect, the example of how iconoclastic religions deal with the image could potentially be helpful. According to these religions, the Invisible manifests itself in the world not through any specific individual image but through the whole history of its appearances and interventions. Such a history is necessarily ambiguous: it documents the individual appearances or interventions of the Invisible (biblically speaking, signs and wonders) within the topography of the visible world, but at the same time it documents them in a way that renders all these appearances and interventions relative and avoids the trap of recognizing one specific image as *the* image of the Invisible. The Invisible remains invisible precisely by virtue of the multiplication of its visualizations.

One example is Orhan Pamuk's novel *My Name Is Red* (2001), which features a group of artists searching for a place for art within an iconoclastic culture, namely that of sixteenth-century Islamic Turkey. The group is composed of illustrators commissioned by the powerful to ornament their books with exquisite miniatures; these books are subsequently placed in governmental or private collections. These artists are not only increasingly persecuted by radical Islamic (iconoclastic) adversaries who want to ban all images; they are also in competition with the Occidental painters of the Renaissance, primarily Venetians, who openly affirm their own iconophilia. Yet the novel's heroes are unable to share this iconophilia, because they do not believe in the autonomy of images. They thus assume a consistently honest iconoclastic stance without abandoning the terrain of art. A Turkish sultan, whose theory of art would actually serve as a good model for contemporary curatorial practice, shows them how to do this. According to the sultan,

> An illustration that does not complement a story, in the end, will become but a false idol. Since we cannot possibly believe in an absent story, we will naturally begin believing in the picture itself. This would be no different than the worship of the idols in the Kaaba that went on before Our Prophet, peace and blessings be upon him, had destroyed them.... If I believed, heaven forbid, the way these infidels do, that the Prophet Jesus was also the Lord God himself,... only then might I accept the depiction of mankind in full detail and exhibit such images. You do understand that, eventually, we would unthinkingly begin worshiping any picture that is hung on a wall, don't you?[3]

Western art—and especially modern art—traditionally struggled with illustration and narrative to create an autonomous image independent of any history. This struggle was repeatedly misinterpreted as iconoclastic, because religion was usually understood as a master narrative. But Christianity had already appropriated and neutralized the iconoclastic gesture operating within the image itself; in the Christian tradition the image of destruction and destitution—Christ on the cross—is transformed quasi-automatically into an image of the triumph of that which has been destroyed. Our iconographic imagination, which has long been trained by the Christian tradition, does not hesitate to recognize victory in the image of defeat. In fact, defeat here is a victory from the start. Modern art has benefited significantly from the adoption of iconoclasm as a mode of production. In the context of modern art, iconoclasm has become subordinate to iconophilia; the image's symbolic martyrdom has only strengthened belief in it. Indeed, the avant-garde staged a martyrdom of the image that replaced the Christian image of martyrdom. The avant-garde subjected traditional painting to all sorts of tortures that recall first and foremost the tortures to which the saints were subjected, as depicted in paintings from the Middle Ages. Thus the image is—symbolically and/or literally—sawed, cut, fragmented, drilled, pierced, dragged through the dirt, and left to the mercy of ridicule. The iconoclastic gesture is instituted here as an artistic method less for the annihilation of old icons than for the production of new images—or, if you will, new icons and new idols that reaffirm the indestructible autonomy of the image.

But digitization of the image makes it dependent on at least one history—the history of its own visualizations—as an individual appearance among many other such appearances of the same invisible digital data. To reflect on this history means to practice the more subtle iconoclastic strategy proposed by the sultan: to turn the image back into an illustration. The narrative's strategy is to tell the history of the visualizations of the Invisible. We have known at least since Magritte that when we look at an image of a pipe we are not regarding a real pipe but one that has been painted. The pipe as such is not present; instead, it is depicted as absent. But we are still inclined to believe that when we look at a painted pipe, we directly confront "an image of a pipe as such." We see the images as perfectly incarnated, as being there—even if the depicted object is absent. Thus the image becomes an idol. But the digitized image is not present; rather, it documents and illustrates the absence of the invisible original.

In this sense, digitization manifests the general conditions of perceiving an image that would otherwise remain hidden and overlooked. The art of the 1960s already began to reflect this situation and to investigate the ambiguous relationship between the image as autonomous artwork and as document or illustration. Artistic projects, performances, and actions conceived of or realized by artists have regularly been documented, and, by means of this documentation, represented in exhibition spaces and museums. Thus the illusion could arise that we are still dealing with the traditional self-sufficient, autonomous image. However, such documentation simply refers to art without itself being art. Art is understood as being both invisible and the narrative about a certain history of its visualizations, but it is not seen as being any of these visualizations themselves. This type of documentation is often presented in the framework of an art installation for the purpose of narrating a certain project or action. Traditionally executed paintings, art objects, photographs, or videos can also be utilized in the framework of such installations. In such cases, artworks admittedly lose their conventional status as art. Rather, they become documents or illustrations of the story narrated by the installation. One might say that today's art audience increasingly encounters art as *documentation*, which provides information about the artwork itself, be it art project or art action; but in doing so the documentation confirms the absence of the artwork. When Marcel Broodthaers presented his *Musée d'Art Moderne, Département des Aigles* at the Kunsthalle in Düsseldorf in

1973, he placed the label "This is not a work of art" next to each of the presented objects in the installation.

One can thus say that the relationship between the invisible and the visible that structures the digital image is prefigured not only by the iconoclastic religions but also by certain iconoclastic artistic and curatorial practices that aimed at manifesting art in an apophatic way (using the term of Byzantine theology)—for example, as being invisible. Here the figure of the curator comes back into play; not because the curator displays an image, but because he tells a story that undercuts the importance of this image and makes it refer to the Invisible. The curator can only exhibit an image by including it in a more general framework, by developing a certain curatorial project, and by telling a story of this project. Even if a curatorial project consists of showing certain images as autonomous images, it necessarily betrays this initial intention because it demonstrates the dependence of the images at least on the curatorial project itself, so that every curatorial project instead abuses the image and makes it profane. The curator is the agent of art's profanation, its secularization, and its profane abuse; but at the same time the curatorial work reveals the dependence of the image on the hidden Invisible. The widespread opinion that an artwork in a museum is "dead" can be understood as meaning that there it loses its status as an idol; pagan idols were venerated for being "alive." The museum's iconoclastic gesture consists precisely in transforming "living" idols into "dead" illustrations for art history. One can therefore argue that even the traditional museum curator has always subjected images to double abuse. On the one hand, images in the museum are aestheticized and transformed into art; on the other hand, they are downgraded to illustrations of art history and thereby dispossessed of their art status. In this sense, curatorial practice allows the opportunity to reflect on the double status of the digital image, which remains obscure as long as this image circulates in open networks of information—by analogy between art as a code and the digital code as such. That is why time and again we see attempts to bring the digital image into the traditional exhibition space—after the digital revolution was long praised as a liberation from the art exhibition, the art museum, or any closed space of contemplation. The exhibition space is needed here not to demonstrate the strength of the digital image but to reflect on its weaknesses.

The space of a museum exhibition or an artistic installation is often despised today because it is a closed space, in contrast to the open space of contemporary media. But the closure that an exhibition effects should not be interpreted as the opposite of "openness." With closure, the exhibition creates its own "outside," its setting, and opens itself up to this outside. Closure here does not stand in opposition to openness but rather is its precondition. The space of media, by contrast, is not open, because it has no outside; it is rather total, all-inclusive. Art practice that is conceived as a machine of infinite expansion and inclusion is also not an open artwork but the artistic counterpart of the imperial hubris of contemporary media. The museum exhibition can be made into a place of openness, disclosure, or unconcealment precisely because it is situated inside finite space and it contextualizes and curates images and objects that also circulate in outside space; in this way it opens itself up to the outside. Images do not emerge into the clearing of Being of their own accord so that their original visibility can be abused by the "art industry," as Heidegger describes it in "The Origin of the Work of Art."[4] Rather, this very abuse makes them visible.

Notes

[1] Giorgio Agamben, *Profanations,* trans. Jeff Fort (New York: Zone Books, 2007), 57.

[2] Walter Benjamin, "The Work of Art in the Age of Mechanical Reproduction," in *Illuminations: Essays and Reflections,* ed. Hannah Arendt, trans. Harry Zohn (New York: Schocken, 1968), 217–51.

[3] Orhan Pamuk, *My Name is Red,* trans. Erdag M. Göknar (New York: Alfred A. Knopf, 2001), 109–10.

[4] Martin Heidegger, "The Origin of the Work of Art." in *Poetry, Language, Thought,* trans. Albert Hofstadter (New York: Harper & Row, 1971), 15–87.

2: Digital Sampling and Analogue Montage

Diedrich Diederichsen

WHAT MAKES A GIVEN CONSTELLATION or phenomenon an adequate object of media studies or media theory? I will attempt to answer this overarching question with regard to two specific constellations. The implicit as well as explicit answer to that question would be: the overlapping of the change in the use of a new technical medium with general political and cultural change. The challenge here is not to resort to the frequent habit of reduction that privileges one of the two spheres over the other and attempts to explain the second sphere with categories of the first. Media theory and media studies contend with a specific overdetermination of their objects in a field (the Humanities in a broader sense) in which, especially recently, the call for technical and scientific explanations has become increasingly louder. Nevertheless, I will argue here for the dignity of political and cultural arguments vis-à-vis technical and technological phenomena or cultural-technological constellations. The object I have chosen for my discussion here, sampling, is especially tricky, for it refers to several phenomena and has become a buzzword for a variety of discourses since the late 1980s.

German media theory is generally characterized by two mutually exclusive tendencies. One, part of a tradition that runs from Martin Heidegger to Friedrich Kittler, is more inclined toward an ontology of media and the mediated. The second tendency is rather a media sociology, which in its best manifestation is part of the tradition of Siegfried Kracauer; at its worst it is not interested at all in the technical or technological status of the media but is rather concerned with the effects of their use by companies, corporations, and so-called creative artists on our children and their education, on the social fabric, and on the health of public life in general. Missing in both of these epistemological queries is a perspective on the connection between the two—between the famous *technical a priori*, as the first school calls it, and its social implementation, of which the second school only studies the symptoms. What is missing thus forms what can be described as a combination of the goals and methods of the Frankfurt School with a technology-based critique of media worthy of its name.

I will concentrate here on a phenomenon that can be described within a particular triangle consisting of first, a techno-historical condition, namely digitality; second, a mass-produced commodity, that is the sampling computer or the so-called sampler from the AKAI 900 and AKAI 1100 onward; and third, a specific social and cultural methodology in rap and hip-hop. Or, in other words: the interface, its often hidden technical ontology, and the social cultural and artistic needs and ideas of concrete and specific people—artists and their audiences. The core period of the phenomenon in question (sampling in the field of digitally produced, recorded, and organized music, especially in the field of hip-hop) occurred from the mid-1980s to the mid-1990s. By "sampling" I refer here to a process that has become internationally known by this name and is, simply described, the process of digital recording by literally sampling data from the sound to be recorded at a certain sampling rate. However, this process is predominately associated in public discourse with the use, quotation, and alteration of recorded digital data within digital audio production. The term has developed a life of its own, in which its technical dimension and its aesthetic, cultural, and social use are hopelessly intertwined. However, we need not lament this situation as the result of the improper use of terms but rather can look at this result as the symptom of exactly the state of affairs I refer to here. I contend that the specific social and cultural use of a technology and its marketing via a certain functional interface can no longer be described from one epistemological perspective alone.

Sampling was thus a very loaded term in discussions in the field of music and art during the 1990s, beyond its role in hip-hop culture. It seemed to magically cover various problems ranging from the issue of falsification and forgery to questions of the legitimacy of contemporary concepts of authorship, quotes, and quotations. In addition, the term was ubiquitous in various discourses that framed these cultural and aesthetic themes with the solid factual category of a technological situation: digitization.

On the other hand, in purely aesthetic and artistic terms, all these problems have been around for a very long time, excepting the digital media involved. They concerned the use of already finished or found material in the arts and raised questions as to whether the material was made in a specific way or by a specific author and to what extent these aspects were supposed to be recognized. These problems arose because there was a technological element in the production of all art; handcraft or handwriting, for example, could no longer be seen as the single source of artistry. Debates from the twentieth century (which were never conclusively terminated) returned. But they also returned in a different fashion; they no longer posed questions about the seemingly categorically soft debates around aesthetic responsibilities and their limits. Rather, it was as if the same aesthetic problems had now found a new techno-scientific hard base, even though the true shift, if I may anticipate one of my theses here, took place, not in the use of new technology, but instead in the way in which its employment by specific users gave these aesthetic questions a new social and political base.

The early days of the digital age witnessed a rather pessimistic counter-concept to the more optimistic use of sampling, namely the equally ubiquitous term "simulation." We will explore in a moment how these terms reappear as antagonists with respect to the specifics of musical practice. But I prefer to first examine an earlier term that, like sampling, contains a similar mixture of aesthetic normativity, technological and political objectivism, and artistic practice, and that functioned in early debates about technology-based art as a precedent to sampling: montage. Montage was itself a rather technologically optimistic idea that seemed to connect artistic, aesthetic notions with hard technical necessity and with the progressivist notion of the objectivity of a newly arrived medium or format. One might thus locate sampling in yet another triangle between the progressivism of montage and the regressivism of simulation, between the notion of being able to lay your technologically advanced hand on the building of the future and the notion of not being able to lay your hand on anything; that is, no longer being able to grasp anything at all under digital conditions.

Montage was, like shock, one of the magic formulas of modernism. It was supposed to magically induce a certain connection or reconciliation: the reconciliation of technological, political, and aesthetic progress. It thus defined progress as the harmonic interplay of two trans-subjective (if not quite objective) vectors: technology and history on the one hand and the subjectivity of artistic production and reception on the other. The famous critical and at the same time pessimistic categories "culture industry" and "spectacle" stood simultaneously for two unbridgeable antagonisms between art and mass culture on the one hand and between social and technological progress on the other. However, they always located their optimistic counterpart in montage, especially in the first half of the twentieth century.

Of course, very different normative and descriptive discourses evolved around the term. There was the emphatic notion of montage as a new opportunity for the democratic or Soviet masses to participate in production, or at least to gain direct and better-controlled access to the material. And there was the rather prosaic reduction of practice to merely the result of media-technological circumstances. Montage in cinema is thus just what one must do, in a very conservative narrative format, but it is not necessarily an enabling tool. There are other inconsistencies: montage is in some versions the very location of disintegration and unreconcilable separation; in others it is the practical synthesis of antitheses.

But some ideas proved to be quite stable. At first one observes that montage was always understood as a both enlightening and enlightened (and thus critical) procedure, leading to an enlightened and critical usage of the means of art and design. In montage, the suture is visible and intentionally disclosed. It, along with the original sources and their contexts, can be recognized, and thus the aesthetic practice itself is evident. Original sources are clearly designated as material like any other material; nothing is more primordial or primary than anything else. Regardless of how one reads the point of this kind of montage, it is not the origin that matters but rather the combination. Montage is thus the true origin. At the same time, one can read it in a completely different manner, arguing that there is no hierarchy in the degrees of origin. Both arguments lead to the collapse of the category of the primary in the arts.

But the recognizably disclosed artificiality of technology-based art is the result not only of a new use of new means and media but also of an employment that deliberately does not cover over its mechanics by declaring its results to be natural, mimetic, or masterful. On the contrary, the position and the means of the producer are marked and thus designated in order to be debated and discussed. In this sense montage indicates the use of new technology for good ethical, political, and aesthetic reasons. But, of course, this implies that the reasons for this use of technology were already articulated or could have been articulated without the technology, since they referred to ethical and aesthetic criteria of the critical and Enlightenment tradition that did not necessarily require the existence of a technology that would later help implement these criteria in artistic practice. Following this line of argument, however, one would need to ignore, for example, the dialectical relationship between the increased illusionism of photography and film and the anti-illusionism of the idea of montage in early Soviet cinema and photo collage, since these are constellations that would not have been imaginable in general normative critical aesthetics. Even if one concedes that, to a degree, these traditions (as, for example, in Greenberg and Adorno) are always based on a specific normative idea of the relationship of artistic practice to its media support, these practical complexities can not be deduced from a general critical relationship to the material and media. With regard to our problem of digital sampling, we can assume that there will also be problems as to how either critical intellectual traditions on the one hand or the historical experiences with montage on the other could be applied to its technical reality.

The notion of a technological reality as an ontologically superior level (or a level of superior cognition) was also already widespread when the discourse of montage first arose in various ways as, for instance, the Marxist idea of a reflection of production relations and as the futurist notion of a new age of war, metal, and speed. They had in common a tendency to see objectivity in technology as an escape route from bourgeois subjectivity and the discourse of sensitivity, rarity, the decadent, the delicate, the connoisseur, and the master. The most important aspect of this second form of montage (which I'll term futurist for reasons of simplicity) is that progress is no longer determined by aesthetic, political, or ethical norms but by technological facts. In this version, humanism and art are only posterior, if of any importance at all, and artists have arrived at an ideological concept of objectivity. Illusionism is now no longer a problem; it can even be the aim of montage as the enrichment of artistic forms that do not plan to break with illusionism.

But perhaps we can posit a third version of montage optimism, which can be constructed from diverse writings by Walter Benjamin, among others. The dialectics of construction and destruction extend the idea of the other two versions, which are either anti-illusionistic or try to increase illusionism by well-made montage. For Benjamin it is of importance that every act of montage is connected with a simultaneous act of demontage, that wherever a continuum is interrupted with a cut and connected with another continuum, the original continuum will be destroyed. In this way, a false idyllic image of the world is ruined, and for Benjamin, this destruction is certainly justified, because it is a false ideological continuity. In this version montage not only connects two halves in a visible and thus anti-illusionist way but also demonstrates that the new connection has replaced an old one and that this is justified.

We can thus resume here three basic positions with regard to montage: first, the marking of the cut in an anti-illusionist sense; second, the improvement of illusionism by new technology; and third, the addition of Soviet-leftist and futurist-apolitical montage in Benjamin and others; in other words, anti-illusionism plus destruction of the old continuum.

The three positions are still with us, but no longer in the context of the avant-garde. These days the basic idea of montage has become a popular function of all computer software in the "copy and paste" function. The first position, in which the suture is marked in a critically enlightened manner, has become a standard of ironic bourgeois culture that has been the province of talk-show hosts after Brecht. The second version, the anti-humanist improvement of illusion, has also left the world of manifestos behind and instead has become the standard overwhelming aesthetic of the culture industry. In the old days of montage, it was unclear whether there would ever be something akin to a culture industry, but in the *Dialectic of Enlightenment* (in the chapter of the same name), Adorno remarked upon montage as a decisive feature not only of the products but also of the forms of presentation in the culture industry. Even the third position, termed here "Benjaminian" for reasons of simplification, was prevalent during the entire twentieth century, especially in the neo-avant-garde movements of the 1950s, such as Cobra and situationism, in the work of Rauschenberg, and in the sometimes involuntarily comical and literal application of the so-called art of décollage. It seemed to eventually disappear with pop art, although I would argue that, in the 1960s, Benjaminian montage disintegrated into two parts. The first part entails pop art and, later, photorealism and other hyperrealist art forms, all of which have in common the tendency to present technically supported, highly realistic or indexical material in the art context. In this kind of technologically supported *readymade* in the context of art, the only montage would be between this hyper-real stuff and the classical or conventional suspension of reality in the White Cube. The second part involves the strategies of the simultaneously evolving concept of art as the presentation of the pure cut; a cut that happens without pasting anything, that is the pure exposition of the intellectual tool of displacement (without displacing anything *from* somewhere *to* somewhere else), a strategy that, one might say, is emblematically represented by Piero Manzoni's "Socle du Monde." Thus the methods of montage, as euphoric attempts to conquer or appropriate the tools and technologies of the culture industry, have reached a hyper-criticality or a maximum of self-enlightenment, in which artistic criticism and enlightenment in the face of their real disempowerment have reached a stage of self-fetishization (to exaggerate matters just a bit).

Montage was thus already thoroughly digested when it was finally inherited by pop music. Central to classical montage was the impulse to build and construct connections and disconnections and to homogenize and de-homogenize different levels and various stages of the material within the art work itself. Pop music, on the other hand, basically pasted itself into the world. It was crucial for pop music from its beginning in the postwar period—and this can be described as a radicalization of ideas by the culture industry and by avant-gardes—that the work of art, the performance, the song, and the image of the star be taken into the world, leaving the protected area of art. This strategy can perhaps also be found in earlier forms of popular music and art forms, but in the postwar music world it was industrialized and professionalized, enabling the triumph of a second culture industry after the film industry, and at the same time creating the basis for the hopes of the historical countercultures since the 1950s, in so far as they were connected to pop music.

In this scenario the role of producers, performers, and authors of pop music was only a minor issue. Their responsibility was rarely very extensive, and the success of the pop-music montage of artificial and worldly material was closely related to the passivity and non-consciousness of those involved—their not knowing what they were doing, their specific enthusiasm about their ignorance, and their eagerness to become a cool medium and to be completed by an outside world. However, in the internal language of the pop-music world, people disguised this situation with very traditional ideas of authorship, intentions, masters, and geniuses. Only when, in the mid to late 1970s, methods and styles inspired by conceptual art and other secondarist practices entered the internal discourses of pop-music journalism were the older models weakened. Now there was open talk about the prefabricated and the always already quoted in pop discourse on the one hand, and, on the other hand, pop's relationship to its social base and reality, absent the precise knowledge of how to deal with the situation aesthetically and productively.

Another clear dichotomy developed in the late 1970s: a futurist-posthumanist-electronic-new-media discourse versus rock, which rather furiously pasted and quoted as part of the continuum from punk to post-punk. This electronic quasi-futurism was at first located between an admiration of the machine as a means to access higher knowledge, often in a spiritualist sense (as in Tangerine Dream and Pink Floyd), and an affirmation of the machine as a signature of civilizing progress and modernity and of social conflicts solved by technology (as in Kraftwerk). Both were distant echoes of the electronic music debates in avant-garde music of the 1950s, with the addition of the social and political ties that bound pop-music practice to contemporary youth and underground culture. Both models were clearly holistic and hostile to montage in their aesthetics. This continued to play a role in most of the so-called synth pop of the early 1980s, which was now partly digital. The face of bricolage and amateurism that shaped pop music for so long was supposed to be left behind by holistic and atmospherically closed sounds.

But this electronic disposition also became an element of the first self-reflexive pop music in a broader sense during the era of punk and new wave. The period that was shaped by the fundamental rupture in the relationship between method and material, object and manufacture, is also known as the digital revolution. From this moment, the electronic production of sound fell under a different paradigm. It no longer followed the discourse of the endless richness of possibilities that had shaped the first electronic revolution, especially in the field of avant-garde music of the 1950s, and it was no longer about new and extended tone and sounds. Rather, digital electronic production promised easy access to sounds along with generic sounds, always important for pop music. Above all, it promised the perfect imitation of sound that heretofore had to be produced by human instrumentalists, especially drummers. In a word, it promised simulation. Seen from a critical perspective, simulation was the digital cousin of illusionism in the role of the bad boy.

Thus the development of electronic pop music toward the wholly reactionary seemed, in a double sense, to have been fulfilled by a new illusionism. The synthesizer-oriented music of the 1970s was already illusionist in its production of illusions of continua that made cuts and construction invisible (or, rather, inaudible), but that still occurred at least in an obviously artificial and electronic sense. On top of that another illusion now was to be perfectly produced, namely the simulation and emulation by digital electronic technology of a specific non-electronic instrument. The earliest interfaces that made the digital *dispositif* of production we know of as sampling accessible advertised their product with the claim that it could perfectly simulate "real instruments." When we observe a musician who samples single saxophone tones from someone else's saxophone solo and then per emulation creates from this a saxophone solo on his MIDI keyboard interface, we see simply the nadir, or the zero degree of montage.

But at this very nadir of montage, with the sad tool of simulation that sampling would be if one were to believe in the ideas of those who marketed the first sampling tools, suddenly something new could happen. You could use the sampler for something else, something traditionally seen as even less creative: you could use it for quoting. The cutting and pasting of alien sources to your own material could be reproduced without any loss in quality: in an illusionist manner, one could say. This combination (the improvement of the illusionist dimension on one hand and the improvement of the cutting and pasting possibilities on the other) was akin to a revival of the technologically euphoric situation of the old montage. And, as then, the disempowerment of a type of artist who had been hegemonic for a long time once again coincided with the empowerment of a new technological tool that was metonymically connected to technological progress per se. The trinity of aesthetic, technological, and political progress, the heart of the historical euphoria over montage, was repeated in the early texts celebrating sampling as a tool—at first, of course, with regard to hip-hop.

The sampling euphoria of the late 1980s and early 1990s revealed a relationship between cultural epoch and technological tool. The early sampling devices, built by AKAI, were soon called "quoting machines." Although they were built and marketed in the beginning as simulation machines, as digital quoting devices they were seen as the adequate technological equivalent of postmodernism, the machine for the administration of inauthenticity. But herein lies the big difference between sampling and montage. This quoting machine was born from simulation, not from the disclosure of heterogeneity; not from the seam, but from the seamless—and still it was considered a critical tool. How was this possible? One answer perhaps lies in the different types of continuity and different types of interruption. The seamless continuity that was demystified and dismantled and, in some deployments, also reconstructed by montage was the stream of hegemonic ideology. In the postmodern period, one can reverse this, although this might be a sort of exaggeration. Fragmentation is not only normative but also, in a way, a hegemonic figure of making sense of social contradictions. The artificial construction of new continuities based on material that has been violently fragmented in the first place can be seen from this perspective not only as a counter-hegemonic measure, but, since at least with hip-hop, we are talking about cultural material from African diasporic culture, also as a truly postcolonial practice.

A closer look reveals that in both montage and sampling there were diverse cultural processes at work whose relationship to the technological materiality of sampling was at best vague. The quoting machine was used for very different purposes: there were subversives and pranksters outside hip-hop, such as Negativland or KLF, the movement of plunderphonic music that continues today with artists like Jason Forrest aka Donnersummer, and of course the movement of "bastard pop," which was composed of wild, copyright-flaunting mixes of other people's contemporary music. All worked with samples as fully and deliberately recognizable elements that once gained were again made recognizable as such by being cut and pasted into new contexts. In most cases, this was done in order to critically expose the decontextualized sound object, to make fun of it or to attack and expose the illusionist streams of continuity in music (although the critical element decreases with phenomena like bastard pop). One finds a more sophisticated version of these strategies in the contemporary work of people like Terre Thaemlitz, whose aim is among others "to attack the spectacle of melody."[1] But these were more or less the classical strategies of montage and collage, whose aesthetic and communicative mechanism was not materially altered by digitization—except that they had become much easier.

In the field of hip-hop, sampling replaced or took over the function of the most visible novelty in 1980s pop music, namely the cut-and-mix methods of hip-hop DJs. Their spectacular effects were now produced in a contemporary manner without the artistry and the very Benjamin-like use of outmoded media (the turntable). But it was also still possible to digitally expose cuts and montages and their intentions in hip-hop, and for the artists, it was obviously desirable to refer offensively and deliberately to the quoted material they used. Interestingly, the use of quotes and cuts in hip-hop had a different, if not entirely antagonistic, meaning compared with the tradition of leftist montage (be it Benjaminian or Soviet art and propaganda), but it was also not congruent with any other historically known use. In hip-hop the aim of montage was not to attack false ideological continuity or to remove hegemonic sound objects from their context but rather to reconstruct former violently interrupted continua in the history of African-American and African diasporic history as music history and to put the musical traces of that history back into the context of contemporary black music. This aim was evident at least between 1987 and 1993 in numerous musical and aesthetic documents, and it was explicitly formulated by several artists (Gang Starr, for example). It spoke in several deliberately recognizable samples of reggae, historic funk, and jazz.

This version of the hip-hop sample reconstructed the former and (for political reasons) interrupted unity in an openly non-natural way. But this reconstruction is not (at least not primarily) about an enlightening and informative impulse toward this history. It is also not about an uncanny reconstruction, which is very important, since other loop-based digital music and its predecessors in minimal music often are about the uncannily absent but hyper-precise author of accentuation and rhythm. But since digital sampling is capable of reproducing (without a doubt in an illusionist way) the original physical properties of the sampled jazz and soul originals, the impression of an uncannily emptied beat does not appear.

The continuities in hip-hop loops are meant to be warm and of a certain regular irregularity that we associate with the human qualities of a groove as opposed to machine-like beats in techno and minimalism. At the same time, they are clearly artificial (by way of the repetitive qualities of the loop) and meant to be recognized as used and found material. However, their appropriation is not an aggressive gesture toward the material but one of a friendly reclamation of a collective ownership based on the collective memories around musical elements (breakbeats, instrumental parts, and so on) that were connected with a genre and a style rather than with individuals (although copyright laws will never reflect this). One can even say that certain styles of African diasporic music have been manipulated in the past in order to make them more generally accessible; especially long repetitive funk and groove-oriented pieces have been edited to make them more songlike. Sampling in hip-hop has also really or symbolically reverted to this by reconstructing the original function and the autonomy of repetitive groove structures from archival material. To use the metaphor of science-fiction fantasy, we could say that sampling in hip-hop is analogous to the scientists' creation of dinosaurs in Jurassic Park: it creates a living format out of fragmented genetic information from a sunken world.

What we have here is a case that can not be described by media ontology. The main claim of the perspective that digital data have no indexical link to what they record and can thus be described as simulation might be ontologically true but is convincingly countered by a social practice that can by no means be described as the belief of manipulated people in the act of simulation. Nor can it be described as a purely social phenomenon based on the life conditions of its producers. Rather, it can be depicted as evolving around postcolonial ideas of fictitious reconstruction, invented pasts, reconstructed history, and so on. All these ideas are already based on the specific usage of media, including new media. However, it can not be portrayed only as an artistic project, based on the mastery of an art form and its specific media; the AKAI sampler series has developed the usage I am talking about collectively rather than as the project of a single artist. And, finally, it also does not fit into critical traditions and their idea of a critical use of montage because of its preference of the seamless over the seam, the continuity of the loop over the exposure of the cut and so on. On the other hand, it does expose its own constructed nature; rather than hiding the historical sources, it proudly claims them.

All of these classical and new media-related descriptions of a media technology and its specific use thus fail, and we are left with the question as to what this media use signifies politically in the tradition of a political and critical interpretation of specific media-use phenomena such as montage and its various ideologies. Here one would have to take two points into account. The first is that the use of samples in hip-hop is mainly limited historically and stylistically to a strand of hip-hop based on diasporic identity politics between 1987 and 1995, and every critical judgment would have to include a discussion and a judgment of these politics (for which this, unfortunately, is not the appropriate forum). The second is that, despite its original limitation to US and African-American diasporic identity politics, we can see globally an adoption of digital cultural politics in current international hip-hop in relation to various other diasporic peoples throughout the world. In this way, the sampled and reconstructed loop from historical music has become something like a sign or a genre relating to a style or a type of identity politics, but not necessarily to their specifics, as it did in its first instance in African-American hip-hop of the 1980s and 1990s. This genre is only in its initial stages, and we can currently see digital diasporic histories and their specific media and data politics in other, mainly visual, formats as well.

Notes

[1] From a conversation between Thaemlitz and the author.

3: Remixability

Lev Manovich

I.

THE DRAMATIC INCREASE in the quantity of information, an increase greatly accelerated by the Internet, has been accompanied by another fundamental development. Imagine water running down a mountain. If the quantity of water keeps increasing, it will find numerous new paths, and these paths will keep getting wider. Something similar happens as the amount of information continues to grow, except that these paths are also all connected to each other and they go in all directions: up, down, and sideways. Some of the new paths that facilitate the movement of information between people, listed in no particular order, include SMS, the forward and redirect functions in E-mail clients, mailing lists, Web links, RSS, blogs, social bookmarking, tagging, publishing (as in publishing one's playlist on a Web site), peer-to-peer networks, Web services, Firewire, and Bluetooth. These paths stimulate people to draw information from all kinds of sources into their own space and to remix it and make it available to others, as well as to collaborate or at least play on a common information platform (Wikipedia, Flickr). Barb Dybwad introduces the apt term "collaborative remixability" to designate this process: "I think the most interesting aspects of Web 2.0 are new tools that explore the continuum between the personal and the social, and tools that are endowed with a certain flexibility and modularity which enables collaborative remixability — a transformative process in which the information and media we've organized and shared can be recombined and built on to create new forms, concepts, ideas, mashups and services."[1]

If the traditional twentieth-century model of cultural communication described the movement of information in one direction from a source to a receiver, in the current era the reception point is just a temporary station on information's path. If we compare information or a media object with a train, then each receiver can be compared to a train station. Information arrives, is remixed with other information, and then the new package travels to other destinations where the process is repeated.

We can find precedents for this "remixability," for instance, in modern electronic music, where remixing has become the key method since the

1980s. More generally, most human cultures developed by borrowing and reworking forms and styles from other cultures; the resulting "remixes" were incorporated into other cultures. Ancient Rome remixed ancient Greece; the Renaissance remixed antiquity; nineteenth-century European architecture remixed many historical periods including the Renaissance; and today graphic and fashion designers remix numerous historical and local cultural forms together, from Japanese manga to traditional Indian clothing. At first glance it may seem that this traditional cultural remixability is quite different from the "vernacular" remixability made possible by the computer-based techniques described above. Surely, a professional designer working on a poster or a professional musician working on a new mix is different from somebody who is writing a blog entry or publishing her bookmarks.

But this conclusion is false. The two kinds of remixability are part of the same continuum. For the designer and musician (to continue with the example above) are equally affected by the same computer technologies. Design software and music composition software make the technical operation of remixing very easy; the Internet greatly increases the ease of locating and reusing material from other periods, artists, designers, and so on. Even more importantly, since companies and freelance professionals in all cultural fields, from motion graphics to architecture to fine art, publish documentation of their projects on their Web sites, everybody can keep up with what everybody else is doing. Therefore, although the speed with which a new original architectural solution begins to appear in the projects of other architects and architectural students is much slower than the speed with which an interesting blog entry is referenced in other blogs, the difference is quantitative rather than qualitative. Similarly, when H&M or The Gap "reverse engineers" the latest fashion collection by a high-end design label in only a few weeks, it is part of the same new logic of accelerated cultural remixability enabled by computers. In short, the person who simply copies parts of a message into the new E-mail she is writing and the large media and consumer company that recycles the designs of other companies are doing the same thing—they are practicing remixability.

Remixability does not require modularity, but it greatly benefits from it. Although earlier precedents for remixing in music can be found, it was the introduction of multi-track mixers that made remixing a standard practice. With each element of a song—vocals, drums, and so on—available for separate manipulation, it became possible to remix the song; that is, to change the volume of some tracks or substitute new tracks for old ones. According to *DJ Culture* by Ulf Poshardt, the first disco remixes were made in 1972 by DJ Tom Moulton. As Poshardt points out, "Moulton sought above all a different weighting of the various soundtracks, and worked the rhythmic elements of the disco songs even more clearly and powerfully... Moulton used the various elements of the sixteen or twenty-four track master tapes and remixed them."[2]

In most cultural fields today there is a clear-cut separation between the libraries of elements designed to be sampled—stock photos, graphic backgrounds, music, software libraries—and the cultural objects that incorporate these elements. For instance, a graphic design may use photographs that the designer bought from a photo stock house. But this fact is not advertised; similarly, the fact that this design (if it is successful) will be inevitably copied and sampled by other designers is not openly acknowledged by the design field. The only fields in which sampling and remixing are done openly are music and computer programming, where developers rely on software libraries for writing new software.

Will the separation between libraries of samples and "authentic" cultural works blur in the future? Will future cultural forms be made deliberately from discrete samples designed to be copied and incorporated into other projects? One might imagine a cultural ecology in which all kinds of cultural objects, regardless of the medium or material, are made from Lego-like building blocks. The blocks come with the complete information necessary to easily copy and paste them—either by a human or a machine—into a new object. A block knows how to couple with other blocks, and it even can modify itself to enable such coupling. The block can also tell the designer and the user about its cultural history—the sequence of historical borrowings that led to the present form. And while the original Lego system (or a typical twentieth-century housing project) contains only a few kinds of blocks that make all the objects one can design with Legos rather similar in appearance, computers can keep track of an unlimited number of different blocks. At the minimum, they can already keep track of all the possible samples we can choose from all the cultural objects available today.

The standard twentieth-century notion of cultural modularity held that artists, designers, or architects make finished works from a small vocabulary of elemental shapes or other modules. The scenario I am entertaining proposes a very different kind of modularity that may appear to be a contradiction in terms. It is modularity without an *a priori* defined vocabulary. In this scenario, any well-defined part of any finished cultural object can automatically become a building block for new objects in the same medium. Parts can even "publish" themselves and other cultural objects can "subscribe" to them the way one subscribes now to RSS feeds or podcasts.

When we think of modularity today, we assume that the number of objects that can be created in a modular system is limited. Indeed, if we build these objects from a very small set of blocks, there is a limited number of ways in which these blocks can be combined. (Although, as the relative physical size of the blocks in relation to the finished object becomes smaller, the number of different objects that can be built increases: think of an IKEA modular bookcase versus a Lego set.) However, in my scenario, modularity does not involve a reduction in the number of forms that can be created. On the contrary, if the blocks themselves are created using one of the many computer-designed methods already developed (such as parametric design), every time they are used they can modify themselves automatically to ensure that they look different. In other words, if pre-computer modularity led to repetition and reduction, post-computer modularity can produce unlimited diversity.

I argue that such "real-time" or "on-demand" modularity can only be imagined today after online stores such as Amazon, blog-indexing services such as Technorati, and architectural projects such as the Yokohama International Port Terminal by Foreign Office Architects and the Walt Disney Concert Hall in Los Angeles by Frank Gehry visibly demonstrated that we can develop hardware and software to coordinate a massive number of cultural objects and their building blocks: books, blog entries, construction parts. But whether we will ever have such a cultural ecology is unimportant. We often look at the present by placing it within long historical trajectories. But I maintain that we can also productively use a different, complementary method. We can imagine what will happen if the contemporary techno-cultural conditions that are already firmly established are pushed to their logical limit. In other words, rather than placing the present in the context of the past, we can look at it in the context of a logically possible future. This "look from the future" approach may illuminate the present in a way not possible if we only "look from the past." The sketch of a logically possible cultural ecology I have offered is a little experiment in this method: futurology or science fiction as a method of contemporary cultural analysis.

So what else can we see today if we look at the situation from this logically possible future of complete remixability and universal modularity? If the scenario sketched above looks like cultural science fiction, consider the process that is already happening on one end of the remixability continuum. Although, strictly speaking, it does not involve increasing modularity to help remixability, ultimately its logic is the same: to help cultural bits move around more easily. I refer here to a move within Internet culture today from intricately packaged and highly designed "information objects" that are hard to take apart (such as Web sites created in Flash) to "straight" information (ASCII text files, feeds of RSS feeds, blog entries, SMS messages). As Richard MacManus and Joshua Porter argue,

> Enter Web 2.0, a vision of the Web in which information is broken up into "microcontent" units that can be distributed over dozens of domains. The Web of documents has morphed into a Web of data. We are no longer just looking to the same old sources for

information. Now we're looking to a new set of tools to aggregate and remix microcontent in new and useful ways.³

And it is much easier to "aggregate and remix microcontent" if it is not locked to a design. A straight ASCII file, JPEG, map, sound, or video file can move around the Web and enter into user-defined remixes such as a set of RSS feeds; a cultural object in which the parts are locked together (such as a Flash interface) cannot. In short, in the era of Web 2.0, "information wants to be ASCII."⁴

If we approach the present from the perspective of a potential future of "ultimate modularity/remixability," we see other incremental steps toward this future that are already occurring. For instance, Orange, an animation studio in Amsterdam, has established a team of artists and developers around the world that is collaborating on an animated short film; the studio plans to release all of their production files, 3D models, textures, and animation as Creative Commons open content on a extended edition DVD.⁵

Creative Commons offers a special set of sampling licenses that "let artists and authors invite other people to use a part of their work and make it new."⁶ Flickr offers multiple tools that combine multiple photos (not broken into parts—at least so far): tags, sets, groups, Organizr. The Flickr interface thus positions each photo within multiple "mixes." Flickr also offers "notes" that allow users to assign short notes to individual parts of a photograph. To add a note to a photo posted on Flickr, one draws a rectangle on any part of the photo and then attaches text to it. A number of notes can be attached to the same photo. I read this feature as another sign of the modularity/remixability mentality, as it encourages users to mentally dismantle a photo into separate parts. In other words, "notes" break a single media object—a photograph—into blocks.

In a similar fashion, the common interface of DVDs divides a film into chapters. Media players such as iPod and online media stores such as iTunes break music CDs into separate tracks, making a track into a new basic unit of musical culture. In all these examples, what was previously a single coherent cultural object is broken into separate blocks that can be accessed individually. In other words, if "information wants to be ASCII," content wants to be granular. And culture as a whole? Culture has always been about remixability, but now this remixability is available to all participants in the Internet culture.

Since the introduction of the first Kodak camera, users have had tools to create massive amounts of vernacular media. Later they were given amateur movie cameras, tape recorders, video recorders, and so on. But the fact that ordinary people have had access to tools of media production for as long as professional media creators have did not seem to play a big role until recently; the media pools of the amateur and those of the professional did not mix. Professional photographs traveled between the photographer's darkroom and the newspaper editor; private pictures of a wedding circulated between members of the family. But the emergence of multiple and interlinked paths that encourage media objects to easily travel between Web sites, recording and display devices, hard drives, and people has changed things. Remixability has become practically a built-in feature of the digital networked media universe. In a nutshell, what is perhaps more important than the introduction of a video iPod, a consumer HD camera, Flickr, or yet another exciting new device or service is how easy it is for media objects to travel between all these devices and services—which now all become just temporary stations in media's Brownian motion.

II.

While the topics of remixability and modularity are connected, it is important to note that modularity is something that does not apply only to RSS, social bookmarking, or Web services. We are talking about the logic that extends beyond Web and digital culture.

Modularity has been the key principle of modern mass production. Mass production is possible because of the standardization of parts and how they fit with each other—that is, modularity. Although there are precedents for mass production, until the twentieth century they remained separate historical cases. But soon after Ford installed the first moving assembly lines in his factory in 1913, others followed, and soon modularity permeated most areas of modern society.[7] Most products we use are mass-produced, which means they are modular, that is, they consist of standardized mass-produced parts that fit together in a standardized way. Modernism also applied the modular principle outside the factory. For instance, as far back as 1932—long before IKEA and Lego sets—the Belgian designer Louis Herman De Kornick developed the first modular furniture suitable for the smaller council flats[8] being built at the time.

Today we still live in an era of mass production and mass modularity, and globalization and outsourcing only strengthen this logic. One commonly evoked characteristic of globalization is greater connectivity. Places, systems, countries, organizations, and so on are becoming connected in ever more numerous ways. Although there are ways to connect things and processes without standardizing and modularizing them (and the further development of such mechanisms is probably essential if we ever want to move beyond the grim consequences of living in a standardized modular world produced by the twentieth century), for now it is much easier just to go ahead and apply twentieth-century logic. Because society is so used to it, it is not even thought of as one option among others.

In the fall of 2005 I attended a Design Brussels event where the designer Jerszy Seymour speculated that once rapid manufacturing systems become advanced, cheap, and easy, designers in Europe will have a chance for survival. Today, as soon as some design becomes successful, a company wants to produce it in large quantities—and its production goes to China. Seymour suggested that when rapid manufacturing and similar technologies are installed locally, the designers will become their own manufacturers and everything will happen in one place. But obviously this will not occur tomorrow, and it is also not at all certain that rapid manufacturing will ever be able to produce complete, finished objects without humans involved in the process, whether in assembly, finishing, or quality control.

Of course, the modularity principle has not remained unaltered since the beginning of mass production a hundred years ago. Think of just-in-time manufacturing, just-in-time programming, or the use of standardized containers for shipment around the world since the 1960s (over 90% of all goods in the world today are shipped in these containers). The logic of modularity seems to permeate more layers of society than ever before, and computers—which are great for keeping track of numerous parts and coordinating their movements—only help this process.

The logic of culture often runs behind changes in the economy. Thus, while modularity has been the basis of modern industrial society since the early twentieth century, we have only begun in the last few decades to see the modularity principle on a large scale in cultural production and distribution. Although Adorno and Horkheimer wrote about the "culture industry" back in the 1940s, it was not then—and it is not today—a truly modern industry.[9] In some areas, such as the production of Hollywood animated features or computer games, we see more of the factory logic at work with the extensive division of labor. In the case of software engineering (that is, programming), software is put together to a large extent from already available software modules; but this is done by individual programmers or teams who often spend months or years on one project—a situation quite different from the Ford production line that assembled one identical car after another. In short, cultural modularity today has not reached the systematic character of industrial standardization circa 1913.

But this does not mean that modularity in contemporary culture simply lags behind the industrial modularity that is responsible for mass production. Rather, cultural modularity seems to be governed by a different logic than industrial modularity. On the one hand, "mass culture" is made possible by a complete industrial-type modularity on the levels of packaging and distribution. In other words, all the material carriers of cultural content in the modern period have been standardized, like the production of all goods—from the first photo and film formats at the end of the nineteenth century to game cartridges, DVDs, memory cards, interchangeable camera lenses, and so on. But the actual making of content was never standardized in the same way.[10] So while mass culture involves putting together new products—films, television programs, songs, games—from a limited repertoire of themes, narratives, and icons using a limited number of conventions, this is done by teams of human authors on an individual basis. And while more recently we have seen a trend toward the reuse of cultural assets in commercial culture—that is, media franchising (characters, settings, icons that appear not in one but a whole range of cultural products—film sequels, computer games, theme parks, toys, and so on), this does not seem to change the basic "pre-industrial" logic of the production process. For Adorno, the individual character of each product is part of the ideology of mass culture: "Each product affects an individual air; individuality itself serves to reinforce ideology, in so far as the illusion is conjured up that the completely reified and mediated is a sanctuary from immediacy and life."[11]

On the other hand, what seems to be happening is that the users themselves have been gradually "modularizing" culture. In other words, modularity enters into modern culture from the outside, so to speak, rather than being built-in, as in industrial production. In the 1980s musicians began to sample music that had already been published; TV fans started sampling their favorite TV series in order to produce their own "slasher films"; game fans started creating new game levels and other kinds of game modifications. And of course, from the very beginning of mass culture in the early twentieth century, artists have sampled and remixed mass cultural products; think of Kurt Schwitters, collage, and in particular the photomontage practice that became popular right after the First World War among artists in Russia and Germany. This continued with pop art, appropriation art, and video art.

Enter the computer. In *The Language of New Media*[12] I named modularity as one of the principles of computerized media. If the modularity principle was previously applied to the packaging of cultural goods and raw media (photo stock, blank videotapes, and so on), now computerization modularizes culture on a structural level. Images are broken into pixels; graphic designs, film, and video are broken into layers. Hypertext modularizes text. Markup languages such as HTML and media formats such as QuickTime and MPEG-7 modularize multimedia documents in general.

In short: culture has already been modular for a long time. But at the same time, it has never been modular. In my view, this is unquestionably a good thing.

Notes

[1] "Approaching a definition of Web 2.0," *The Social Software Weblog*, http://socialsoftware.weblogsinc.com/search/?q=%22approaching+a+definition+of+web+2.0%22 (accessed 25 Jan. 2009).

[2] Ulf Poshardt, *DJ Culture*, trans. Shaun Whiteside (London: Quartet Books, 1998), 123.

[3] "Web 2.0 Design: Bootstrapping the Social Web," *Digital Web Magazine*, http://www.digital-web.com/types/web_2_design/ (accessed 25 Jan. 2009).

[4] The modern information environment is characterized by a constant tension between the desire to "package" information (a Flash design, for instance) and the desire to strip it of all packaging so that it can travel more easily between different media and sites.

[5] http://orange.blender.org (accessed 25 Jan. 2009).

[6] http://creativecommons.org/about/sampling (accessed 25 Jan. 2009).

[7] "An assembly line is a manufacturing process in which parts (usually interchangeable parts) are added to a product in a sequential manner using optimally planned logistics to create a finished product," http://en.wikipedia.org/wiki/Assembly_line (accessed 25 Jan. 2009).

[8] Council flats are low-cost rental apartments for low-income families, provided by the British authorities.

[9] Theodor W. Adorno and Max Horkheimer, "The Culture Industry: Enlightenment as Mass Deception," in *Dialectic of Enlightenment: Philosophical Fragments*, ed. Gunzelin Schmid Noerr, trans. Edmund Jephcott (Stanford, CA: Stanford UP, 2002), 94–136.

[10] Adorno writes: "The expression 'industry' is not to be taken too literally. It refers to the standardization of the thing itself—such as that of the Western, familiar to every movie-goer—and to the rationalization of distribution techniques, but not strictly to the production process . . . it [culture industry] is industrial more in a sociological sense, in the incorporation of industrial forms of organization even when nothing is manufactured—as in the rationalization of office work—rather than in the sense of anything really and actually produced by technological rationality." Theodor W. Adorno, "Culture Industry Reconsidered," *New German Critique* 6 (Fall 1975): 12–19.

[11] Adorno, "Culture Industry Reconsidered," 12–19.

[12] Lev Manovich, *The Language of New Media* (Cambridge, MA: MIT Press, 2001).

4: New Media Aesthetics

Carsten Strathausen

I.

THE DECEPTIVELY MODEST GOAL OF THIS ESSAY is to give substance to its title. What does the aesthetics of new media look like? Is there just one or are there many? And why should we care? These questions are difficult to answer not least because of the vagueness of the terms employed. Besides "new media," scholars also refer to "digital media," "multi-media," "emergent media," and so on.[1] Although "new media" is by far the most popular and frequently used among them, its meaning still remains nebulous. Indeed, one of the most persistent issues in new-media studies over the last decade has been the effort to define what exactly we mean by "new media." "New" is a relative term, of course. Five hundred years ago, the printed book was a decisively new medium, as were photography and film in the nineteenth century. Likewise, video and television art of the 1960s were (and still are) considered "new media" both in the art market and in art history departments. This led to a serious terminological confusion even among experts once the existence of digital media had to be taken into account.[2] Symptomatic of the confusion is Lev Manovich's elaboration of as many as eight different definitions of new media—"more can be invented if desired," of course.[3]

A different picture emerges once we turn toward the other major term in use today, namely "digital media." Contrary to "new," the adjective "digital" is absolute and not relative. It refers to the structural organization of a particular technology regardless of its historical emergence and use. This is not to deny that the digital mode of communication predates electronic media in general and the computer in particular. There are a vast number of ancient communication systems that qualify as digital, such as writing and musical notation, both of which translate a polymorphous smear of sound (that is, spoken or sung sounds) into a set of distinct and limited elements (be it the twenty-six letters we call the alphabet or our twelve-tone musical scale). Digital systems of communication have been around for a long time. Nonetheless, "digital" remains a technical term with a clear-cut definition. It differs from "analogue" in that the latter sends a signal that remains proportional (or analogous) to the message it transports, whereas the former does not. Analogue media (such as the gramophone or traditional photography) both register and adapt to the spatial and temporal specificity of their forwarded message. In contrast, the digital signal dissects the same message into a limited number of discrete and codified elements that bear no intrinsic relationship to the original message and thus disregard its physical particularities altogether. With this distinction in mind, we might say that "new media" discourse situates itself within a historical process and is thus "continuous" in the mathematical sense of the term, whereas any discourse oriented along the lines of "digital studies" implicitly posits a discontinuous history by emphasizing the radical newness of computer technology. "Digital studies," in other words, insinuates a logic of discrete states of being that does not allow for any grey zones in between. The hype about virtual reality (VR) during the 1990s was exemplary in this regard. We were told that everything already had been or soon would be left behind through digital technology, not only the human body and our traditional notion of materiality (Hans Moravec, Ray Kurzweil), but also reality and the real itself (Jean Baudrillard).[4]

Much of this rhetoric quieted down after the Y2K bug turned out to be as much of a chimera as the "digital revolution" had been before it. The burst of the dot.com bubble in 2001 led most critics to exchange their erstwhile revolutionary vocabulary for a more historically nuanced one. Unfortunately, however, the pendulum swung back all too quickly from one extreme ("we are living in a radically new age") to the other ("there is nothing new going on at all"). Virtually every critic today repeats the truism that "new" media imply the existence of "old" media, meaning that nothing is new forever, nor has it ever been, strictly speaking, absolutely "new" to begin with. Instead, everything occupies a shifting place on a chronological scale of historical contingency that informs both its manifest "birth" and its potential "future." This constitutive intertwinement of new and old media is what Bolter and Grusin have termed remediation, and nothing, they claim, exists prior to it: "All mediation remediates the real."[5]

For example, the computer's GUI is dominated by traditional metaphors related to books (Web *pages*), pictures *(icons)* and architecture *(windows)*, all of which serve to familiarize us with a new technology whose real operational mechanism (that is, code) usually remains hidden and out of sight. Indeed, Lev Manovich develops *The Language of New Media* explicitly with reference to the history and language of film and the avant-garde.[6] For Manovich, computers are not primarily catalysts for new forms but mainly strengthen already existing ones: "In short," he claims, "the avant-garde vision became materialized in a computer."[7] Thus what Bolter and Grusin call remediation, Manovich calls remapping: "Software renders it possible to remap old media objects into new structures, that is, to transform media into what I call meta-media."[8] Friedrich Kittler agrees: "New media do not make old media obsolete: they assign them other places in the system."[9] This means that the content of one medium is always just another medium, that "the medium is the message," as Marshall McLuhan famously put it. Most new-media critics thus tend to focus on the similarities and continuities leading from the old to the new, from Italian frescos to VR environments, from the development of the Morse code to that of the digital.[10] "The impact of new media . . . is evolutionary, not revolutionary," as David Thorburn and Henry Jenkins succinctly summarize their central premise.[11] Given this strong historical orientation to contemporary discourse on new media, the vast majority of publications can be subsumed under the prominent subfield "media archaeology," a term first used by Erkki Huhtamo and Siegfried Zielinski during the 1990s. Huhtamo understands "media archaeology" as the scholarly effort to situate contemporary media practice within the vast field of its historical predecessors. As early as 1996, he warned against the "mythologization of interactivity" by pointing out that "interactive technology provides no more than a frame of opportunities which is always filled by specific applications and ideological ideas."[12] The overall goal, according to Huhtamo, is for media archaeology to "find a wider and more multifaceted social and cultural frame of reference" that moves beyond the immediate present.[13]

Although Zielinski pursues a parallel approach with similar objectives, his methodology is more refined than Huhtamo's. Zielinski considers the central goal of media archaeology the effort to decentralize: "I try not to homogenize or universalize the historic development of the media," Zielinski wrote in 1996. Instead he seeks to appreciate "the previous technical and aesthetic and theoretical richness of the development of artifacts of media development."[14] In his more recent *Deep Time of the Media*, Zielinski reiterates that media archaeology does *not* seek to establish a new master trope for defining new media. Nor does it seek to find the one technological invention whose rediscovery will require a complete rewriting of media history. On the contrary, Zielinski insists that such master tropes or killer inventions do not exist. It follows that "notions of continuous progress from lower to higher, from simple to complex, must be abandoned, together with the images, metaphors, and iconography that have been—and still are—used to describe progress."[15] Instead, we need to investigate the vast number of disparate inventions, theories, and practices that constitute the (contingent, contradictory, convoluted) history of the media. Once this happens, Zielinski predicts, media archaeology will lead to a "body of individual anarchaeological studies [that] should form a *variantology* of the media" (*DTM*, 7).

Zielinski thus reverses the critical trajectory of Bolter and Grusin's study on remediation. The goal of media archaeology is precisely not to "seek the old in the new, but [to] find something new in the old" (*DTM*, 3). Zielinski's emphasis on historical discontinuity and media incompatibility also puts him at odds with Manovich's central claim that new media are meta-media because they use old media as their primary material. While Manovich focuses on the ways in which digital "culture is now busy re-working, recombining and analyzing the already accumulated media material,"[16] Zielinski, by contrast, seeks to "uncover dynamic moments in the media-archaeological record that abound and revel in heterogeneity" (*DTM*, 11). Manovich relies on the history and aesthetics of cinema to come to terms with that of the computer, whereas Zielinski deliberately bypasses established media history in the hope of discovering old theories and practices whose decisive feature is to have as little as possible in common with today's digital culture. His goal is not to build a bridge between the old and the new but to emphasize the historical and epistemological abyss that separates them. As Thomas Elsaesser puts it, "A media archaeologist would therefore notice above all what is missing or has been suppressed and left out in our genealogical chart."[17]

We might want to call Manovich's approach a genealogical account of new media and Zielinski's a properly archaeological one. Both methodologies have their strengths and weaknesses, of course. Genealogists like Kittler and Manovich have been accused of streamlining the past and thus limiting the inherent possibilities of new media aesthetics.[18] However, a rigorously pursued archaeological approach in new media studies faces the opposite danger of getting lost in the abundance of historical detail. Its major challenge remains to situate the disparate pieces it finds within a coherent analytical framework useful for us today.[19] Although Zielinski certainly ranks among the most accomplished media theorists today, he too struggles with this problem. He repeatedly assures his readers that he has "by no means made a random selection" in his efforts to dig out forgotten theories, objects, and practices in media history. Instead, he chose to include in his study only that which "has had enduring, rather than ephemeral, effects" (*DTM*, 36).

If this is true, however, then the central ambition of media archaeology, namely to access the various "curiosities" of media history without an immediate concern for how they contribute to our present condition, becomes questionable. We all know from personal experience that we need to know what to look for in order to find it. Google or any other digital search engine is utterly worthless to those unable to categorize the object of their inquiry. Our various cultural archives only collect what they deem relevant for a particular period within a given set of parameters. To look for something outside any and all parameters is impossible. Zielinski faces the same problem: he attempts to find medial leftovers in the dustbin of history (that is, those theories, objects, and practices that our culture has hitherto considered irrelevant or worthless), while at the same time he tries to establish their cultural relevance for us today. The first step of the process requires media archaeologists to abandon the very methodology of linear progress and "re-mediation" they are subsequently forced to embrace in a second step.

Zielinski himself recognizes the dilemma and proposes to let his archaeological gaze fall where it may, unrestrained by and free from the "power" of traditional modes of classification:

> The paradox that arises when engaged in this work [of media archaeology] is that one is dependent upon the instruments of cultural techniques for ordering and classifying, while, at the same time, one's goal is to respect diversity and specialness. The only resolution of this dilemma is to reject the notion that this work is groundbreaking, seminal: to renounce power, which one could easily grasp, is much more difficult than to attain a position where it is possible to wield it. (*DTM*, 27)

Zielinski's achievements notwithstanding, his solution "to renounce power" strikes me as the worst possible one—not only because it is literally impossible, but also because wielding power wisely is about the most difficult thing imaginable. The effort to grasp power constructively constitutes the primary challenge for scholarly discourse, and if Zielinski were to live up to his own advice, his investigation of what he calls "a collection of curiosities" would fall prey to the postmodern chaos of mere particulars.

To avoid this fate, media archaeology needs to generate some kind of universal principle or general objective able to both guide its investigative process and guarantee the relevance of its findings. The archaeological emphasis on "searching" and "surprises" (*DTM*, 27) must be accompanied by a second step of binding together the found material into a coherent collective of sorts. *Both* steps (of deterritorization and reterritorization, if you wish) are indispensable for a meaningful study of the media. Zielinski's effort to "maintain tension and movements within developing processes" (*DTM*, 258) is a necessary but ultimately insufficient step toward achieving this larger objective. For some important questions remain: What specific insights does this tension yield? What exactly do we learn from media archaeology and how does it change our relationship to the media? How does media archaeology help us improve our way of being in the world? (If it does not, why bother?)

These questions are, of course, political questions.[20] Like any other epistemological inquiry, media archaeology is political to the core, "a necessarily political enterprise," as Geoffrey Batchen puts it.[21] In his recent *Reassembling the Social*, Bruno Latour spells out this two-step approach with regard to contemporary social theory. The first step, he argues, is to account for all possible actors in the world, not just those that traditional sociology has been willing to recognize. That tally needs to be expanded, opened up to other participants and new influences. In terms of new media, this step calls precisely for the kind of media "variantology" Zielinski seeks to establish. Latour's second step, however, is to create a common world out of this heterogeneity, a world in which everybody can coexist peacefully and live a fulfilling life. Latour rightly emphasizes that this is a political task and not an academic-analytical one. Faced with the question: "What are the [political] *assemblies* of those [material] *assemblages?*" he calls upon the left to endorse a positive rather than a merely critical view of politics, one steeped in questions of (political) representation and (social) cooperation to achieve a common goal.[22]

Similarly, media archaeology cannot simply focus on expanding our critical understanding of historical media but must also demonstrate the productiveness of its findings for social theory and practice. Insofar as media archaeology calls for a genuine discovery of the old in order to reimagine the new, it must embrace rather than suspend the political dimension of its project. This means, however, that new media studies must recover some of its earlier enthusiasm about the emancipatory potential of new media—an enthusiasm that has been dismissed all too quickly as "naive" or "utopian" over the last decade. There was nothing "naive" at all about the way in which the 2008 Obama presidential campaign used the Internet to help raise the most money ever for a presidential candidate. Or the way in which it quickly released fact-checks and counter-statements on-line in order to combat Fox News allegations that Obama "palled around" with terrorists or supported legislation to enforce sex education for preschool children, and so on. Likewise, on-line communication and virtual communities are anything but fictional. They are real in the sense that they structure people's lives and influence their political views and social behavior.[23] We may all agree that the 1990s hype about the digital revolution was exaggerated and promised more than it could possibly achieve. But it was nonetheless based on what is utterly lacking today: an overall directive and purpose for why media studies matter. Media archaeology in its present form has no politics. To be sure, it destabilizes our contemporary assumptions about the "nature" of the media; it surprises us with new possibilities and forgotten practices; and it allows for innovative juxtapositions between the old and the new, the magical and the technical. But it neglects to tell us what exactly we hope to accomplish in political terms via these juxtapositions.

The reason for this lacuna in contemporary media archaeology, I believe, stems from its underlying epistemological framework, a strange mixture of Foucaultian discourse analysis and Marxist cultural studies. This mixture is strange not only because Foucault (much like Deleuze) always kept a sizable distance from Marxism, but also because both Foucault and Marxists focus on the analysis of power relations within society and thus implicitly contradict Zielinski's methodological effort "to renounce power." For Foucault, there is no outside of power. All resistance to power is just another effect of power itself. Huhtamo's and Zielinski's frequent references to Foucault's *The Archaeology of Knowledge* thus seem to rest on a lopsided interpretation of that particular text, for it appears as if Foucault had sought to establish the "autonomy" of discursive rules and epistemic ruptures considered apart from their material conditions or their influence on human agency—that is, considered apart from politics and the political.

The opposite is true: a strict opponent of structuralist thought, Foucault refused "to analyze scientific discourses in their succession without reference to something like a constituent activity," and he considered it impossible "to free the history of thought from all taint of subjectivity."[24] Instead he emphasized the productivity of power and the fact that discursive regulations "are not so much limitations imposed on the initiative of subjects as the field in which that initiative is articulated."[25] This emphasis on the active involvement of human agents is crucial for Foucault's project, because it alone guarantees the possibility of political change. Rather than renouncing power, media archaeology would profit from revisiting Foucault's own turn from archaeology to genealogy, from (what appeared to be) a disinterested analysis of epistemic rules and discursive networks to (what has always been) an analysis of the real power wielded by speaking and acting subjects in history. Even Foucault's final lectures at the Collège de France, "The Hermeneutics of the Subject," testify to his lasting interest in questions of human agency that have little in common with the scholarly search-and-rescue operation that characterizes much of contemporary media archaeology.[26]

The second epistemological influence that informs media archaeology—Marxist cultural studies—is more pronounced in genealogical as opposed to archaeological accounts of new media. The major reference point (in studies by Henry Jenkins, David Thorburn, and John T. Caldwell, for example[27]) is the work of Raymond Williams—a good choice, since Williams sought to liberate cultural developments from the simplistic economic determinism that governs traditional Marxism. Still, the problem remains that, generally speaking, a Marxist-inspired cultural critique (particularly in Adorno's or Jameson's variation) tends to be too suspicious of technological innovation to recognize the positive political potential of new media. The reason why "there is no neo-Marxist network theory that critically engages with new-media culture," as Geert Lovink rightly points out, lies in the failure of "the aging 1968 generation to grasp the Internet and take it serious[ly] as an object of theory."[28] Indeed, Hans Magnus Enzensberger lamented the lack of a leftist media theory as early as 1970, and neither his critique nor his utopianism has lost validity since then:

> The New Left of the sixties has reduced the development of the media to a single concept—that of manipulation.... The current theory of manipulation on the left is essentially defensive; its effects can lead the movement into defeatism.... A revolutionary plan should not require the manipulation to disappear; on the contrary, it must make everyone a manipulator.[29]

The new media require such manipulation; otherwise their progressive potential is squandered. New-media studies, whether in its genealogical or its archaeological garb, is called upon to determine the (political, cultural, social) goal of this manipulation and the way in which it can be achieved. In a word, it needs an aesthetics.

II.

This brings us to the second part of my title. Given the increasing influence of "new media" and computer-based art, a group of science-oriented critics has emerged who insist on a decisive rupture between analogue and digital media. As a consequence they juxtapose classical art and aesthetics with contemporary media theory and practice. The nascent aesthetics of new media is variously named "rational aesthetics" (Claudia Gianetti) or "info-aesthetics" as well as "post-media aesthetics" (Lev Manovich) or "techno-aesthetics" (Peter Weibel).[30] Peter Weibel, for example, associates classical aesthetics with a two-centuries-old tradition based on a "static concept of Being, which excludes or negates, *a priori*, the nature of media art, in particular that of the moving image—its dynamic, its immateriality and its temporality."[31] Likewise, Claudia Gianetti contrasts the "aesthetic model based on the Romantic and idealist tradition" with "a rational aesthetic" based on cybernetics and the history of science:

> The fundamentals of one aesthetics [connected to the new media] are anchored in rational methods. Here, the reflection about art is supposed to be based on scientific procedures in order to produce objective results. The other model is oriented toward the truth of art. Thus, it refuses to reduce aesthetic experience to causal or objective relations. Since this approach is based on subjective experience, it cannot be equated with the exact sciences.[32]

"Rational," "info-," or "techno-" aesthetics is thus informed by the history of science and engineering rather than that of philosophy and politics. Its heroes are Boscovich, Boole, Turing, and Bense instead of Aristotle, Kant, Hegel, or Adorno. For Weibel and Gianetti, the rift between these two traditions cannot and must not be bridged, because doing so would allow the old to assimilate the new without leaving a trace.

It is difficult to disagree with Weibel's basic idea that we are witnessing a radical change in our understanding and experience of art. An interactive video installation is simply *not* the same as a traditional or "autonomous" work of art. The latter calls for a critical intellectual response by an individual and disinterested spectator, whereas the former requires the spectators to engage with it and each other. Those visitors who lounged about in the Great Hall of the Tate Modern under the milky sun of Olafur Eliasson's *Weather Project* in 2003 would not have done so in the Louvre while studying the *Mona Lisa*. There is simply no space, both literally and figuratively, for such communal behavior in front of traditional images in the museum, meaning that new media art is slowly beginning to change the nature of the museum itself. "Exercising the integration of the spectator, or rather, the spectating act itself, as part of the museum's undertaking has shifted the weight from the thing experienced to the experience itself," Eliasson rightly claims.[33]

Along similar lines, the German photographer Thomas Struth, in his recent series "Museum Photographs," tries to incorporate the act of reception into the artwork itself. Struth's expressed goal in this series was to undo what he calls the "fetishization" of famous paintings: "I wanted to remind my audience that when these art works were made, they were not yet icons or museum pieces."[34] By making photographs that depict people looking at paintings, Struth aims to emphasize the process of reception as a key element of art. Thus the act of perceiving an artwork becomes part of the work itself. Clearly, the tension between stasis and mobility sustains Struth's photographs; it is the tension between the timelessness of classical painting and the spontaneity of modern photography, between being and becoming.

As these examples demonstrate, one can easily embrace Weibel's emphasis on art's essential mobility and flux without having to advocate scientific rationality as the sole or privileged way toward establishing a contemporary aesthetics. Although the history of modern science certainly has much to add to the Western philosophical tradition of thinking about time and experience, it neither can nor should replace that tradition. Insofar as rational aesthetics, in Giannetti's words, concentrates on "scientific procedures in order to produce objective results" about art,[35] it simply misses the crucial effect of much contemporary art, which is behavioral and not rational. We get a distorted picture of new media aesthetics if we concentrate too much on the technological aspects of media art at the expense of its phenomenological effects on the user. "The essence of technology is nothing technological," Martin Heidegger once remarked, and Gilles Deleuze similarly argues that "the machine is always social before it is technical."[36] What matters in digital imagery is not just its new ontological status of zero-dimensionality, as Kittler argues, but the epistemological and behavioral adjustments this new ontology demands from the viewer. And these adjustments are motoric and not just cognitive. They require action rather than contemplation. Lev Manovich captures this point perfectly when he states that "new media change our concept of what an image is—because they turn a viewer into an active user. As a result, an illusionistic image is no longer something a subject simply looks at.... The new media image is something the user actively *goes into*.... *New media turn most images into image-interfaces and image-instruments.*"[37]

I believe that this recognition of the increasing importance of the human body constitutes the point zero of new media (or digital) aesthetics.[38] After all, the word digital comes from the Latin "*digitus*," meaning fingers or toes—a reminder that our own limbs provided the very first digital tools available to us long before the computer was invented. This crucial dialectical exchange between body and technology is truncated by the self-declared "hardware-fanatic" Kittler,[39] whose "obvious technological determinism"[40] reduces the body to a passive receptacle programmed by the media: "One knows nothing about one's sense prior to the media providing models and metaphors," he states categorically.[41] I am critical of this view *not* because Kittler and Weibel emphasize the role of technology in contemporary culture—which is important and needs to be done—but because they do so at the expense of the entire Western aesthetic tradition. In other words, they ontologize the difference between the analogue and digital without giving due consideration to the phenomenological and epistemological effects of new technologies on our perceptual system that, after all, serves to bridge this difference. We need to learn not only how to write computer code, as Kittler continues to insist, but also how to deal with our affective response to the increasing speed of technological change. Once we do that, the focus of new media aesthetics no longer rests exclusively on technology alone but shifts to the relationship between computer hardware and human cognition as channeled through our perceptual system.

The renewed focus of new media aesthetics on the phenomenological body reminds us that there is no ontology separated from epistemology.[42] This is a constructionist argument, of course, but one that is crucial for new media aesthetics. Kittler's claim that digital data are real literally means nothing. For as long as such data remain locked away in the virtual space of the computer, it does not signify *for us*. However, as soon as we access this data, whether in the form of numbers, language, or images, we enter a particular ontological-epistemological system, one that has material effects and enables or restricts socio-political action. This is precisely what a Foucault-inspired media archeology must always remember: all technology, including the digital, is forced to operate within a particular order of knowledge that both limits and facilitates its effects. Of course, the digital is different from the analogue. But this difference does not signify or mean anything unless it becomes productive—unless it is *made* productive in and through human action. And since there is no metasystem, no meta-ontology above and beyond all others, it follows that this productivity is inevitably bound by the epistemological *a priori* and the ontological borders of the particular thought-system or medium you have chosen, be it mathematics or language or something else, because these systems are mutually exclusive. "The idea is that disparate systems of thought are not mutually expressible," as the philosopher of science Ian Hacking summarizes the issue:[43]

> We cannot reason as to whether alternative systems of reasoning are better or worse than ours, because the propositions to which we reason get their sense only from the method of reasoning employed. The propositions have no existence independent of the ways of reasoning towards them.[44]

In other words, there is no transcendental point of view, no position that remains completely unaffected by its object of study or the ontological-epistemological framework supporting it. "Truth is immanent, and there is no higher. We must speak from within a theory, albeit any of various," Willard van Orman Quine concludes.[45] This is precisely what cybernetics and systems theory have taught us as well: regardless of where exactly you draw the distinction (between culture and nature, between analogue and digital media), the crucial point is that you *cannot not* draw one, because no thought is all-comprehensive. But as soon as you have drawn a distinction, you have actively created the very reality you claim to passively observe or describe.

The same holds true for our analysis of technology and the media, neither of which is reducible to its scientific essence as imagined by Kittler and Gianetti. In this sense, new media aesthetics should be proud of not being "objective," in spite of the current trend toward a more "scientifically" oriented mode of aesthetic criticism. Instead, new media aesthetics should look sideways at what has been overlooked and languishes at the periphery of our visual field. Media archaeology can certainly help us find such forgotten objects and practices. Yet it remains the task of new media aesthetics to develop the proper ontological-epistemological (and thus political!) framework that emanates from these finds.

Notes

[1] For an excellent introduction to "new media," see Wendy Hui Kyong Chun, "Introduction: Did Somebody Say New Media?" in *New Media, Old Media: A History and Theory Reader*, ed. Wendy Hui Kyong Chun and Thomas Keenan (London: Routledge, 2006), 1–10.

[2] To wit, we should distinguish between at least three historico-technological dimensions that define "new media": the chemical and mechanical production of images in the nineteenth century (photography and film); the electromagnetic production and transference of images in the middle of the twentieth century (TV and video); and, finally, the coupling of electromagnetic technology with digital computation as it occurs in contemporary computers.

[3] Lev Manovich, "New Media from Borges to HTML," in *The New Media Reader*, ed. Noah Wardrip-Fruin and Nick Montfort (Cambridge, MA: MIT Press, 2003), 13–25, here 16.

[4] Hans Moravec, a professor of Robotics at Carnegie Mellon University, has argued over the last decade that by the year 2030 the processing power and memory capacity of computers will have increased sufficiently for them to match the intellectual performance of the human brain. See Hans Moravec, "Robot: Re-Evolving Mind," http://www.frc.ri.cmu.edu/~hpm/project.archive/robot.papers/2000/robot.evolution.html (accessed 25 Jan. 2009). Pushing the timeline back to the year 2050, the inventor Ray Kurzweil similarly contends that by that time machines will not only be more intelligent than humans but will have achieved a status of self-consciousness comparable to our own. Ray Kurzweil, *The Age of Spiritual Machines: When Computers Exceed Human Intelligence* (New York: Penguin, 2000). See also Jean Baudrillard, *The Perfect Crime*, trans. Chris Turner (New York: Verso, 1996).

[5] Jay David Bolter and Richard Grusin, *Remediation: Understanding New Media* (Cambridge, MA: MIT Press, 1999), 59.

[6] Lev Manovich, *The Language of New Media* (Cambridge, MA: MIT Press, 2001).

[7] Lev Manovich, "The Avant-Garde as Software," http://www.manovich.net/ (accessed 25 Jan. 2009).

[8] Lev Manovich, *Black Box, White Cube* (Berlin: Merve, 2002), 85; all translations are my own unless otherwise credited.

[9] Friedrich Kittler. "The History of Communication Media," www.hydra.umn.edu/kittler/comms.html (accessed 25 Jan. 2009).

[10] Timothy Druckrey insists that "virtual space inhabits the history of representation—and particularly the representation of perspective—right from the start," while Paul Willeman contends that "interactivity has always been a feature of any representational media." Timothy Druckrey, "Preface," in *New Screen Media: Cinema/Art/Narrative*, ed. Martin Rieser and Andrea Zapp (London: BFI, 2002), xxi–xxiv, here xxii; Paul Willeman, "Reflections on Digital Imagery: Of Mice and Men," in *New Screen Media*, 14–26, here 14. There are, indeed, countless monographs and anthologies that situate the new media in the context of ancient art and non-digital practices—too many to discuss in the context of this essay. Exemplary are Oliver Grau, *Virtual Art: From Illusion to Immersion*, trans. Gloria Custance (Cambridge, MA: MIT Press, 2003) and his more recent *MediaArtHistories* (Cambridge, MA: MIT Press, 2007). Others, like Rachel Greene in her *Internet Art* (New York: Thames & Hudson, 2004), explore contemporary computer-generated art works with reference to the invention of the telegraph, photography, the historical avant-garde, and pop and video art during the 1960s.

[11] David Thorburn and Henry Jenkins, "Introduction: The Digital Revolution, the Informed Citizen, and the Culture of Democracy," in *Democracy and New Media*, ed. David Thorburn and Henry Jenkins (Cambridge, MA: MIT Press, 2003), 1–20, here 5.

[12] Erkki Huhtamo, "Time Traveling in the Gallery: An Archeological Approach in Media Art," in *Immersed in Technology. Art and Virtual Environment*, ed. Mary Anne Moser (Cambridge, MA: MIT Press, 1996), 232–68, here 258.

[13] Erkki Huhtamo, "From Kaleidoscopomaniac to Cybernerd: Notes toward an Archaeology of the Media," in *Electronic Culture: Technology and Visual Representation*, ed. Timothy Druckrey (New York: Aperture, 1996), 296–303, here 302.

[14] Siegfried Zielinski, "Media Archaeology," *ctheory* (1996), http://www.ctheory.net/articles.aspx?id=42 (accessed 25 Jan. 2009), section 8.

[15] Siegfried Zielinski, *Deep Time of the Media: Toward an Archaeology of Hearing and Seeing by Technical Means*, trans. Gloria Custance (Cambridge, MA: MIT Press, 2006), 5. All subsequent references to this title appear in the body of the text using the abbreviation *DTM* and the page number.

[16] Lev Manovich, "The Avant-Garde as Software," 4.

[17] Thomas Elsaesser, "Early Film History and Multi-Media: An Archaeology of Possible Futures," in Chun and Keenan, *New Media, Old Media*, 13–25, here 18.

[18] For a well-balanced critique of Kittler's work, see Geoffrey Winthrop-Young and Michael Wutz, "Translator's Introduction," in Friedrich A. Kittler, *Gramophone, Film, Typewriter*, trans. Geoffrey Winthrop-Young and Michael Wutz (Stanford, CA: Stanford UP, 1999). With regard to Manovich, Mark B. N. Hansen claims that Manovich tends to "reduce new media to a mere amplification of what came before" (32). "Unable to think beyond the cinematic metaphor, [Manovich] can only reify the empirical state of new media today and thereby validate it as the ontology of new media per se" (34). This, in turn, severely limits the "possibilities for alternative aesthetic deployments of the digital" (36). Mark B. N. Hansen, *New Philosophy of New Media* (Cambridge, MA: MIT Press, 2004). A different yet related critique is voiced by Steve Dixon, who charges Manovich with over-emphasizing the formal, technological aspects of the new media at the expense of their specific aesthetic content. According to Dixon, Manovich's approach "encapsulates an indiscriminate techno-postmodern aesthetic theory of infinite (yet always-already recycled) possibilities and 'technology for technology's sake' that has tended to mar rather than advance critical understandings of the relationships between technology and art." Steve Dixon, *Digital Performance* (Cambridge, MA: MIT Press, 2007), 5.

[19] In his preface to the English translation of Zielinski's monograph, Timothy Druckrey warns that media archaeology must not succumb to "a form of material retrieval—as if the preservation of materiality was tantamount to preserving history itself" ("Foreword," viii). See also the short but incisive comments on media archaeology by Geoffrey Batchen, "Electricity Made Visible," in Chun and Keenan, *New Media, Old Media*, 27–44, here 44 n. 60.

[20] I use the term "political" here in Ernesto Laclau and Chantal Mouffe's sense as a "discursive space" charged with negotiating the "validity" of popular demands

within a given society. See Ernesto Laclau and Chantal Mouffe, *Hegemony and Radical Democracy* (London: Verso, 1984).

[21] Geoffrey Batchen, "Electricity Made Visible," 39.

[22] Bruno Latour, *Reassembling the Social: An Introduction to Actor Network-Theory* (Oxford: Oxford UP, 2005), 260.

[23] This is the central argument in Tom Boellstorff's excellent study *Coming to Age in Second Life: An Anthropologist Explores the Virtually Human* (Princeton: Princeton UP, 2008).

[24] Michel Foucault, *The Archaeology of Knowledge*, trans. A. M. Sheridan Smith (New York: Pantheon, 1972), 201.

[25] Foucault, *The Archaeology of Knowledge*, 209. Philipp Sarasin's commentary is to the point: "One thoroughly misunderstands the Foucault of the *Archaeology* if one sees him retreating to the analysis of 'autonomous' discourses which are then, on top of it, misunderstood as linguistic entities. At stake in the *Archaeology* is the attempt to uncover a special layer of rules that function as content-related classification patterns in order to generate recognizable things for the involved subjects and to structure their world—precisely within the frame of very material, and following Foucault's beliefs, non-discursive technical, institutional, and medial conditions, dependencies, and relations." Philipp Sarasin, *Michel Foucault zur Einführung* (Hamburg: Junius, 2005), 113; my translation.

[26] Michel Foucault, *The Hermeneutics of the Subject: Lectures at the Collège de France, 1981–1982* (New York: Picador, 2005).

[27] See David Thorburn and Henry Jenkins, "Introduction: The Digital Revolution, the Informed Citizen, and the Culture of Democracy," 1–20; John Thornton Caldwell, "Introduction: Theorizing the Digital Landrush," in *Electronic Media and Technoculture*, ed. John Thornton Caldwell (New Brunswick: Rutgers UP, 2000), 1–31.

[28] Geert Lovink, *My First Recession* (Rotterdam: V2_Nai, 2003), 13.

[29] Hans Magnus Enzensberger, "Constituents of a Theory of the Media," in Druckrey, *Electronic Culture*, 62–85, here 66, 68. The English translation was first published in 1970 in the *New Left Review* 64 (Nov./Dec. 1970).

[30] Cf. Claudia Gianetti, *Ästhetik des Digitalen: Ein intermediärer Beitrag zu Wissenschaft, Medien- und Kunstsystemen* (Vienna: Springer, 2004), 33; Peter Weibel, "Transformationen der Techno-Ästhetik," in *Gamma und Amplitude: Medien- und kunsttheoretische Schriften*, ed. Rolf Sachsse (Berlin: Philo & Philo Fine Arts, 2004), 13–64; Lev Manovich, "Info-Aesthetics," http://www.manovich.net/IA (accessed 25 Jan. 2009).

[31] Weibel, "Transformationen der Techno-Ästhetik," 14.

[32] Gianetti, *Ästhetik des Digitalen*, 33.

[33] Olafur Eliasson, "Seeing Yourself Seeing," in *Olafur Eliasson*, ed. Madeleine Grynsztejn, Daniel Birnbaum, and Michael Speaks (London: Phaidon, 2002), 127.

[34] Struth, qtd. in Phyllis Tuchmann, "On Thomas Struth's 'Museum Photographs,'" http://www.artnet.com/magazine/features/tuchman/tuchman7-8-03.asp (accessed 25 Jan. 2009).

[35] Giannetti, *Ästhetik des Digitalen*, 33.

[36] Martin Heidegger, "The Question Concerning Technology," in *The Question Concerning Technology and Other Essays*, trans. W. Lovitt (New York: Harper & Row, 1977), 4; Gilles Deleuze and Claire Parnet, *Dialogues*, trans. Hugh Tomlinson and Barbara Habberjam (New York: Columbia UP, 1987), 126. Another critic, Charlie Gere, puts it this way: "Digital refers not just to the effects and possibilities of a particular culture. It defines and encompasses the ways of thinking and doing that are embodied within that technology. . . ." Charlie Gere, *Digital Culture* (London: Reaction Books, 2002), 13.

[37] Manovich, *The Language of New Media*, 183.

[38] This is also the central argument of Mark B. N. Hansen's recent work, particularly in his *Bodies In Code: Interfaces with Digital Media* (London: Routledge, 2006). Likewise, Katherine Hayles has insisted on the crucial importance of embodiment in contemporary culture. See Katherine Hayles, *How we Became Posthuman: Virtual Bodies in Cybernetics, Literature, and Informatics* (Chicago: U of Chicago P, 1999).

[39] Cf. Kittler's remarks at http://www.literaturhaus-stuttgart.de/archiv/rueckschau65.htm (accessed 1 Apr. 2008).

[40] Winthrop-Young and Wutz, "Translator's Introduction," xxxiv.

[41] Friedrich Kittler, *Optische Medien: Berliner Vorlesung, 1999* (Berlin: Merve, 2002), 28; my translation.

[42] Bruno Latour, for example, refers to "the impossible distinction, contradicted every day, between ontological and epistemological questions." Bruno Latour, *Politics of Nature: How to Bring the Sciences into Democracy*, trans. Catherine Porter (Cambridge, MA: Harvard UP, 2004), 41.

[43] Ian Hacking, *Historical Ontology* (Cambridge, MA: Harvard UP, 2002), 169.

[44] Hacking, *Historical Ontology*, 175.

[45] Willard van Orman Quine, *Theories and Things* (Cambridge, MA: Harvard UP, 1981), 21–22.

Part 2: From Aura to Distraction

5: Aura, Virtuality, and the Simulacrum

Sabine Eckmann

I.

IMAGES CONCEIVED BY MEANS of digital technologies have become more widespread than those created by employing more conventional analogue technologies. These common electronic images are more often than not disregarded, seen as disembodied "Photoshop" reality without any remnants of immediate or authentic experience. Such images, it is frequently argued, instead attest to the digital condition in which simulation has replaced the world of phenomena.[1] According to this assessment, the virtual quality of these images abandons a crucial relationship to our physical environment and immerses the viewer in a world in which the distinctions between subject and object, time and space, and reality and fiction have completely disappeared. In a similar vein, digital images have been characterized as no longer images, as they are based on calculated algorithmic systems that are seen not only as an insufficient alternative to factual referents but also as producing renderings that are devoid of spatial qualities and essentially flat.

Such criticism voiced within the context of aesthetic theories is specifically targeted at representations that are considered within the frame of fine art, and it strongly suggests that digital imagery does not in principle satisfy notions and demands for the work of art, or, more precisely, is counter to dominant understandings of what art should be or do. While we may, for example, claim that abstract paintings are indexical of artistic subjectivity and figurative ones a mediation or reflection of the world in which we live, digitally conceived images, whether representative or abstract, if we take them literally, refer to not much more than a mathematical code that transcends linear time and actual space. Hence, according to the argument against digital art, the human gesture is ultimately broken and destroyed by the computer.[2] The alleged immateriality of the digital is conceived of as threatening the materiality of art and, consequently, its very existence. In this context, Paul Virilio called attention to an aesthetic of disappearance, denying digital images perceptions of aura in the sense of an original and unique experience.[3] However, Virilio also gave this a positive twist by underscoring the degree to which digital images increase our skepticism about the reality of the real as they emphasize its unreal qualities. According to Virilio, only through perceptions of the non-seen as created by digital technologies are we able to grasp the ontology of things, that is, their very capacity to disappear (338, 339).

Yet many critics do not share Virilio's concern about the unstable visibility of the real. On the contrary, the immateriality of the digital, embodied in the loss of "real" time and "real" space and in the fusion of reality and fiction, and its limitations, which allow for endless variability yet impede creative innovation, fundamentally necessitate artworks that not only consciously thematize these conditions, as Florian Rötzer argues, but also transform art's own qualities.[4] Under these circumstances, art, according to Rötzer, should rather bond with anti-fiction yet also satisfy new desires for auratic experiences and, in contrast to the theatrical world of digital culture, concentrate on itself, its very own qualities, rather than continue to embrace the spectacular that so much of contemporary art brings to visualization. Instead of delving into what Frieder Nake has called the new image-world of floating unrealism, Rötzer encourages artworks that, on the one hand, reflect on themselves in order to revitalize an autonomous aesthetic realm, and on the other hand, support documentary and anti-fictional impulses.

Peter Weibel, however, has argued that under what he terms the "post-media condition" various established art forms as well as new digital art and other visual media interpenetrate each other, dissolving as distinct manifestations rather than maintaining singular realms of creativity.[5] While attesting to the fact that digital images are synthetically created and based on numbers, he contends that more than anything else they provide "the look of the real" and constitute creations of a new reality. This hybrid ontological register consisting of reproductions and dematerialized fantasy imagery is manifested in the form of digital incarnations.[6] In this context, new qualities of the digital, such as its tactile dimension and its capacity for immersion through virtual environments, are highlighted. And for the engaged and most often active onlooker, this means that affect and experience take the place of contemplative, static, and fixed aesthetic perceptions. Weibel's concept of the aesthetic linkage of fantasy and the imaginary—illusion and fiction on the one hand, and the objective and calculated worlds of mathematical codes in the digital artwork on the other hand—calls not only for a more precise differentiation of the relation between fact and fiction, reality and illusion, the real and the virtual, but also for a consideration of how these dichotomies have generally played out in past non-digital aesthetic practices.

However, there is no history that examines digital art in relation to the legacy of the art that occupies a space in between the conventions of realist art and forms of abstraction, or documentary traditions and subjective expression. Given this lack of art historical inquiry, I would like to explore the meaning and use of the virtual as it currently exists and connect it to the art historical model of the simulacrum, as an alternative to the concept of original and copy. The virtual is often conceptualized as both dependent on and independent of experiential reality. However, it is, in its broadest sense, what in a variety of ways aesthetic practices embrace per se insofar as they imitate, idealize, criticize, and reflect upon experiences of the everyday. Accordingly, some critics do not distinguish the virtual as something that is solely indebted to digital art and contend, for example, "that the virtual imaginary has always been a fundamental part of European culture . . . ; it has repeatedly attempted to capture the aura of the unutterable."[7] The persistent and frequent use of the term "virtual" in the 1990s and at the turn of the millennium reflects, moreover, the extent to which computers and the Internet have influenced writing on art and visual culture, especially since the two fields have traditionally had little common terminology. Often the virtual may even refer to a variety of situations, sites, and places that are outside everyday experiences. Donald Preziosi, for example, calls the museum a virtual site.[8]

The Merriam-Webster dictionary defines the virtual image as "an image (as seen in a plane mirror) formed of points from which divergent rays (as of light) seem to emanate without actually doing so."[9] Virtual images, according to this definition, create illusions. This notion of the virtual encompasses what we traditionally understand much art to do. Denis Berthier's explication of the virtual in his *Méditations sur le réel et le virtuel* departs from it, however.[10] In this work he elaborates on the virtual, considering its electronic manifestations, and he summarizes it as that which is not real and material but which displays full qualities of the real. Like Weibel's definition of the virtual as electronic images that present us with the look of the real, Berthier's allows us to understand that new conceptions of the real may emanate from a virtual object. Such creations may be seen as compatible with experiential reality and tied to presence. Hence these traceless digital counterfeits, according to Norbert Bolz, accomplish both: they liberate us from reality and force us to reflect on the very nature of the real.[11] Bernhard Waldenfels, in contrast, has argued that virtual images create spheres of experience that belong to the domain of the "as if" world and thus neither abandon the realm of fiction nor augment the sphere of the real and material.[12]

Given these fuzzy relations of the virtual to fiction and illusion as well as to the real and material, we may preliminarily presume that digitally conceived artworks display qualities of imagination and simulation that may affect perceptions of the real. Yet we should not fail to remember that electronic artworks are also virtual insofar as they create images, construct installations, and generate environments that are, given the mathematical code on which they are based, the purest embodiments of fictions. This is also true for those works in which the observer experiences an artwork that simulates reality through immaterial means, as in Jeffrey Shaw's *Legible City* (1988–91). What is then genuine in virtual electronic images is that they allow for a range of instances of coexistence of fiction, illusion, and perceptions of the real. In contradistinction to the fictitious painted image on the one hand and analogue photography with its emanation of an indexical referent, as in the instance of Barthes's punctum, on the other, digital art is capable of simultaneously enabling multiple perceptions of fiction and fact, illusion and reality, immateriality and materiality.

However, this blurring of categories that articulate and negate experiential reality immediately prevents the formation of an analytic trajectory of virtuality from earlier visual incidents that have fashioned shifting associations between the artwork and the external world they mediate, between the aesthetic object and the spaces of experience to which they accord meaning and signification. Yet the relationship between the real and its copy has been a central concern in theoretical discourse about the nature of art ever since Plato. As the art historian Michael Camille has shown, this narrative track has repressed a conceptualization of the history of the simulacrum so as not to undermine the prevailing art historical concept embedded in the dichotomy of model and copy, original and reproduction, image and likeness. Yet the simulacrum as term and practice has progressively grown in significance since the 1960s, the decade that increasingly illuminated symptoms of the breakdown of the solidity of the real, not least through the increase of technological art forms such as photography and video, which had at that time only recently gained fine-art status.[13] According to Camille, the simulacrum in art is comprised of a false likeness that is actually built upon difference and dissimilarity. Such artwork commonly considers an anticipated subject position of the beholder and, through perceptual manipulation for example, creates a simulacrum that has the appearance of an original. Given this concept, Gilles Deleuze emphasized in 1990 that the simulacrum erases any distinction between model and copy, original and reproduction, as it is a copy for which no original exists or, alternatively, an original that foregoes reproduction.[14] Michel Foucault predicted as far back as 1977 that notions of resemblance, imitation, and faithfulness toward an original would increasingly become meaningless. In this vein both Deleuze and Félix Guattari conceptualize images as incarnations rather than imitations, as affects and materialities rather than reflections and copies.[15] For our investigation into the very nature of digital art, the simulacrum, I contend, opens up avenues for discussing the quality of digital images as a new chapter in a not-yet-written history of art, as it thematizes both false likeness and difference. Hence the notion of the "simulacrum" is an important supplement to the blurry and often all-encompassing concept of "virtual(ity)." Since the simulacrum allows us to theorize the creation of new realities that resemble those we commonly experience yet at the same time are not grounded in them, it frees us from the common relation between original and copy. Considering the growing discourse that articulates the unstable and constructed nature of the real, I propose that the concept of the simulacrum is an appropriate tool for examining the specificity of digital art and its relation to the dissolution of the dichotomy of the authentic and its reproduction, both of which have progressively lost meaning and relevance in the history of twentieth- and twenty-first-century art.

II.

In his essay "The Work of Art in the Age of Mechanical Reproduction" (1935–36), Walter Benjamin theorized the artwork in light of its condition of reproducibility and not only famously argued for its consequent loss of aura but also deemphasized the more traditional copy-original dichotomy. Concurrently he established, I contend, a new notion of the original that includes reproducibility in a variety of ways and complicates the concept of a simple copy. If any and every artwork can always be envisioned and accessed as reproduction, as Benjamin argues, then the value and quality of the original changes dramatically; namely, it loses its significance in relation to the status of the work of art. The original as such simply doesn't matter anymore. Of importance here is not only that the artwork's unique presence in time and space has been diminished, but also, according to Benjamin, that new art forms informed by reproducibility, such as photography and film, have the capability of triumphing over older forms of illusionism, as in realistic painting. When Benjamin's cameraman deeply penetrates his object in order to divide it into multiple and heterogeneous fragments, then he accomplishes both: on the one hand, he creates a higher degree of illusion than is possible for the painter-magician, as he breaks into his object rather than just copying it. On the other hand, because of the numerous fragmentations that are part of this process, the nature of this creation may also be theorized as a new original that is built upon false likeness. Or, put differently, he produces a simulacrum that may coexist in different times and spaces at once.[16] In order to visualize this in a figurative manner, we may, for example, picture images of body parts that are separated from their proper body and have a presence of their own. We may furthermore assert that the loss of organic coherence, along with the absence of such categories as copy and original, also involves radical changes that affect the reception of such works. If we trust Benjamin, these mechanical simulacra replace individualized and contemplative perceptions with collective and often distracted attention.

Simulacra that transcend original and copy consequentially also transform notions of aura, a concept that has regained discursive significance since the emergence of digital technology in the 1990s.[17] Benjamin has described aura in relation to the viewer's perception of the artwork as containing a mysterious and magical unapproachability that disintegrates once the work acquires commodity status in a nomadic exhibition context. More importantly, however, Benjamin recognizes that the very existence of analogue technologies of reproduction such as photography alter art's ontological homogeneity, that is, its factual and unique presence, and therefore its existence as original. As a consequence, any artwork can now be reanimated in many different situations, indefinitely shifting its appearance, meaning, and content in a variety of exhibition and publication contexts. Following this logic, the uniqueness of an artwork and its auratic effect decreases to the degree to which the artwork's potential and factual availability increases. The artwork's proper context, its permanent presence in the here and now, is, according to Benjamin, as much tied to the notion of aura as are historical concepts that embrace rather than eradicate individualized creativity and artistic authorship; in short, aura is closely connected with the idea of an artwork as an index of human subjectivity and art as the sphere of human freedom. Yet instead of the painter-magician who creates imaginary worlds that are unique, stable, and homogenous, the post-auratic artist provides aesthetic encounters that are interwoven with, yet also detached from, experiential reality. Manipulations, deformations, and inventions position these works in between fact and fiction, and original and copy, blurring these boundaries to such an extent that we might very well call these works simulacra. On the one hand, then, we may contend that the presence of such modern artworks is mediated and deferred, accounting for the impossibility of auratic experiences. On the other hand, Benjamin also insisted that an incredulity about the objectivity of the material world, which he saw at work in the medium of photography, is inherent in auratic works. Thus we have to consider the unique and factual existence of the auratic work while also taking into account its subjective and fictitious aesthetic qualities. Hence Benjamin's notion of aura is not incompatible with the concept of the simulacrum, since it too traverses between unique existence and fiction as well as factual world and illusion. Consequently, we might say that the qualities of digital art enable new auratic perceptions, as these works foreground false likeness that more often than not results in new creations that bear resemblances to the external world.

Theodor W. Adorno determined that the artwork's content, that which transcends the artwork and at the same time establishes its objective fixity, is its auratic quality. Like Benjamin, Adorno also mourned the decline of aura in the modernist artwork. According to Adorno, for the onlooker the moment of aura realizes itself in the act of identification with the artwork, which in the age of art's autonomy has become impossible, as artwork and external world are linked through a dialectics of negativity. Drawing upon Benjamin, and perceiving parallels to atmospheric qualities of nature, Adorno likened an auratic experience to the "breathing of aura" and to "beautiful semblance."[18] Accordingly, we are asked to understand an auratic experience as a non-mediated one that calls for the meeting of self-identical identities, meaning that neither the artwork nor the aesthetic experience refers to anything outside itself.[19] In this context, and as a condition for aura, critic Dieter Mersch underscores the significance of an experience with alterity, which is what endows such auratic encounters with existence. According to Mersch, technical media, from photography to moving images to digitization, by contrast contribute irrevocably to a representation of presence as deferred and mediated.[20] Mersch, like many others, contends that it is precisely the immaterial nature of digital products that prevents experiences with existence and, by extension, aura. Yet he also argues that contemporary artworks that draw upon event aesthetics, such as happenings, enable experiences with alterity and non-repeatable occurrences. These time-based artworks present us with new materializations of aura through encounters in real time. Whenever an active onlooker experiences herself and others in a performative aesthetic situation, she may understand this as a form in which aura becomes visible as subject and object encounter self and other in a unique situation. Yet these auratic experiences are, in contrast to Adorno's concept of the artwork, based on multiplicity and ever-new meanings as opposed to the self-sufficient object of art. Art in Mersch's sense is indebted to a process of becoming, as are perceptions of the external world.

However, the concept of the simulacrum opens up another space through which to re-envision aura: since the simulacrum abandons the dichotomy of original and copy, making a differentiation between technological and man-made artistic creations redundant, we must also understand it as non-reproducible. In this sense qualities of the digital are theoretically not unlike Adorno's notion of the self-identical character of art that carries traces of empirical reality. In addition then to artworks that are based in temporal situations and may enable aura through performative encounters between subject and object and among various subjects, we may also understand the simulacrum as a register of uniqueness that may enhance moments of aura—that is, experiences with existence and otherness. Many visual artists have, since Benjamin's elaborations, assimilated his notion of aura to such a degree as to alter the ontology and the content of artworks, bringing about new forms of perception that embrace moments that hark back to aesthetic experiences of aura, though through means of theatrical staging. With minimalist installations in the 1960s, artists such as Donald Judd, Dan Flavin, and Robert Morris created "open structures" (to use Umberto Eco's terminology) to contest the reproducible object character of the artwork by insisting on perceptual modes that take place in a specific space and call for a certain time span of engagement. The completed work of art as entity in itself is transmuted into a contingent structure that achieves its constitution as artwork only through the active yet transitory perception of an individual observer, somewhat akin to Benjamin's analysis of the perception of architecture. Benjamin analyzed the perceptual experience with architecture as one that is both tactile and optical and calls for a distracted observer. This means that the encounter with an architectural site is not so much driven by the intention to engage with a particular aesthetic object whose significance and content ask for deciphering; on the contrary, the aesthetic experience is one in which neither object nor subject is constituted through a fixed frame but is established through unfocused movements and distracted experiences. Minimalist structures, although in their prefabricated and serial existence reflexive of technological processes of industrial production, are brought into being as artworks through these unspecified and performative encounters many times and by many different viewers without ever existing as the same artwork, so that over and over again they acquire new meaning and furnish distinct aesthetic experiences that are unique and thus revitalize the notion of aura.

Moreover, critics such as Nicolas Bourriaud have recently argued with respect to Benjamin's concept of aura that aesthetic experiences in such environments, yet also in events by artists like Rikrit Tiravanija, produce situations of interpellation in order to create unfettered forms of the social. The environments in which events like cooking and eating take place are distinguished by a lack of conventional aesthetic coherence, resembling everyday situations rather than artistic forms. They constitute themselves as artworks through the time span of the moment in which the observers together experience their surroundings and each other. This unpredictable event forms a moment of lived and authentic time—that is, according to Bourriaud, aura. Benjamin (and maybe even more so Adorno) would most likely object to the fact that, in both minimalism and recent performative environments, the artwork itself lacks any permanence, fixity, and unique existence, as it can be constituted only fleetingly. Moreover, the mode of intersubjective and distracted perception, as it applies to such projects as Tiravanija's, is seen by Benjamin as the enlightening potential of technological art forms in contrast to those that employ or rely on the arbitrariness of the everyday. Yet we should not forget that theorists such as Mersch have associated the existence and perception of aura with artworks that are freed from technological means, like the ones created by Tiravanija, asserting that the usage of electronic media forgoes aura.

By comparison, many of the new digital artworks more often than not resemble completed works of art rather than open structures, yet they still require an observer to actively and most often physically engage with them. One of the most prominent examples of such interactive digital art produced in the last decade is Jeffrey Shaw's *Legible City* (1988–91). For this work Shaw transformed the plan of three different cities—Amsterdam, Manhattan, and Karlsruhe—into a computerized projection that screens the actual buildings in these cities in the form of monumental letters and words. Nevertheless, as if Shaw distrusts language and logical content, his installation projects these textual architectures in the form of surreal visualities.[21] *Legible City* relies for its completion as artwork on a viewer turned user or player. The player in Shaw's work rides on a stationary interface bicycle to which a small computer screen is attached that simulates the user's position as she navigates the virtual city and its ground plan. With the handlebars and pedals, the user controls her speed and direction, while the computer projects her movements through the virtual terrain onto a large screen for other viewers to witness. Only through the movement of the user on the bike is it possible to experience the city; without it we can see only one static image. The Manhattan project (1989) uses eight different personal narratives about the city from which the player can choose, while the Amsterdam (1990) and Karlsruhe (1991) versions of *Legible City* only employ letters that are identical in scale and location to the actual buildings in these cities. These texts are largely taken from archival documents. In all three versions, the city appears as an actual structure, transformed into letters and words, that a user can explore on a bike, and also as an immaterial and virtual site. The user-generated images of words and sentences about the specific places resemble the original and the historical while at the same time undermining it through alterations that create a new order of real. In fact, Shaw asks us to newly consider the complex and ambiguous relations between the real and the simulated and to reflect on both phenomena as probable forms of visual representation. His city visualizations evoke an original yet are reworked to such an extent that they acquire independence from the historical sites. In short, they are simulacra built upon false likeness. The projections generated by the user-players are obviously also simulacra insofar as they are created in the realm of virtual projections. More importantly, as the movement of every user is necessarily distinctive, the projected images of the cities remain to a large extent exclusive, so that we can make a case here for the uniqueness of digital art and hence its auratic character.

III.

More recent artworks—performative environments and installations—also dwell on the concept of the simulacrum while either employing or mediating electronic media. In contrast to artworks that may be seen as thematizing a relation between original and copy, those by Olafur Eliasson and Michel Majerus, I want to argue, not only coalesce fact and fiction, materiality and illusion but also complicate notions of permanence and reproducibility, opening paths for the gestation of new auratic appearances and experiences. Like Shaw, both Eliasson and Majerus employ in their work elements—the virtual and the real, the simulated, and the historical and material—as distinct but also assimilated spheres in order to probe the new promise of aura through electronic media while also considering its impact on conventional techniques such as painting.

In the summer of 2005, artist Olafur Eliasson collaborated with architect David Adjaye on the installation *Your Black Horizon* (fig. 5.1) which, as part of the Venice Biennale, was located in Adjaye's temporary pavilion on the Isola San Lazarro. After traveling for about twenty minutes from the Biennale grounds to the island on a vaporetto, the visitor quickly entered a black pavilion devoid of windows and completely empty (fig. 5.2). The structure had a thin horizontal opening at eye-level on all four sides, so that the daylight of Venice could illuminate the darkened space. At least, so it seemed at first. However, since the colors of the light changed dramatically, the observer swiftly suspected some kind of technological manipulation to be at work. In fact, installed just below the horizontal gap were fiberglass optics that produced the colors and their fast-changing pace. It took thirteen minutes to watch the whole color spectrum before it repeated. On a text panel placed outside the pavilion the concept of the installation was revealed. Eliasson and his team recorded the light conditions and color intensities of Venice from sunrise to sunset. They then calibrated their findings electronically and condensed them to a thirteen-minute time span. The installation itself neither reveals the technological processes and materials involved nor lays open the hybrid and confusing perception of technological operation and fast-paced simulation on the one hand (the electronic light and color recreation that compress a day into thirteen minutes) and nature (the light of Venice) on the other. Additionally, as Eliasson has explained, the electronic color creates an after-image of the complementary color: "The notion of the after-images depends on what kind of retinal material you might carry with you, in your eye, and of course the retinal material is not just physiological, it's also our memory and what our brain puts into the eye that we project. An after-image, unlike taking in an image, is a projection. The concept that you are in fact constituting your surroundings by looking at it is something I found generous in the sense that the person looking is becoming the producer of her/his own surroundings."[22] Yet the individualized creation and perception of new surroundings, of the not-yet-seen, did not end there. Upon leaving the pavilion, the observer also perceived the factual light of Venice with heightened consciousness as something that was invisible before. The installation thus starts and ends with perceptions of and investigations into the phenomenology of nature, in this case the specific light and colors of Venice. Seen from an art-historical perspective, Eliasson surely could not have chosen a more contested and more myth-founding theme: many histories of Renaissance art still dwell more on artistic visualizations of the magical and mysterious light

Fig. 5.1. Olafur Eliasson, Your Black Horizon, *2005. Pavilion built by David Adjaye. Used with permission.*

Fig. 5.2. Olafur Eliasson, Your Black Horizon, *2005. Installation view at Thyssen Bornemisza Limited Edition Pavilion, 51st Venice Biennale, 2005. Photo: Cameraphoto Arte, Venezia / T-B A21.*

of Venice as explications for artistic accomplishment than on Renaissance rationality and scientific curiosity, which, as dialectical backdrop, establish Eliasson's fascination. Maybe more than anywhere else in the Western world, Venice and its light are perfectly suited for illustrating concepts of nature as fully penetrated by cultural constructions such as nature as mystery and, by implication, the artist as genius, both of which Eliasson challenges with *Your Black Horizon*.

The visitor's encounter with a black box, without even taking into consideration the artificial light and color rotations, already implicates the sphere of technological virtuality as experienced in the many black boxes that museums today use in order to display films, video art, and virtual realities. The observer, however, quickly loses her secure position as a technologically savvy art expert and is challenged instead, as with the Brechtian stage, to sort through the virtual and material, fiction and fact. However, slowly, and in contrast to Brechtian aesthetics, the electronic images take over the visitor's perception, drawing her into an intense sensory experience. Despite her knowledge about the technological apparatus, she does not succeed in rationalizing the experience but rather engages with perceptual challenges. In contrast to Eco's notion of the open artwork and contingent minimalist structures that allow the aesthetic subject to participate in the meaning and significance of artworks, Eliasson guides the process of aesthetic experience quite intentionally. After exiting the installation, the somewhat blinded visitor is taken hold of by nature. On the one hand, she is now involved in connecting to the natural light of Venice and its magical qualities, which are exposed as mere construction, much as the virtual simulacrum inside the black box also operates like a reflector. On the other hand, the dialogical entanglement of two registers, that of nature and that of the simulacrum, of actuality and of dissemblance, stimulate unique and, in that sense, auratic perceptions in relation to the light of Venice, first as the result of an after-image projected in the pavilion and then as an individualized perception of Venice outside. Eliasson's effort to deconstruct or maybe even de-mediate notions of nature unveils nature in order to allow individual and short-lived glances at its very existence. Yet both perceptions are materializations of the light of Venice. And both exist as independent creations, remaining separate from each other as opposed to a relation of original and copy. Rather, they are built upon difference and false likeness in such a way that they both thematize and complicate our notion of the phenomenon of the light of Venice. Eliasson puts into motion a guided process of enlightening and individualized perceptions that include moments of unique auratic experience. Drawing on both digital art and experiential reality, the installation illuminates nature as construct and at the same time does not close the door on the possibility of nature as nature. Furthermore, technology is more than a means to simulate nature; technology appears as an associate to nature, both of which enable and disable perceptual cognition and unique visual experiences.

IV.

Equally reflective of the condition of art-making in relation to advanced technology are the massive colorful surfaces and installations of the late Michel Majerus, which not only use digital imagery, like the early arcade video game *Space Invaders,* but also displace the aesthetics of popular virtual realities onto the fictional sphere of painting. Comparable to the surrealist meeting of an umbrella and a sewing machine on a dissecting table, in Majerus's artworks digital imagery encounters pop and mass culture as well as that which once counted as high art. Appropriately, Majerus's paintings always call attention to the changed status of art in the age of digital technologies, as in his *product* (2002), which assimilates digitized fonts with abstract gestural painting.

Recently Daniel Birnbaum observed:"Majerus mediates the way that digital methods of picture production seem to alter space, the very space of representation itself, producing a strange sense of emptiness and a visual dissonance."[23] Birnbaum compares, for example, the heterogeneous spatial fields of the wall installation *eye protection* (1999) to a computer screen and sees the visual logic of computer games at work in Majerus's *yet sometimes what is read successfully, stops us with its meaning, no. 2,* which consisted of various paintings and was installed in a cinema for the 1998 *Manifesta 2* in Luxembourg. Spatial ruptures, mismatched iconographies, empty backgrounds on which images or objects float, and the lack of any homogeneity and coherence are reason enough for Birnbaum to conclude that Majerus's art demonstrates the ontological status of painting under the condition of electronic media. Tilman Baumgärtel comes to a similar conclusion when he writes that "we might get a better understanding of the pictures of Majerus" if we consider them "as a form of painting that has also taken new digital design methods aboard without making a great to-do about it."[24] Although I do not object to this thesis, I am skeptical of considering Majerus's endeavors solely as a mediation if not transformation of digital aesthetics into the sphere of expanded painting; Majerus invested too much energy converting canvases into spatial and experiential objects. He employed, for example, layers of panels that intrude from the wall into the exhibition space; he installed canvases as massive objects in their own right; he combined canvases and floor objects into fully fledged installation pieces, all of which endow this new form of painting—complex and multilayered representations of time and space—with stability and presence, yet also with fleetingness and contingency. Not only do these artworks expand the frame of conventional painting in order to assert a spatial presence as materialities in their own right, but they also circumvent perceptual immersion due to their massive scale, which necessitates not only a multiplicity of viewing angles but also distinguishes them from the virtual images they depict. Furthermore, Majerus not only appropriated and transformed the iconography and aesthetic languages of electronic media but also persistently commented on and employed diverse painterly styles that, as incarnations of artistic invention, become meaningless and instead acquire the status of exchangeable image-worlds. His objects therefore demonstrate that he is investigating the condition of painting in the age of electronic media while also scrutinizing the state of electronic media in relation to the medium of painting, which, more than any other art form, is employed to foreground uniqueness and otherness. Majerus's twist on painting and the digital is evident in such canvas objects and assemblages as *donkey kong* (1996) and *it's cool man* (1998), in which Game Boy images and symbols struggle against the intrusion of abstract painting and vice versa. In such ways Majerus creates new worlds, in which electronic media and high art visualizations coexist in an experiential space that alienates both virtual and fictional domains in order to establish new manifestations of simulacra.

Monumental installations, such as *bring the next line up* (2000; fig. 5.3), measuring approximately 13 x 27 x 24 feet (410 x 900 x 764 cm), are not convincing as translations (or better, copies) of the computer screen into a three-dimensional space, nor can the use of diverse painterly styles, such as hard edge on the one hand and trompe l'oeil on the other, necessarily be seen as the mediated results of digitization. Tellingly, the installation itself is produced by using paint on the wall and digital printing. What is at stake is the fact that Majerus reworks both painting-turned-into-permanent-objects and the visualization strategies of digital media, playing them out against each other, yet also entangling them.

In *bring the next line up*, Majerus transforms the virtual and dematerialized world inside an electronic screen into a tangible object that resembles a platform, yet is also distinguished iconographically as interactive and part of the virtual world via free-floating phrases and words such as "bring the next line up," "forgot" and "just when I nearly had the answer." The viewer of the installation, although required to walk around it in order to read the text and apprehend its spatial dimensions, is not permitted to enter the installation on the platform. However, it is unclear whether Majerus wanted to signify that the virtual-turned-real shuts us off as individuals, exposing virtuality as immaterial, or that the virtual-turned-art calls for unapproachability and distance. Similarly, a large-scale die that formally seems to belong to the electronic device sits as an unrelated fragment on the right side of the installation, making us wonder if we should attribute this incoherence to the effects of virtual image-worlds or see the displaced die as symbolizing creative freedom within contemporary art practices and reclaiming the authorial artist. On the one hand,

Fig. 5.3. Michel Majerus, bring the next line up, *2000. © Estate Michel Majerus, 2000, Courtesy neugerriemschneider, Berlin. Installation View: Taipei Biennale, 2000.*

Majerus turned the user-friendly computer screen, with its potential for experiencing new visual worlds, into a monumental art object that asserts objecthood. On the other hand, the artwork also refuses to do what we usually expect modern painting to do: expose the materialities of paint and carefully conceived color compositions as indices of artistic subjectivity, creativity, and skill. We may even want to understand Majerus's text, "just when I nearly had the answer," as commenting on the challenges posed by the creative process.

The other elements of the installation—the frame of a screen and the screen itself—are formally also heterogeneous, mixing characteristics that are specific to the medium of painting with those used in the realm of digitization. Both penetrate experiential reality as a location for the visualization of such collisions. Along with Clement Greenberg we may claim them as impurities that are stretched to their very limits in order to eventually generate a new form. For example, the frame and the screen are separated from each other by an enormous spatial distance measuring twenty-seven feet, as if the depth effects of perspectival painting had turned material. The trompe l'oeil rendition of a hand with a pointed index finger, however, translates into painting the visual strategies of electronic games in which objects appear to intrude into the space of the viewer rather than descending into the background, as with illusionistic painting conventions.

It doesn't matter, as Majerus himself once pointed out, if he paints the walls or canvases himself or employs digital technologies.[25] By displacing and mixing conflicting methods of image-making, by engaging the parameters of fact (the three-dimensional space that his installations inhabit), illusion (the iconography of popular virtual worlds and their representation), and fiction (the painterly interpretation of these image-worlds by the artist), Majerus's artworks can as much be conceptualized as a new and different genre, with the artist in the role of creative competitor, as they can be comprehended—considering the trajectory of painting in the twentieth century—as a climax of non-form. Yet it is more than obvious that this hybridization of various image-making strategies, which embrace and dislocate the design of electronic media into the materiality of space, connect visual worlds that, seen together, nevertheless scrutinize what we commonly call the real. This critical engagement produces another order of reality in which fact and fiction, the material and immaterial, time and space, exist together. Hence *bring the next line up* looks like some kind of copy of a virtual game, yet its deviation from any precise form of imitation registers it as image without any resemblance. Like the simulacrum, Majerus's installation makes the distinction between original and copy superfluous and even uninteresting. On the contrary, what sparks our fascination with the installation is an aesthetic experience that is built upon false likeness, bringing about new and unique perceptions (as with aura) that mediate the effects of a digitized world.

In order to specifically thematize this specific form of the simulacrum, Majerus often included textual references that comment on the implications of digital culture on the creative process. For example, *if we are dead so it is* (2000; fig. 5.4), his skateboard rink object that measures 9 x 30 x 138 feet (3 x 10 x 46 m), demonstrates this compellingly. Majerus warns the user as she enters the rink that engaging with the field of mathematics means to risk getting erased as an "I." The installation, however, not only cautioned about possible fatal effects of digital media on subjectivity but also criticized the authorial artist with the line "fuck the intention of the artist," while concurrently indicting the functioning of the American art market as one focused on the individual and unique artwork. This work is similar to most of Majerus's other works in its aesthetic strategy of involving simultaneously the painterly manipulation of digital imagery and the digitization of everyday objects; both are realized within a massive spatial field that the visitor may enter in order to encounter dissimilar registers of the visual and textual. Unlike minimalist installations, the large scale of *if we are dead so it is* blurs the boundaries between art and the everyday. Rather than enhancing contingent and individualized perceptual experiences this work may be seen to materialize Bourriaud's concept of aura in his theory of relational aesthetics: Majerus's manifestation of the everyday—the skateboard rink—underemphasizes aesthetic structures,

Fig. 5.4. Michel Majerus, if we are dead, so it is, *2000. © Estate Michel Majerus, 2000, Courtesy neugerriemschneider, Berlin. © 2009 Artists Rights Society (ARS), New York / VG Bild-Kunst, Bonn. Installations View: Michel Majerus, Kölnischer Kunstverein, Cologne, 2000.*

thereby strongly enabling, motivating, and creating a space for new social relations. "The aura of art," according to Bourriaud, "no longer lies in the hinter-world represented by the artwork, nor in form itself, but in front of it, within the temporary collective form that it produces by being put on show."[26] While *bring the next line up* explores the potential of auratic and unique perceptions via its emphasis on new visual hybridizations that challenge experiential reality with new concepts of existence, the banal object of *if we are dead so it is* probes aura as a temporary production of social interaction and inter-subjective experience.

Needless to say, neither Majerus nor Eliasson attempts to reestablish or restore aura in an unreflected, homogeneous, or unified manner. They have in common very experimental, diverse, and unique deployments of digital technology that penetrate experiential reality, and practice art in such a way that virtual worlds, individualistic art-making, and subjective and collective perception coexist. In the work of both artists aura is illuminated as unique existence. Whereas Eliasson creates moments of auratic experience that dwell on an interchange between the virtual regimes of the visible and sensible as well as those facilitated by nature, Majerus produces environments in which he opens avenues to new perceptions of aura through forms that hybridize digitization and more conventional modes of representation. Although he altered the status of the nomadic canvas by creating permanent objects that fittingly belong to both art and the everyday, his penetration of the aesthetics of virtualization with a variety of painterly styles, ranging from abstraction to figuration, allows for and at the same time challenges concepts of aura. Eliasson empowers perceptions and creations of new aesthetic realms, while concurrently altering already-constructed ones. Similarly, Majerus bends the mediums of painting and digital image-worlds in order to create a new universe, one that elucidates the prospective coexistence of manmade and machine-calculated imagery, material and immaterial worlds, and virtual orders that together establish unique perceptual sensations. And although Majerus repeatedly called upon the "now" to describe his endeavors, his works simultaneously evoke and revoke aura; presence and absence manifest themselves at the same time.

Majerus and Eliasson both consciously reflect on reality and fiction, fantasy and illusion as qualities and strategies supplied by virtuality. This new logic allows for an excavation of allegedly dispensable notions that embrace originality and individual agency in relation to artist and onlooker, as repeatedly stressed by critical writings on modern and contemporary art. Rather than attempting to exert control over the external world via artistic means, both artists generate images without resemblance, causing the distinction between original and reproduction to appear futile, and thereby also contributing to a critical thematization of this art-historical model. We may then locate Majerus's and Eliasson's creations within another, new, register of creation, that of the simulacrum permeated as much by the factual world as by the virtual one.

Notes

[1] Holger van den Boom, "Digitaler Schein—oder: Der Wirklichkeitsverlust ist kein wirklicher Verlust," in *Digitaler Schein: Ästhetik der elektronischen Medien*, ed. Florian Rötzer (Frankfurt am Main: Suhrkamp, 1991), 183.

[2] Florian Rötzer, "Mediales und Digitales: Zerstreute Bemerkungen und Hinweise eines irritierten informationsverarbeitenden Systems," in Florian Rötzer, *Digitaler Schein*, 18–19.

[3] "Die Ästhetik des Verschwindens: Ein Gespräch zwischen Fred Forest und Paul Virilio," in Florian Rötzer, *Digitaler Schein*, 334–42.

[4] Florian Rötzer, "Mediales und Digitales," 9–80.

[5] Peter Weibel, "Zur Geschichte und Ästhetik des digitalen Bildes," in *Bilder in Bewegung: Traditionen digitaler Ästhetik*, ed. Kai-Uwe Hemken (Cologne: DuMont, 2000), 214.

[6] Weibel, "Zur Geschichte und Ästhetik des digitalen Bildes," 210.

[7] Franz Krahberger, "Virtuality Goes Reality," http://ezines.onb.ac.at:8080/ejounal/pub/ejour 97-II/buecher/bably.vitual.html (accessed 25 Jan. 2009).

[8] Donald Preziosi, "Collecting/Museums" in *Critical Terms for Art History*, ed. Robert S. Nelson and Richard Schiff (Chicago: U of Chicago P, 1996), 411.

[9] Online Edition of *Merriam Webster Dictionary and Thesaurus*, http://search.eb.com (accessed 25 Jan. 2009).

[10] Denis Berthier, *Méditations sur le réel et le virtuel* (Paris: Editions L'Harmattan, 2004).

[11] Norbert Bolz, "Wirklichkeit ohne Gewähr," in *Texte zur Medientheorie*, ed. Günter Helmes and Werner Köster (Stuttgart: Reclam, 2002), 327.

[12] Bernhard Waldenfels, "Experiment mit der Wirklichkeit," in Helmes and Köster, *Texte zur Medientheorie*, 318.

[13] Michael Camille, "Simulacrum," in Nelson and Schiff, *Critical Terms for Art History*, 35–48.

[14] Camille, "Simulacrum," 35–37. See Gilles Deleuze, "The Simulacrum and Ancient Philosophy" and "Plato and the Simulacrum," in *The Logic of Sense*, ed. Constance V. Boundas (New York: Columbia UP, 1990); Michel Foucault, "Theatrum Philosophicum," in *Language, Counter-Memory, Practice: Selected Essays and Interviews* (Ithaca, NY: Cornell UP, 1977).

[15] Gilles Deleuze and Félix Guattari, *What Is Philosophy?* (New York: Columbia UP, 1994).

[16] Walter Benjamin, "The Work of Art in the Age of Mechanical Reproduction," in *Illuminations*, ed. Hannah Arendt, trans. Harry Zohn (New York: Schocken, 1969), 217–52, here 229 and 230.

[17] Nicolas Bourriaud, *Relational Aesthetics* (Paris: Les Presses du Réel, 1998), 61.

[18] Theodor W. Adorno, *Ästhetische Theorie*, ed. Gretel Adorno and Rolf Tiedemann (Frankfurt: Suhrkamp, 1974), 73 and 408–9; my translation.

[19] See also Dieter Mersch, *Ereignis und Aura: Untersuchungen zu einer Ästhetik des Performativen* (Frankfurt am Main: Suhrkamp, 2002), 11 and 185.

[20] Mersch, *Ereignis und Aura*, 110.

[21] www.jeffrey-shaw.net/html_main/frameset-works.php3 (accessed 25 Jan. 2009) and *Jeffrey Shaw—A User's Manual: From Expanded Cinema to Virtual Reality*, ed. Anne-Marie Duguet, Heinrich Klotz, and Peter Weibel (Karlsruhe: ZKM, 1997).

[22] *Thyssen-Bornemisza: Art Contemporary Pavilions*, Brochure (n.d.), 18.

[23] Daniel Birnbaum, "Search Engine: The Art of Michel Majerus," *Artforum* (Feb. 2006): 171.

[24] Tilman Baumgärtel, "Super Mario and the Night of the Visual," in *Michel Majerus: Installationen 92–02 / Installations 92–02*, ed. Peter Pakesch, Gijs van Tuyl, Robert Fleck, Veit Görner, and Marie-Claude Beaud (Cologne: Walther König, 2005), 233.

[25] In conversation with the author, Berlin, Jun. 2003.

[26] Bourriaud, *Relational Aesthetics*, 61.

6: What Does It Mean to Read Online? On the Possibility of the Archive in Cyberspace

Michel Chaouli

I.

EVERY REFLECTION ON ELECTRONIC LITERATURE—on those texts that depend on computers for their literary effects and are of little use when printed—must come to terms with a massive blind spot in its field of vision that keeps it from analyzing or even recognizing its object adequately. This blind spot is the concept of literature itself. An analysis of "electronic literature" guided by the concept of literature cannot help but find "literature" in the electronic medium; it presupposes what it should set out to find. Thus many electronic texts, particularly those that mean to be challenging or avant-garde (Mark Amerika's "Grammatron," for example[1]), read as though they were written in response to a demand that literature had issued to modern technology. Breaking with the *conventions* of literature, which is the norm for electronic literature, changes nothing about the fact that the *idea* of literature continues to remain intact. In fact, the more electronic literature and its criticism insist on undermining literary tradition (by being "experimental," "difficult," and so on), the more they work to preserve the very category of literature.[2] The effect of what is supposed to be radically new is ultimately judged by what is tried and true. Beginning an analysis of computer-based verbal artworks with the concept of literature thus risks two distinct failures: it can easily misrecognize the truly artistic innovations of electronic writing, and, conversely, it is apt to overlook the shifts that the electronic medium may provoke in literature itself.

But if we provisionally set aside the concept of literature, we allow new questions to be asked. For example: What are the consequences for art (and therefore also for verbal art) that arise from the specific methods of electronically saving and sending data? What conclusions can we draw about the production and the processing of meaning? What are the effects of the new electronic medium on memory? Do processes like reading and writing change and, if so, how?

If we begin our analysis with the properties and effects of electronic media, then we are more likely to treat literature as an open question rather than a known entity. Instead of asking what literature looks like when it is processed by a computer, we could ask how literature—whether in print or on the screen—reacts to the existence of new technologies of writing and reading. What are the effects on literature if, for example, everyone who knows how to write can, by simple means, transmit texts of every kind—internal memos, love letters, jokes, invitations, obituaries, and also poetry—to a potentially unlimited number of readers? Would the poem need to be composed differently than it was before? We would of course like to know whether the electronic medium will afford us the same mysterious pleasures of reading that lead us back to literature, whether stories can be told using the computer with the same sophistication that we know from Flaubert or Flannery O'Connor. We would then be measuring the new with an old yardstick. But if we turn things around and think about how the medium affects art, we would be prepared to ask, with Walter Benjamin, whether through the invention of electronic data processing and communication the *entire nature* of art has not also changed.[3]

II.

The World Wide Web is often described as a distributive, non- and even anti-hierarchical network that (like Deleuze's rhizome) resists centralization and in which no single node controls the others.[4] Seen globally, the Web has neither central memory storage nor a central processor, yet in principle every data bit is saved in a single location that is tagged with a unique Universal Resource Locator.[5] And each individual processing of data performed with the help of a program is not distributive but rather is managed from one location.[6] (By *data* I mean the processing instructions as well as the variable bits to be processed.) Because of this unique data storage, the medium has two important advantages. First, distribution can be more tightly organized. The sender can minimize what in publishing is called wastage, because data is processed and sent only when requested. The advantage to users is that they can receive data entirely independently of location, as long as they are equipped with a receiver within range of the network. Senders and receivers of data therefore find each other more easily and efficiently than in the media of print and film (which handle distribution through bookstores and movie theaters). The second advantage of unique data storage over other storage media lies in the fact that here data can always be changed. This shortens the feedback loop and makes possible the constant correction and updating of data. Instead of having to wait for the second, improved, edition of a book, which might never appear, the author of a Web site can always bring the text up to date.

At first glance, unique data storage looks like the sort of technical detail of interest mainly to engineers and programmers, yet it turns out to have profound implications for concepts that have stood at the core of poetic and aesthetic theories. For in a strict sense unique data storage obviates the concepts of original and copy, not because digital duplication is so flawless that it erases the line between original and copy, but rather because there are no "copies" on the Web. Each instance of data retrieval is unique; it causes the representation of particular data in a particular configuration at a particular address. It copies nothing. There are, then, only originals that possess the strange capability of appearing any number of times and in the most distant corners of the net. In other words, there are new kinds of entities that concepts like "original" and "copy" have a difficult time grasping.

We can take this a step further, for with the abolition of original and copy, the very concept of "work" begins to weaken. Although Benjamin regards the copy with a certain melancholy, he does not denounce it because he knows that the idea of the original and its permanence depend on the copy. The concept of an enduring original is produced through the same operation—technical reproducibility—that also calls the copy into being. Hence reproduction undermines his concept of the aura while leaving the idea of the work of art intact. Reproduction sabotages a certain *conception* of the artwork, namely the auratic work of art, but not the artwork itself.[7] "In principle a work of art has always been reproducible," Benjamin establishes in the very beginning of the text (which aptly enough is known as the "artwork essay").[8] In the electronic medium *reproducibility* itself is lost, and without it we lose not only a work's aura but also the work itself. Why this is so becomes clearer when we examine the significance of the second feature of unique data storage, the mutability of data.

The "historical testimony" of an artwork depends for Benjamin on its "authenticity" and its "substantive duration." The loss of this auratic testimony occurs when authenticity and substantive duration (for instance in an image) are separated through repeatability and transience (for instance in the reproduction of the image in a magazine).[9] But what happens when these characteristics are short-circuited, when the unique work disappears and substantive duration can only be guaranteed through repeatability? The electronic medium has confronted us with this situation by offering *permanent mutability* instead of duration. To appreciate how far-reaching the consequences of this technical feature really are, consider the fact that one of the great achievements of technical reproduction lies in expanding the historical and geographical range of texts, which is to say their cultural life expectancy. One of the consequences of printing many copies of a manuscript in book form lies in a massive externalization of individual and social memory, which gains in reliability with the number of its copies. The more perfect copies of *Oedipus Rex* are in circulation, the less likely it is that the text will suffer the same fate as some of Sophocles's other plays. (What is true of books also goes for lithographs, photographs, films, records, CDs, and so on.) The substantive duration of social memory—of culture—is bolstered by redundancy. The data *carrier* may fall victim to decay; the data itself remains readable, provided that it has been copied often enough.

Technical reproducibility promotes—even makes possible—the idea of the work for another, more important reason. Copies are only copies when they refer to the same original, that is, when they are seen as reproductions of the same object despite differences (in the technical means of reproduction, in social function, and so on.). What is at stake is the distinction between reproduction and reproducibility: while reproduction creates copies, and thus redundancies, reproducibility creates, so to speak, the transcendental condition for the possibility of reproduction. This condition is nothing more than the idea of the autonomous and completed work, which guarantees the continuity of reference through necessarily mutable copies. The fact that the differences between the reproductions of a painting (in postcard form, as a poster, or in a magazine) are at all recognizable, the fact that one can discover the same novel through completely different material representations of a verbal work (in book form, on cassette, as CD-ROM) rests on the idea of a lasting, identical, unchangeable work. You begin to notice how powerful this idea is when you confront a work that lacks textual stability, as for example with Hölderlin's lyrical poetry or Joyce's *Ulysses*. Our confusion in such cases is entirely justified, since technical reproducibility assumes fixed data. In order to be copied, the work must hold still. Reproducibility precipitates, as it were, a phase shift in the work's state from fluid to solid. The elastic process of writing, painting, singing, and so on, in which the elements can always be reordered, hardens into a rigid configuration, now ready for innumerable reproductions. Work in progress turns into work. The transience of a developing not-yet-object solidifies in the permanence, completeness, and authenticity of the artwork.

In contrast with print (as well as other technologies of reproduction based on it), the Web in principle allows mutability to be a *permanent* feature of texts. It thus manages to combine flexibility and publishing in ways not yet achieved in any other medium. This fundamental and, as we shall see, groundbreaking characteristic of the medium results from the interconnection of two technologically different properties. The extraordinary agility of digital storage, which makes possible the swift deletion and reorganization of electronically fixed bits undetectable to the reader, becomes a distinguishing feature of published texts through computer networks.[10] In the pre-electronic world, changeability and publication remained for the most part strictly separated; the author polished his composition privately and in publishing relinquished it, making it into a work and himself, retroactively, into its author. By contrast, in the electronic world, the moment of "printing," in which a specific state of data becomes suspended, is simply a point on a continuous time line; data retrieval offers nothing more than a snapshot of the permanently changeable data stream.

This flexibility appears to invalidate an old allegation against writing, indeed the primary reproach raised against it. Besides the separation of the word from its author, which is to say the externality of script, Plato laments precisely its inflexibility; texts are silent and static when they are questioned. "Besides, once a thing is committed to writing, it circulates equally among those who understand the subject and those who have no business with it."[11] The printed book is constantly accused of indiscriminately recording both truths and lies, which, according to Walter Ong, earns it the dubious honor of being burned: "There is no way to refute a text.... This is one reason why 'the book says' is popularly tantamount to 'it is true.' It is also one reason why books have been burned. A text stating what the whole world knows is false will state falsehood forever, so long as the text exists."[12] When lies are printed, they lie as long as their material carrier exists; only when this carrier is burned, ripped apart, pulped, banned, or confiscated do the lies fall silent. Compare this with electronic data processing and storage, where in most cases you only have to press the *delete* key to achieve the same effect. The difference between the ways print and electronics handle changes in the status of truth is especially noticeable to those authors who write electronically and publish in print—that is, most of the authors active today. James O'Donnell, for instance, states: "There is scarcely a page I have published in a decade and a half of scholarly writing that I would not now change if I could. Words that I know to be inadequate and in some cases untrue continue to speak for me. I am no longer the person I was when I wrote them, but I am still somehow their author."[13] The fact that the mutability of texts threatens their durability is fine with O'Donnell: "If the world is in constant flux, then surely the descriptions of that world should find a way to change to reflect that changed world."[14]

III.

If one wanted to comply with O'Donnell's seemingly persuasive demand to synchronize descriptions of the world with the world's constant change, one would abolish the central mode of storage in all print cultures, thereby robbing culture of large parts of its archive, that is, its social memory. The archive is not composed of the ongoing flow of words but is rather made up of arrested descriptions, of "halted speech," as Jan and Aleida Assmann write.[15] This halting of speech—its temporal standstill, its *im*mutability—distinguishes it as a medium that affords points of reference beyond the here and now in life's endless succession. A description that is remembered or written down (and how strongly print cultures tend toward the writing of descriptions is demonstrated in words like "Beschreibung" and "description") is necessarily asynchronous to the world it describes and consequently allows for the difference between present and past—and thus for temporality as such—to come into being. The temporal references in writing, speech, ritual acts, indeed in all media that store social knowledge always differ from the present, if only because they require reference to the past in order to be understood. (Derrida's *différance* captures exactly this temporal shift.) Only then is memory possible and only with memory are both the recourse to a past that is recognized as past and the anticipation of the future possible. Without the halted speech of memory, we could neither recognize nor make sense of differences in perceptions.[16] We cannot imagine culture without memory, as culture is little more than a fuzzy concept for the processing of privately and collectively stored information. "Memory is the origin and basis of culture," as Aleida and Jan Assmann put it.[17] For this reason every culture develops what are called hypomnestic storage technologies, that is, technologies that archive communications in a medium *external* to the body, thereby making increasingly more complex communications—indeed culture itself—possible.[18]

What are the consequences for the archive when communication is conducted through a network of computers? One does not need to be a media-determinist like Marshall McLuhan or Friedrich Kittler to be able to foresee or at least anticipate the tremendous consequences of the electronic medium. In his book about the psychoanalytic archive, which simultaneously provides an outline of a psychoanalysis of the archive, Jacques Derrida registers the invention of electronic communication and memory technologies as an "archival earthquake."[19] The devastating consequences of this earthquake would be predictable, according to Derrida, if one imagined Freud, his proponents, and his opponents communicating not via snail-mail but rather through other technologies—phone cards, portable tape recorders, computers, printers, fax machines, televisions, teleconferencing and *above all* E-mail. In such a case, he writes, the psychoanalytic archive would be "unrecognizable" to us (16). The archive, as Derrida demonstrates, is more than a simple accumulation of traces of the past: "The technical structure of the *archiving* archive also determines the structure of the *archivable* content even in its very coming into existence and in its relationship to the future. The archivization produces as much as it records the event" (17). Because the archive not only assigns storage space to each piece of data but also controls the possibility of its recall, and because the writing technologies of the archive also always determine its reading technologies, only what the archive regards as an event can be processed as a past event. One can recall only what has been stored and is storable. Therefore the archiving function of the archive—its hypomnestic technology—generates the trace of the past that is to be archived by recording, arranging, and keeping it ready for recall. The historical testimony of past events and, as a result, the possibility of opening up references to the future depend on the technological conditions of storage, as storage always also includes ordering. As Derrida might put it, to bring out the political stakes, it also includes giving an order.

Derrida tells us that the new communication media, "above all e-mail," cause the archive to quake, but just how this happens we have not yet learned. What interests us is a topography of the shaken archive and of hypomnestic memory as we find it *after* the intervention of electronic media. We may safely assume that such a description would have a rather ambiguous, perhaps even paradoxical status, since it attempts to secure evidence of this violent change by archiving the quaking of the archive. In order to achieve this, the archiving archive must position itself next to or above the trembling archive and yet remain untouched by its trembling. Or it must, itself trembling, register the trembling of the tremor. It is the problem of the seismograph, which needs to be *both* linked to the earthquake (for otherwise there would be nothing to record) *and* independent from it (for otherwise there would be no baseline against which the agitation of the earth could be measured). Derrida approaches this uncertain space by singling out one medium, E-mail, from a range of modern media that could scatter the handwritten or printed archive of psychoanalysis to a point at which it would no longer be recognizable.[20]

As to the importance of E-mail over other media, Derrida remains rather vague. Why is E-mail to be privileged? "Because electronic mail today, even more than the fax, is on the way to transforming the entire public and private space of humanity . . . It is not only a technique, in the ordinary and limited sense of the term: at an unprecedented rhythm, in quasi-instantaneous fashion, this instrumental possibility of production, of printing, of conservation, and of destruction of the archive must inevitably be accompanied by juridical and thus political transformations" (17). Without going into further detail and without taking up a discussion of causality, Derrida connects the new regulation of private and public space to a quality of E-mail that is often remarked upon, namely its speed. The speed of E-mail transactions is often so great that it appears to us as immediate and therefore as an absence of speed—and, hence, as an absence of time and space. Why speed gives E-mail (in pronounced contrast to the fax, where the impression of immediacy is actually even stronger) such a capacity for change remains unclear. This rough description of electronic mnemonic devices leads Derrida to a diagnosis of the expected "juridical and thus political transformations" that achieves nothing more than a repetition of a commonplace: "These affect nothing less than property rights, publishing and reproduction rights" (17).

Because Derrida is one of the few philosophers who inform readers about the way their writings have come about (about the occasion for writing a given text as well as the technological circumstances of the writing process), the text itself gives us indications of the considerable explanatory gap between what it diagnoses, namely the quaking of the archive itself, and how it analyzes the material conditions and philosophical consequences of this quake. It is worth listening when Derrida "tinkl[es] away" on his "little portable computer" (25), because there the technical structure that is so decisive for his analysis of the modern archive, shaken by E-mail, becomes apparent. For right under his fingertips, the small Macintosh metamorphoses from a digital computer into an engraving tool and printing press ("I became aware of this . . . almost a year before inscribing and printing on my computer the first word of what I am saying to you here . . ." [25]), and E-mail offers, to return to the passage I quoted earlier, the possibility of printing ("d'impression"), that is, of impression and imprint. The fact that it is not a printer that is hooked up to a computer, but rather the computer itself, that carries out these inscriptions and impressions becomes apparent when Derrida ponders the exact moment of archiving during the process of writing. When exactly did the words he wrote while tinkling away on his computer on a sunny California morning a few weeks earlier become archived?

> Was it not at this very instant that, having written something or other on the screen, the letters remaining as if suspended and floating yet at the surface of a liquid element, I pushed a certain key to "save" a text undamaged, in a hard and lasting way, to protect marks from being erased, so as to ensure in this way salvation and *indemnity*, to stock, to accumulate, and, in what is at once the same thing and something else, to make the sentence available in this way for printing and for reprinting, for reproduction? (25–26)

This is a rhetorical question, which should have remained open-ended. At precisely the point where the difference between electronic archiving on the one hand and handwritten and printed archiving on the other could have been worked out to reveal the topography of the archival earthquake—at the very point where one should have been able to register the transformative power of E-mail—electronic writing simply becomes yet another kind of engraving, inscribing, printing. If the computer, hooked up to a network, merely creates "new models of recording and impression, or printing" (26), then it is difficult to understand why this reconfiguration of print would cause the archive of the "impressed and imprinted" word to come unhinged.

Derrida makes it clear not only just how deeply the conceptual terminology of psychoanalysis is determined by handwriting and print (by the Freudian impression)[21] but also how this is the case with deconstruction itself. Deconstruction's critical leverage depends largely on the fact that the archive, even the electronic one, is imagined along the lines of the mechanics of printing technologies: only then can one make a distinction like "the *pressure* of the *printing,* the *impression,* before the division between the printed and the printer" (18), a distinction whose analogue logic is useless for understanding the structure of digital data. Having recourse to the traditional imagery of the earthquake fits this pattern as well, because an earthquake, as disturbing as it may be to the foundation, conforms to the very analogue mechanisms that make the operation of mechanical writing machines possible. The earthquake may shake everything else, but it does *not* shake the seismograph, to the extent that the latter records the tremors faithfully (that is, analogically). Even when the earthquake wreaks utter destruction, it leaves intact the logic of inscription, for the tremors are understood in *analogy* to an analogue process that can differentiate between the printed and the printer. In the end, the earthquake is for Derrida nothing more than a kind of writing or printing. Despite its melodrama, the metaphor of the archival earthquake in fact serves to level the differences between electronic data and print, between digital and analogue communication. Just as in his early works speech turned out to be a kind of inscription, here Derrida turns digital bits into analogue inscriptions, making them available to the archive of deconstruction.

The question that is evaded by such an analogization of the non-analogue is whether electronic communication is at all compatible with the concepts of archiving.[22] E-mail leads us down the wrong path here, because it renders invisible the most radical consequences of its own technology. Following McLuhan's slogan, according to which old media appear as the content of new media, E-mail simulates epistolary correspondence. For example, it differentiates between sender and receiver, author and reader (distinctions made automatically, that is, by the machine). The message's time-stamp, likewise automatically appended and seemingly unchangeable, produces in what appears to Derrida and others to be a "quasi-instantaneous" medium a fixed past and with it a temporality that announces the establishment of a stable archive. Both the designation of fixed points on a temporal axis and the differentiation of reader and author are meant to produce texts whose integrity is in keeping with the standards of epistolary correspondence. But this content is only simulated. McLuhan has warned us of the dangers of focusing too intently on the content of media: "The 'content' of a medium is like the juicy piece of meat carried by the burglar to distract the watchdog of the mind."[23] Technology distracts its users by putting artificial limits on its own capabilities. For instance, when I attempt to edit an E-mail message I have received (a string of bits stored on my computer that I should be able to process), my E-mail program (Eudora, Version 4.3.2) informs me: "Sorry, but you can't change that text." I *can* change that text, I am tempted to respond, but you won't let me. Why does the technology block itself? It can only be because the E-mail message is imagined to be a mailed letter and its writer an author; and texts written by authors (as opposed to writers) are not subject to change after the fact.

In contrast to E-mail, the Web operates according to a model of storage and communication that pushes the possibilities of the electronic medium further than other models of which I am aware, and that can potentially bring the archive of print—and with it literature itself—to a point even more devastating than a quake, namely a standstill. As we have seen, the combination of mutability and publication—a direct consequence of the interconnection of singular storage and universal networking—prevents the establishment of a binding temporality in the reading of Web-based texts. I have argued that concepts like *author* and *work* (and with them *duration* and *authenticity*) are thereby rendered useless and that the very "historical testimony" that for Benjamin constitutes the essence of each unique object is impaired in ways no one was able to foresee. Yet the demise of aesthetic concepts is only one consequence of a further-reaching phenomenon, namely the loss of a guaranteed externalized temporality, which makes both archive and culture possible. We literally do not know how to read a text that, in principle, remains mutable even as we read it. For decades literary theory has encouraged us to free ourselves from such antiquated conceptual baggage as *work* and *author*, but literary theory has not instructed us how we should react to the change in the materiality of communication itself. We can try to make good on Barthes's challenge to turn work into text, provided the verbal structure itself is stable enough that its coherence and permanence persist even after it has been cut into hundreds of *lexia*. But what if that is no longer given? We have yet to develop protocols of reading that do justice to the radically unstable temporality of reception we experience in the electronic medium every day: two queries at the same Web address only a few seconds apart can call up two different sets of data.[24] We react by printing, downloading, and e-mailing Web pages to ourselves. These rituals amount to a belated inscription process and are meant to endow fleeting electronic data with the permanence we expect of archivable material.

There are genres, for example newspapers, that have tried to absorb the shock of this utterly new situation in which the content of digitally stored and universally available data is constantly mutable. Because they specialize in novelty, the possibility of constant "updating" offered by the Web appears to be a benefit to them. To accommodate this change, the paper is imagined to appear not once but many times a day. But the idea of multiple publications fails to account for the fact that, because nothing is printed, what the newspaper records online is a snapshot at any given moment and may have changed by the next. This can cause immense disorientation in the reader, something with which newspapers, especially newspapers "of record" have only begun to grapple. We can observe similar uncertainty among textual genres whose constant updating is in principle accepted (for example encyclopedias and dictionaries), since they see themselves as being up-to-date and thus as temporally unbound. Yet even here it is difficult to know how one should deal with the possibility of constant mutability. How do we read an encyclopedia that can at any moment change without leaving any traces? And how does one refer to the knowledge stored there? Thus far, our crutch has been to introduce temporal markers; the standard citation styles now require writers to provide the date on which they have accessed a site. The citation effectively tells readers: "When I looked, this is what the Web site said; no guarantees for what you will find." These problems are amplified in texts whose meanings are created from the tension between an imagined past and an anticipated future, texts that refer to other internal or external texts, and texts whose complicated temporalities depend on the stability of the sources to which they refer. This group includes not only virtually all literature but also many legal, scholarly, religious, and historiographic texts.

Can literature handle a situation in which its storage medium—writing—forfeits its material permanence?[25] Thus far, electronic texts have mainly attempted to rescue the material duration of writing and thus the concept of the work either by evading the possibilities of electronic communication or by limiting themselves in such a way that the reader is assured of the fixity of data and program. In effect, the new medium has been truncated to behave like the old one. Ironically, the very attempt to free oneself from the constraints of the book through electronic hypertext relies on media conditions (such as permanence of writing and absence of the author) that can be fulfilled much more aptly by the book than by the electronic medium.[26] Whether it is sold on CD-ROM or frozen on a Web site, supposedly challenging hypertext literature is usually published in a form that—like the book—bars the possibility of changing data: *read only memory*. Literature has yet to meet the challenges of *read and write memory*.

*Translation from the German by
Necia Chronister and Tracy Graves*

Notes

A version of this essay, identical in outline and argument, different in wording, was first published in German as "Was bedeutet: Online lesen? Über die Möglichkeit des Archivs im Cyberspace," *Text + Kritik* 152 (2001): 65–74.

[1] http://www.grammatron.com (accessed 25 Jan. 2009).

[2] The traditional concept of literature appears in almost all the secondary literature on the subject, no matter whether this literature argues for or against hyperfiction. For example, see Roberto Simanowski, one of the most well-informed observers in the field: "I . . . examine only those (text) groups . . . that are most

strongly committed to the traditional concepts of author and work," in "Perspektiven einer Ästhetik der elektronischen Literatur," http://www.dichtung-digital. de/Simanowski/5-Okt-99 (accessed 25 Jan. 2009). Simanowski gives no reasons, presumably because the restrictions are taken to be self-evident. There are important exceptions: Janet Murray's *Hamlet on the Holodeck: The Future of Narrative in Cyberspace* (New York: Free P, 1997) and Espen Aarseth's *Cybertext: Perspectives on Ergodic Literature* (Baltimore: Johns Hopkins UP, 1997). Both work with newly developed concepts of literature, which are, nonetheless, still concepts of *literature*.

[3] See Walter Benjamin, "The Work of Art in the Age of Mechanical Reproduction," in *Illuminations*, ed. Hannah Arendt, trans. Harry Zohn (New York: Schocken Books, 1969), 227. Here Benjamin examines the invention of photography.

[4] For example: "As the capacity of hypertext systems to be infinitely recentrable suggests, they have a corresponding potential for being anti-hierarchical and democratic." George Landow und Paul Delany, "Hypertext, Hypermedia and Literary Studies: The State of the Art," in *Hypermedia and Literary Studies*, ed. Paul Delany and George P. Landow (Cambridge, MA: MIT Press, 1991), 3–50, here 29.

[5] The "mirror sites" that reproduce the content of one site in another location are not counter-examples. In order to maintain likeness to the original they are organized dynamically and adapt automatically to the contents of the original memory. Therefore, from the perspective of the user they remain indistinguishable from the original data.

[6] A Java application may be run on a receiving computer, technically speaking, but it will always be managed by the sender. The receiver has the choice to turn Java on or off but not to change the activity of the program.

[7] A questionable line of thought, because reproducibility increases—even makes possible—the aura (as the congestion around the Mona Lisa in the Louvre demonstrates). This is, however, not the place to pursue this line of thought.

[8] Benjamin, *Illuminations*, 10.

[9] Benjamin, *Illuminations*, 13–15.

[10] I cannot broach the important question of *trace* in electronic data storage here. To the extent that electronic data storage requires a material substrate (for instance a magnetic disk), changing the data leaves traces on it. But since the recipients of electronic communication receive information independently from that substrate (calling up data on the Web or reception of an E-mail does not require the sender also to dispatch his or her hard disk), they cannot examine the substrate like a palimpsest for traces. What is more, in the communication of electronic data there is admittedly information transmitted of which the sender is seldom, if ever, aware. This is where a psychoanalytic study of electronic communication would have to follow.

[11] Plato, *Phaidros*, 275e; in English, *Phaedrus and the Seventh and Eighth Letters*, trans. Walter Hamilton (New York: Penguin Books, 1973), 97.

[12] Walter Ong, *Orality and Literacy: The Technologizing of the Word* (London: Methuen, 1982), 79.

[13] James O'Donnell, *Avatars of the Word: From Papyrus to Cyberspace* (Cambridge, MA: Harvard UP, 1998), 41.

[14] O'Donnell, *Avatars of the Word*, 41.

[15] Aleida Assmann and Jan Assmann, "Schrift und Gedächtnis," in *Schrift und Gedächtnis,* ed. Aleida Assmann, Jan Assmann, and Christof Hardmeier (Munich: W. Fink, 1998), 266.

[16] See also Niklas Luhmann, *Die Gesellschaft der Gesellschaft* (Frankfurt am Main: Suhrkamp, 1977), 44–46.

[17] Assmann and Assmann, "Schrift und Gedächtnis," 267.

[18] For more information on "hypomnesis," see H. G. Gadamer, "Unterwegs zur Schrift?" in Assmann, Assmann, and Hardmeier, *Schrift und Gedächtnis,* 15–19. What exactly is meant by "external" cannot always be determined. Are the mnemonic devices of rhyme and rhythm, for example, external? Is tattooing, circumcision, or the dueling scar external? In the context of this essay, it is only possible to raise the question of where the boundary between external storage and internal memory runs, or indeed whether it exists at all.

[19] Jacques Derrida, *Archive Fever: A Freudian Impression,* trans. Eric Prenowitz (Chicago: U of Chicago P, 1996), 16.

[20] He is explicit about the privilege of E-mail: "But the example of E-mail is privileged in my opinion . . ." (17).

[21] See the wonderful passage on Freud's "Notiz über den 'Wunderblock,'" 13–15.

[22] I cannot discuss the problem of the technical conditions of electronic archiving, the security of the material substrate of storage, or its operative accessibility here. There are two distinct problems: first, most electronic media have shown themselves to be relatively sensitive; second, the rapid changes in storage (or writing) technologies have made many reading technologies obsolete, so that today electronic texts that are barely ten years old have, more often than not, become unreadable. See Robert Simanowski, "Die Ordnung des Erinnerns: Kollektives Gedächtnis und digitale Präsentation," http://www.dichtung-digital.de/Simanowski/30-Dez-99 (accessed 25 Jan. 2009), esp. sections 1 and 2.

[23] Marshall McLuhan, *Understanding Media: The Extensions of Man* (New York: McGraw Hill, 1964), 32.

[24] Even simultaneous queries (assuming there to be such a thing as true simultaneity on the Internet) can produce different results depending on the earlier behavior of the reader.

[25] It is also an open question whether literary *criticism* can endure this change. How could it cite texts, if the sources of those texts remain fluid? This also applies to this essay: it cannot offer its readers any assurance that the Web sites it references can be found as they were when it was written.

[26] It is remarkable just how often the iconography of the book, of the page, of turning the page, and so on, appears in those Web sites that engage with *un*printable literature. See, for example, http://www.dichtung-digital.de (accessed 25 Jan. 2009).

7: Please Hold

Juliet Koss

I.

DIGITAL TELECOMMUNICATION, ONE HEARS, takes us everywhere at once when we are nowhere in particular; we can send E-mail messages from New York to an address in St. Louis to be read by someone in Berlin who pictures us sitting at a computer in Los Angeles. As geographic and temporal distances dissolve (the story goes), so, too, does the centrality and uniqueness of the human body, the somatic entity we identify with our inner selves. Fiber-optic cables render haptic experience meaningless; we communicate constantly with others, elsewhere, disregarding our actual, physical location; and we blithely (or even eagerly) replace communication devices with temporary substitutes and ever newer models. Our physical presence is apparently so bereft of significance that we can find mementos of our travels on the World Wide Web, while art historians preparing conference papers and essays can find extraordinary images on the Internet, without ever visiting a slide library—let alone a museum.

A photograph of George W. Bush speaking by telephone with the men and women aboard the Space Shuttle Discovery, published on the front page of the *New York Times* in August 2005, makes the official message clear (fig. 7.1, left). The halting conversation between the president of the United States and the astronauts was replayed on radio and television, its image disseminated in print and over the Internet. One hundred years after the invention of the telephone and almost eighty years after the establishment of transatlantic wireless phone service, the United States government made a phone connection to outer space, and the fact of this telephone call—rather than any particular message it relayed—signified that all was well, technologically speaking.[1] The running man clutching a mobile phone, a built-in "movie clip" that lurks in Macintosh computers, exemplifies the mythical status of the human being in the age of interplanetary communication: this mobile man is dressed for the office, but he has neither hands nor feet, let alone feet that touch the ground—a ground that itself is only suggested by the presence of his cartoon shadow. Efficient communicators, this image suggests, have no need for hands and feet.

Fig. 7.1. George W. Bush talking on the telephone to the astronauts on the Space Shuttle Discovery, photograph by Paul J. Richards/AFP for the New York Times, *2 August 2005; United States Army soldiers stationed in Iraq, photograph by Christoph Bangert/laif/Redux for the* New York Times, *13 August 2005.*

Those who have ever been unwillingly stranded without Internet access or a working computer understand the limitations of this narrative. Such persistent physical ailments as carpal tunnel syndrome, aching backs, sore thumbs, and the unresolved threat of cancer from cell phone use suggest another story, one in which the presence of the human body is reasserted, with the apparent dissolution of time and space, as anything but virtual. Computers, laptops, telephones, and other communication devices in the digital age exist to be held; they make no sense without our fingers on them. (Not for nothing is the mobile telephone called a "Handy" in German.) The body that communicates by virtual means—and perhaps this body most of all—is holding on, both in the sense of engaging an object physically and in the sense of waiting attentively: physically sentient, uncertain, and even hopeful. "Perhaps the only remaining attitude is one of *waiting*," Siegfried Kracauer wrote in 1922. "By committing oneself to waiting, one neither blocks one's path toward faith . . . nor besieges this faith. . . . One waits, and one's waiting is a *hesitant openness,* albeit of a sort that is difficult to explain."[2]

Kracauer was not, on that occasion, writing of telephones, but his words prompt an exploration of the aesthetics of attendance in the digital age. Using the telephone (both object and conduit) as a rhetorical model, this essay takes literally the theme of attentiveness, central to recent art-historical discourse, to consider some of the physical aspects of attending—in the sense of paying attention to the work of art and, more prosaically, waiting.[3] Inspired by the late-nineteenth-century German discourse of *Einfühlung,* or empathy, and with reference to the work of several contemporary artists, it foregrounds the conceptual overlap of the optic and the haptic—the paradox of embodied vision—by attending to the centrality of waiting, or being "on hold," in the digital age. Whether tapping their way through the digital revolution or idly drumming our impatience, the digits of our hands, I argue, mark our bodily presence—often, it seems, while our attention is directed somewhere else.

II.

"When does the telephone become what it is?" asked Avital Ronell in 1989, sixteen years after the invention of the mobile phone (and six years after the first model went on sale in the United States). The telephone, Ronell explained at that time, "presupposes the existence of another telephone, somewhere, though its atotality as apparatus, its singularity, is what we think of when we say 'telephone.'"[4] The phone belongs to a network, in other words, and the existence of this network "abolishes the originariness of site."[5] Yet Ronell herself signs her introduction "AR, area code 415," which in the late 1980s marked her book's own point of origin as San Francisco. With the advent of the mobile phone, such a number means little, for one can now choose an area code just as one can choose an E-mail address: with complete disregard for one's own geographical location.[6] After the digital divide, the "originariness of site" has been rendered irrelevant.

Reality, they say, is a simulacrum, without location or origin, and physical presence is insignificant. The theoretical ground for such an argument was laid some time ago; in the early 1990s Jean Baudrillard famously used this reasoning to maintain that the (first) Gulf War did not take place.[7] A third photograph from the *New York Times* of August 2005 resonates beautifully with this claim: three soldiers in the U.S. Army stationed in Iraq are playing video war games, entertaining themselves as they wait for the so-called "real" war to make use of them (fig. 7.1, right). Basking in the television's purple glow, they seem fully absorbed in its image. For these men, the photograph suggests, the daily reality of the war is that of a video game. But as they sit around waiting for the war to become more physically present, their waiting is itself a literal holding on, a bodily activity of attendance; their hands clutch the consoles that link them to their game. By contrast, the man bathed in golden light in the background, speaking with someone beyond the frame, gesticulates—and holds on to nothing.

One model for the consideration of haptic vision, a kind of spectatorship simultaneously visual and bodily, comes from the discourse of *Einfühlung* (literally, the activity of "feeling into"), developed in Germany in the last quarter of the nineteenth century by researchers and theorists in philosophical aesthetics, perceptual psychology, optics, and art and architectural history, all of whom wished to describe or analyze the embodied response to an image, object, or spatial environment.[8] The interdisciplinary nature of the discourse of *Einfühlung* reflected a relative openness among the humanistic and scientific disciplines; viewers might feel their way into anything from everyday objects or non-referential markings to works of fine art, according to the interests of particular authors. Placing the perceiving eye within the viewer's body, *Einfühlung* described a range of relationships between this body and the work of art, including a tendency to anthropomorphize and a notion of projection we now associate with Sigmund Freud.[9]

We are aware of the power of images to elicit a visceral response; one example would be the discomfort provoked in the squeamish body by images of physically painful events. In 1873 the philosopher Robert Vischer articulated this response to form in abstract terms, arguing that even simple marks could induce physical reactions. Vision itself, in fact, was not always central; the process relied heavily on a network of responses that included spatial understanding, imagination, emotion, and (in some cases) what he termed "artistic reshaping," or the creative aesthetic response. "We can often observe in ourselves," Vischer noted, "the curious fact that a visual stimulus is experienced not so much with our eyes as with a different sense in another part of our body."[10] This sensation occurred with particular intensity along the body's surfaces, Vischer believed, and it provided an explanation for the mystical shivers and goose bumps of aesthetic transport. Along with the destabilization of identity and psychic projection, such bodily sensations on the spectator's skin produced a powerful self-awareness. As the viewer "lost himself" in the work of art, *Einfühlung* articulated a loss of self that simultaneously reinforced a powerful physical sense of selfhood.

The demise of the discourse of *Einfühlung* in the early twentieth century, because of a range of factors that include a gradual loss of interest among art historians and psychologists, preceded forceful rejections of the concept by Wilhelm Worringer in 1908 and, in the 1930s, Bertolt Brecht. Yet *Einfühlung* remained central to the discourse of twentieth-century architecture and was also reframed and transformed, with the birth of cinema and the emergence of visual abstraction, to describe the new forms of spectatorship that were becoming popular in the 1920s. Throughout its variegated history, it has described a potentially uncomfortable destabilization of identity along the viewer's perceptual borders, a sensation at once physical, psychological, and emotional. If German critical theory can helpfully address such current conceptual contradictions as embodied vision, the manner in which such contradictions are experienced in the digital age may in turn assist us in navigating this discourse. The larger aim, then, is to imagine an embodied aesthetics for the digital age.[11]

The appeal of *Einfühlung* lies partly in its interdisciplinary nature and partly in its ability to straddle the categories of "aesthetic" and "non-aesthetic"—in its application, that is, to a range of objects and images, from paintings in the 1880s to the movies in the 1920s. But the question of the history of art history is, at the same time, a question about its current practice. Heinrich Dilly, among others, has traced the links between the emergence of art history as a discipline and the development of photography as a medium, while Horst Bredekamp has argued that photography illustrates "the basic conflict in art history," as the discipline itself "depends largely on the autopsy of the original but . . . questions it also through the lens of photographic-founded knowledge."[12] Photography, that is, has been central to the discipline's development, whether in the form of magic lantern slides or as images illustrating art historical texts. One wonders what the work of art history may yet become in the age of digital media and international conferences.[13]

This brings us back to Kracauer, and to a photograph of a woman at the Femina Dance Palace in Berlin in the 1920s, holding the telephone line while her companion across the table holds only a cigarette (fig. 7.2). Dolled up in a fur coat, stylish hat, and white gloves, she gazes across the table at her companion while apparently listening—or at least linked by telephone to—someone else. Smiling confidently, she also appears fully aware of the camera that shoots her image (which is to say, of herself as an object on view), yet on further inspection it becomes clear that she is not fully engaged in any one of the relationships the photograph apparently documents. The setup is impossible, or at least staged; it provides an overabundance of interpersonal relations that renders each one superficial, a parody of connection. "There are a lot of people these days," Kracauer wrote in 1922,

> who, although unaware of [one another], are nevertheless linked by a common fate . . . These scholars, businessmen, doctors, lawyers, and intellectuals of all sorts . . . often forget their actual inner being in the din of the hustle and bustle . . . But when they do pull back from the surface . . . they are overcome by a profound sadness that ultimately overruns all layers of their being. (*TWW*, 129)

Kracauer calls this emptiness an "*exile* from the religious sphere," a spiritual or intellectual alienation, a sense of "*isolation and individuation*," and "a *relativism* that has been pursued to the extreme" (*TWW*, 130 and 131, emphasis in original). He names five responses to this predicament, two of which (the use of narcotics and the embrace of religion) he dismisses out of hand before demonstrating the limitations of two more: skepticism and the formation of the "short-circuit person," who has a kind of energetic, faked faith.

Kracauer ends his essay by describing the attitude of waiting that is, he argues, the only proper response to the emptiness of contemporary existence. It is, he explains, "an attempt to shift the focus from the theoretical

Fig. 7.2. *Woman on the telephone at the Femina Tanzpalast, Berlin, 1920s. Photograph courtesy of the Getty Research Institute Library, Los Angeles, California (920024).*

self to the self of the entire human being, and to move out of the atomized unreal world of shapeless powers and figures devoid of meaning and into the world of *reality* and the domains it accompanies" (*TWW*, 139). This kind of waiting is an embrace of the real, of physical presence; it opposes the kind of "theoretical thinking" that, he writes, "has led us, to a horrifying degree, to become distanced from reality—a reality that is filled with incarnate things and people and that therefore demands to be seen concretely"(*TWW*, 139–40). Yet the distinction between incarnate things and extreme relativism—between a grounded, fully engaged "entire human being" and a "theoretical self" that operates in an "atomized unreal world"—is today not so stark, if indeed it ever was. One might instead call this seemingly impossible opposition an existential condition, one that is emblematized by the mobile phone: connecting us to others, it both perpetuates our distanced life and remains an actual object to be negotiated daily. A tangle of fiber-optic cables permits our haptic experience, allowing us to wait as a prerecorded voice requests, "please hold; an operator will be with you shortly." The *"person who waits,"* Kracauer meanwhile asserts, possesses "a dauntlessness that manifests itself in the ability to hold on," and this "holding on" can be both literal and metaphorical (*TWW*, 138–39, emphasis in original).

Fig. 7.3. Ventriloquist, telephone, dummy, 1920s, photograph courtesy of Janet Klein; Bell Telephone advertisement, 1939; and Leonhardi hair dye company advertisement, pre-1910.

Another photograph—a calling card if ever one existed—shows a mise-en-abîme of 1920s telephone communication, an infinity loop of inanimate attendance (fig. 7.3, left). Much has been written about the telephone as prosthetic device and its symbolic link to the automaton; here we need only remember that as children Alexander Graham Bell and his brother attempted, at their father's request, to construct a "speaking automaton," but when they finished all it could actually say was "mama" (and, as it happened, their mother was deaf).[14] The automaton, the doll, and the ventriloquist's dummy: these inanimate objects all conflate sensations of empathy and alienation.[15] Staring blankly, they offer a comforting presence while cruelly inflicting a silence both uncomprehending and incomprehensible; they are ideal matches for the telephone. The dummy, here, is on hold—but of course it is the ventriloquist who is holding on.

The problematic relationship between the human body and the telephone, a relationship that may accurately be described as an incompatibility of the animate and the inanimate compounded by an inequality of scale, is suggested by an advertisement for the Bell Telephone System in 1939 (fig. 7.3, center). While we know ourselves to be larger than our telephones, the system is clearly larger than we are, as Ronell suggested. As if to emphasize its own physical needs, Bell's successor, the American Telephone & Telegraph Company, began a marketing campaign in 1981 with the phrase, "Reach Out and Touch Someone." One might argue that the company was promoting exactly what was missing from the experience of talking on the telephone: sex sells, and touching apparently sells better than listening. But such an argument would ignore the bodily experience that actually takes place during a telephone call—the holding, the waiting, and the holding on—and that telephone company advertisements often evoke. "Let your fingers do the walking," a slogan from an advertising campaign run by the same company in the 1970s and 1980s, promoted telephone use by emphasizing the haptic nature of the experience of consulting the phone book, if not that of making the phone call. "Weary from shopping all over town for what you want?" the advertisement queries. "Take the drudgery out of shopping!" Decades earlier the gentleman in an advertisement for the Leonhardi hair dye company had already done so, in his effort to shop discreetly by telephone (fig. 7.3, right).

III.

As our fingers do the walking, as we reach out and touch someone, another set of hands is also holding on, invisible to us, as a photograph from 1910 attests (fig. 7.4). Privy to countless private, anonymous exchanges, the telephone operator works in a room that reflects the intensity of her manual labor; the drawn blinds and the absence of wall decorations prevent visual distraction and thwart potential snoops, keeping optical encounters out of the listening station. The tapestry material draped over the bed at right, meanwhile, evokes the more famous couch of Freud's study: the listening room in which private words were spoken, someone attended, and a fair amount of patience was usually necessary. Like the photograph of the woman on the telephone at the Femina Dance Palace, this image, too, appears on closer inspection to be staged; the wires at the console are apparently not connected to any external line. This operator is plugged in—but to what?

Throughout its history, the telephone has needed operators behind the scenes: mediums for our messages, their recorded voices asking us please, to hold. These operators have almost invariably been women:

> In 1878, the first telephone exchange opened in New Haven, Connecticut . . . Boys operated these early exchanges. [They] shouted at the customers, and it took several boys and many minutes to make a call. Girl operators later replaced the boys. The girls had softer voices, more patience, and nimble fingers.[16]

Girls not only proved more adept at holding on, at being both patient and nimble-fingered; they also could be hired for lower wages. Just as the word "typewriter" originally referred to the woman who worked in an office in the early twentieth century, typing up pages of text, and not to the machine she used, the identification of the telephone operator and the telephone exchange—the person and the object—was also understood.[17] Even today, telephone workers in the United States are generally (poorly-paid) women.[18] They are our benevolent assistants, patiently attending to our connections without jamming the line.

Fig. 7.4. Telephone operator in Ida, Illinois, ca. 1910.

Fig. 7.5. Mark Hansen and Ben Rubin, Listening Post, 2002.
Photograph courtesy of the artists.

That, at least, is the scenario that Mark Hansen and Ben Rubin evoke in *Listening Post* (2002), an installation comprising eight speakers and a grid of little screens, each of which displays a continuous line of words sampled from publicly accessible Internet sites, some of which are also broadcast by a computer-generated voice against a background of post-minimalist music (fig. 7.5). A Donald Judd sculpture for the digital age (Philip Glass and Jenny Holzer might also be cited in connection with this work), the piece was funded in part by Bell Laboratories, the research wing of the telephone company that has supported an extraordinary range of artistic practices for five decades, most famously the collaborative Experiments in Art and Technology projects of Robert Rauschenberg and the physicist Billy Klüver in the 1960s. In *Listening Post*, members of the audience become the operators, listening to (or spying on) the Internet exchanges that are orchestrated into an astonishing beauty.[19]

Relevant here is an observation made by Debra Singer, an associate curator at the Whitney Museum when the work was installed there in 2002. *Listening Post*, Singer has said, "seemed to forge new sculptural possibilities in terms of how Internet art is presented and experienced. It didn't rely on the familiar interface of the computer monitor; instead it's sort of rendered at a human scale, a bodily scale."[20] One might consider such a bodily response to a work of art the incarnation of *Einfühlung* in the digital era: a communal experience of an environment created collaboratively between an artist and a computer scientist on the basis of the anonymous exchanges in Internet chat rooms. But for all the new technology, the model of spectatorship is familiar: an embodied engagement with the work of art.

A literal investigation of technology's obdurate physicality is found in a series of photographs from 2005 by Chris Jordan.[21] Massive in size (about as large as a standard work by Andreas Gursky, Sharon Lockheart, or Jeff Wall), *Cell Phones #2, Atlanta* shows roughly 3,000 cell phones artfully arranged in a trash heap of consumer waste; it is one of a dozen works in the series *Intolerable Beauty: Portraits of American Mass Consumption* (fig. 7.6). Swirls of color render the image a mosaic, or perhaps a Jackson Pollock drip painting, its all-over technique stretching beyond the limits of the frame to an infinite field of high-tech garbage. Much like the human body, objects often make their presence felt most strongly by falling apart.[22] The photograph presents the counter-image of the mobile man with a mobile phone who lives in our laptops: the very real detritus of our virtual lives.

The awareness of the ever-increasing levels of such detritus, and the growing sense of the relation of this detritus to our mobile lives, have conditioned critical no less than artistic practices. With regard to the nomadic lifestyle that is facilitated by and also helps create the garbage that Jordan photographs, Miwon Kwon has written the following ambivalent lament:

Fig. 7.6. Chris Jordan, Cell Phones #2, *Atlanta, from the series* Intolerable Beauty: Portraits of American Mass Consumption, *2005. Photograph courtesy of the artist.*

For many of my art and academic friends, the success and viability of one's work are now measured by the accumulation of frequent flyer miles. The more we travel for work, the more we are called upon to provide institutions in other parts of the country and the world with our presence and services, the more we give in to the logic of nomadism . . . the more we are made to feel wanted, needed, validated, and relevant. Our very sense of self-worth seems predicated more and more on our suffering through the inconveniences and psychic destabilizations of ungrounded transience . . .[23]

The more we seek to emulate a digital cartoon—a running figure, always running onward, with neither hands to hold a cell phone nor feet to touch the ground—the more we need to continue running, to show up somewhere, to prove we still exist, even as mobile bodies that deny their bodies' very existence. Such psychic destabilizations, of course, are also registered somatically, most obviously in the forms of jet lag, exhaustion, and sore backs; for every conference paper edited on an airplane flight, it seems, there is an equal and opposite backache. In this context, one might also consider a related phenomenon that can be termed the double negative of bodily denial: the imagined rings and buzzes of absent mobile phones, phantom corporeal sensations that suggest the extent of the conflation of nomadic selves with digital technology.[24]

IV.

One artist strongly associated with the accumulation of frequent flyer miles, the globally itinerant art star *par excellence,* is Rirkrit Tiravanija who, according to his own press material, "lives and works in New York, Bangkok, and Berlin." If his life exemplifies the nomadic and virtual in the digital age, his work, as if in response to our global psychic and physical destabilization, insistently creates or plays on a sense of homemaking, hospitality, and socializing. Indeed, as Janet Kraynak has wryly noted with regard to his peripatetic existence in the global art network, "The dilemma for [art] criticism is whether Tiravanija's work self-reflexively critiques this phenomenon, or unwittingly reproduces its logic."[25] His medium, most famously, is food, or perhaps one should say hospitality; a photograph of one of his events shows him serving Pad Thai to gallerygoers in New York in 2002. "Since the early 1990s," the Guggenheim Museum proudly announced when awarding him the Hugo Boss prize in 2004, "Tiravanija has explored a new aesthetic paradigm of interactivity. He has cooked and served food to his audiences, set up a recording studio in a museum, reconstructed his apartment inside a gallery for visitors' use . . . and provided opportunities for numerous other everyday activities to occur within art spaces."[26]

An installation and event at the Portikus Gallery in Frankfurt in 2002, presented by Tiravanija in collaboration with Pierre Huygue and the art historian Pamela M. Lee, exemplifies this emphasis on food and hospitality. With the help of numerous assistants, the artists constructed a giant wall of flat loaves of bread, slicing a doorway into it with an electric saw. The architectural incision paid homage to Gordon Matta-Clark's *splitting* in two of a house in suburban New Jersey in 1974, but the event was pure Tiravanija: an array of savory dips was offered to accompany extra loaves of bread at the opening. In the next room, following a lecture by Lee on Matta-Clark's food-based art, the three reenacted Matta-Clark's cuts on a cake specially baked for the occasion (one that evoked suburban Frankfurt more than suburban Englewood, New Jersey) while the film of Matta-Clark's own *Splitting* was projected on the wall behind them. Pieces of cake were then served to all present.

Perhaps most striking about the two cuts—one in Englewood in 1974 and the other in Frankfurt in 2002—was the manner of their documentation. Whereas Matta-Clark had a friend with a movie camera film his destruction of the New Jersey house, switching to black-and-white film when the color ran out, the Portikus event was both more social and, strangely, more virtual. Each participant, and many others in the room, supplemented the photographs and video made by the gallery with their own, rendering the event a festival of digital documentation (fig. 7.7). Tiravanija himself took pictures using the built-in camera on his mobile phone before heading to the airport to catch his next flight.

This essay ends with an entreaty for you to wait, and to continue waiting, provided by a video made by Pierre Bismuth in 2006. *Coming Attractions* is a hypnotic montage of the final moments of movie trailers, a

Fig. 7.7. Pamela M. Lee, Pierre Huygue, Rirkrit Tiravanija, and others. Photograph from Gordon Matta-Clark—In the Belly of Anarchitect *(Frankfurt am Main: Portikus Gallery, 2004). Photograph by Wolfgang Günzel, used with permission.*

slowly pulsating sequence of images, each one promising that something, or perhaps someone, will be coming soon.[27] Initially an amusing paradox—these are advertisements for movies we do not see—or perhaps a parody of a structuralist film, the work soon becomes addictive. One tries to identify the film being advertised, sometimes with the help of sound clues, background images, or added text. (Occasionally a movie is identified with a web address, like an advertisement linking to another advertisement.) Finally, one falls into the rhythm of the film itself, waiting for the next screen to appear while pondering the logic of film advertising, the pleasure of anticipation, and the aesthetics of attendance. The bodily aspect involved in holding on, in seemingly eternal expectation, here attains the level of sexual innuendo. Or, as Kracauer more decorously put it, "It can easily happen that someone who waits in this manner may find fulfillment in one way or another."[28]

Notes

[1] The first telephone call took place in Boston in July 1875 between Thomas A. Watson and Alexander Graham Bell. The first long-distance telephone call took place between Bell (in Boston) and Watson (in East Cambridge) the following October. See Avital Ronell, *The Telephone Book: Technology, Schizophrenia, Electric*

Speech (Lincoln: U of Nebraska P, 1989), 258–61. On the establishment of transatlantic wireless telephone service in 1926, see Mel Heimer, *The Long Count* (New York: Atheneum, 1969), 100.

[2] Siegfried Kracauer, "Those Who Wait" (1922), in *The Mass Ornament: Weimar Essays*, trans. and ed. Thomas Y. Levin (Cambridge, MA.: Harvard UP, 1995), 138, emphasis in the original. Further references to this work will be given in the text using the abbreviation *TWW* and the page number.

[3] For recent art historical explorations of attentiveness and perception, see, for example, Jonathan Crary, *Techniques of the Observer: On Vision and Modernity in the Nineteenth Century* (Cambridge, MA: MIT Press, 1990) and *Suspensions of Perception: Attention, Spectacle, and Modern Culture* (Cambridge, MA: MIT Press, 2000); as well as Michael Fried, *Menzel's Realism: Art and Embodiment in Nineteenth-Century Berlin* (New Haven: Yale UP, 2002).

[4] Ronell, *The Telephone Book*, 3.

[5] Ronell, *The Telephone Book*, 9.

[6] Perhaps the book's most out-of-date assertion: "The telephone presents itself nowadays as a relatively unpretentious thing. It barely belongs to the league of high-tech desires" (Ronell, *The Telephone Book*, 214). But if the book appears to be a technologically dated analysis, it remains at moments still unnervingly relevant in the digital age, as when it asks, "Does the telephone, despite mere appearances, not fundamentally belong to the structure of not-being-at-home, of a being expropriated from a *chez-soi?*" (51). And: "There is something to its not-thereness, destabilizing and implacable at once, it is a place without location from which to get elsewhere, translating into electrical carriages the air or ether waves which convey voices" (305).

[7] Jean Baudrillard, *The Gulf War Did Not Take Place*, trans. Paul Patton (Bloomington and Indianapolis: Indiana UP, 1995).

[8] See Juliet Koss, "On the Limits of Empathy," *The Art Bulletin* 78.1 (Mar. 2006): 139–57, from which this and the following paragraph are taken; repr. in Koss, *Modernism after Wagner* (Minneapolis: U of Minnesota P, 2010).

[9] A mutual interest in the work of Arthur Schopenhauer links the empathy theorists to Freud; see Harry Francis Mallgrave and Eleftherios Ikonomou, introduction to *Empathy, Form and Space: Problems in German Aesthetics, 1873–1893*, ed. and trans. Mallgrave and Ikonomou (Santa Monica, CA: Getty Center Publications, 1994), 8–10.

[10] Robert Vischer, *Über das optische Formgefühl: Ein Beitrag zur Aesthetik* (Leipzig: Credner, 1873), 10; in English, "On the Optical Sense of Form: A Contribution to Aesthetics," trans. in Mallgrave and Ikonomou, *Empathy, Form and Space*, 98.

[11] For a contemporary discussion of embodied aesthetic perception centered more specifically on the viewer's eye—as a conduit of emotions, and specifically tears—as well as of vision, see Andrea Fraser, "Why does Fred Sandback's Work Make Me Cry?" *Grey Room* 22 (Winter 2006): 30–47.

[12] Heinrich Dilly, *Kunstgeschichte als Institution: Studien zur Geschichte einer Disziplin* (Frankfurt am Main: Suhrkamp, 1979), 149; Horst Bredekamp, "A Neglected

Tradition? Art History as *Bildwissenschaft*," *Critical Inquiry* 29 (Spring 2003): 420.

[13] In this context, see Whitney Davis, "How to Make Analogies in a Digital Age," *October* 117 (Summer 2006): 71–98. This topic is also the subject of the series of conferences entitled "Our Literal Speed," organized by Christopher P. Heuer, Matthew Jesse Jackson, and Andrew Perchuk and held at the Center for Art and Media (ZKM) in Karlsruhe in spring 2008, at the University of Chicago in spring 2009, and at the Getty Research Institute in Los Angeles in 2010.

[14] Ronell, *The Telephone Book*, 315. In the winter of 1873, two years before inventing the telephone, Alexander Graham Bell was a professor of vocal physiology in the School of Oratory at Boston University. See *The Telephone Book*, 309 and 330.

[15] Rainer Maria Rilke's description of this process in 1914 beautifully evokes the mysterious power of communication by means of inanimate objects: "At a time when everyone still tried hard to answer us quickly and soothingly, it, the doll, was the first to inflict on us that larger-than-life silence that later wafted over us again and again from space when somewhere we approached the frontiers of our existence. Across from it . . . we first experienced . . . that hollowness of feeling . . . in which one would perish if the whole of gently persistent nature did not lift one, like a lifeless thing, over abysses." Rilke, "Puppen," in *Schriften* 4, ed. Horst Nalewski (Frankfurt am Main: Insel, 1996), 689, my translation. For more on inanimate creatures in the 1920s, see Koss, "Bauhaus Theater of Human Dolls," *The Art Bulletin* 85.4 (Dec. 2003): 724–45; repr. in Koss, *Modernism after Wagner*.

[16] A. W. Merrill, *Book Two: History and Identification of Old Telephones* (La Crosse, WI: R. H. Knappen, 1974), 29, quoted in Ronell, *The Telephone Book*, 301. The citation of Merrill appears to be a reference to Ron Knappen and Mary Knappen, *Price Guide, History and Identification of Old Telephones—A Scrapbook Encyclopedia, Book Two* (Melrose, WI: Ron and Mary Knappen, 1974).

[17] Ronell sees the connection between gender and technology differently: "Technology in some way is always implicated in the feminine. It is young; it is thingly" (*The Telephone Book*, 207).

[18] Or, if they are male, they often live and work in India. For a film documentary exploring the lives and jobs of telephone workers in present-day Mumbai, see *Bombay Calling*, dir. Ben Addelman and Samir Mall (2006).

[19] "It is as if Hal, the haywire computer from Stanley Kubrick's film *2001: A Space Odyssey*, were giving an avant-garde poetry reading with subtitles." Roberta Smith, "Art in Review: Mark Hansen and Ben Rubin—'Listening Post,'" *New York Times*, 21 Feb. 2003.

[20] Debra Singer, quoted in Christopher Hawthorne, "Sound + Vision," *Metropolis*, July 2002, http://www.metropolismag.com/html/content_0702/rub/index.html (accessed 25 Jan. 2009).

[21] Mobile phones have also inspired the creation of works of art that actually make use of their own technology. See Jori Finkel, "An Exhibition Where Paintings Are So Last Century," *New York Times*, 6 Aug. 2006 (section 2, page 24).

22 "The *Zeug* imposes itself on awareness when it ceases to function, at the moment of breakdown. The collapse of the tool in its serviceability is what fixes our attention," Ronell has written (*The Telephone Book*, 44), citing Martin Heidegger. "Not only has the body of mother earth become polluted and mangled but 'the self-assertion of technological objectification is the constant negation of death'" (217). The quotation is from Heidegger, *Poetry, Language, Thought*, trans. Albert Hofstadter (New York: Harper & Row, 1975), 125.

23 Miwon Kwon, *One Place after Another: Site-Specific Art and Locational Identity* (Cambridge, MA: MIT Press, 2002), 156.

24 On this phenomenon, see Brenda Goodman, "I Hear Ringing and There's No One There: I Wonder Why," *New York Times*, 4 May 2006 (section G, page 1).

25 Janet Kraynak, "Rirkrit Tiravanija's Liability," *Documents* 13 (Fall 1998): 37. See also Claire Bishop, "Antagonism and Relational Aesthetics," *October* 110 (Fall 2004): 51–79; and Calvin Tomkins, "Shall We Dance? The Spectator as Artist," *The New Yorker*, 17 Oct. 2005, 82–95.

26 Joan Young, "The Hugo Boss Prize: Rirkrit Tiravanija," Guggenheim Museum Press Release, 25 Feb. 2005.

27 Pierre Bismuth is better known for his work on *Eternal Sunshine of the Spotless Mind*, which in 2005 garnered him (along with Michel Gondry and Charlie Kaufman) an Academy Award for Best Original Screenplay. While the coming attraction operates in the temporality of the immediate future, it also has a history; on this see Vinzenz Hediger, *Verführung zum Film: Der amerikanische Kinotrailer seit 1912* (Marburg, Germany: Schüren, 2001).

28 Kracauer, "Those Who Wait," 138. "This waiting signifies an openness," Kracauer writes, "one that naturally must not in any way be confused with a relaxation of the forces of the soul directed toward ultimate things; rather, quite the contrary, it consists of tense activity and engaged self-preparation" (139).

8: Art, Medium, Progress

Juliane Rebentisch

I.

By 1970 at the latest, art passed a threshold beyond which everything seemed possible and permissible. Quite evidently, however, across the board it now rejects being instructed to concur with the categories of modernist art theory and aesthetics. This is especially true of the concept of medium specificity. In this essay, I shall try to embed the discussion of the aesthetic status of digitality within this context. In regard to the question of the role the modernist call for medium specificity still plays or should play in relation to our concept of art, the use of digital technologies in art since the 1990s has, in my opinion, merely advanced a trend that commenced at least twenty years earlier and has then taken that trend to a peak. This sharpening of focus has meanwhile undoubtedly assumed quite dramatic proportions. For digitality, as precisely those works that try to explore the specificity of the digital demonstrate, is not one aesthetic medium among others; you do not see or hear it directly. In the context of digital technologies, the concept of media loses its connotation of a materiality that can be grasped by the senses (like a canvas or celluloid, for example). Furthermore, digitality can, as it were, consume the older arts; it can be translated into all of them—music, text, and image. It is a medium of convergence that by definition runs counter to the modernist idea of medium specificity. It is therefore no coincidence that digital technologies today are primarily employed in artistic productions that we would term intermedia productions. But, in my view, the phenomenon of intermediality itself already constitutes the significant threshold—more in terms of media aesthetics than of media theory, where the central categories of the aesthetic discourse of modernity inevitably come to nothing.

For the attack on conventional subdivisions of art into the arts meant to call into question the modernist concept of art. The latter centers on the assumption that the production of autonomous art hinges on the technically specialized and historically informed inquiry into the specifics of each individual aesthetic medium. Even before the digital medium of convergence arose, this assumption threatened to collapse, not only because increasingly *different* aesthetic media were incorporated into individual works, but also because the assumption was undermined at an even more fundamental level as well by Duchamp's provocation, for he claimed the concept of art *had absolutely nothing* to do with specific media and corresponding skills. Confronted with hybrid, industrially manufactured, ready-made, and eventually digitally supported post-1970 art, the modernist argument about media specificity entered into such a crisis that its champions today can hardly conceal how inappropriate their arguments are in light of contemporary phenomena—even when they resort to bitter proclamations of the decline and fall of art. We can of course see such crises as an indication that the time for a paradigm shift has come.[1] Accordingly, such a shift has frequently been deemed to be underway in discussions of aesthetic postmodernism in art criticism and art theory. Yet the issue that still bears discussion today is how precisely to define that new paradigm.

I do not believe that aesthetics today should be replaced by media theory. Rather, I consider the unsentimental swan song about art and its discourse, which at times is heard from the vantage point of a theory of new media, to be the affirmative counterpart to a false diagnosis of a crisis. I would maintain that even the use of digital technologies in art participates in a paradigm shift that is prompted by genuinely aesthetic rather than technological motives. With regard to the current position of philosophical aesthetics in Germany, I follow the intuition that the so-called "transgression of the arts," be it digitally supported or not, compels us in general to replace the media-aesthetic paradigm with one based on the aesthetics of experience. My considerations proceed from the diagnostic hypothesis that the resistance that contemporary art puts up to the key categories of modernist discourse do not, as often assumed, call into question the idea of aesthetic autonomy as such but only its objectivistic misunderstanding, such as is expressed in the media-aesthetic line of argument. Through its attack on media specificity, among other things, contemporary transgressive art compels us not to abandon the notion of aesthetic autonomy but to fundamentally reinterpret it.

In this context, I shall investigate both the modernist idea of medium specificity and the related idea of *aesthetic* progress. In fact, both the idea of medium specificity and that of aesthetic progress appear obsolete in light of a situation in which, at least in the visual arts, essentially anything goes. Unlike those who have responded to this situation with renewed talk of the end of art, I propose, from the vantage point of a theory of experience, that we can indeed speak of *aesthetic* progress with regard to the critical relationship between contemporary art and its modernist precursors—not least when it comes to the question of how to understand the aesthetic role of medium specificity.

Needless to say, Adorno is of decisive importance for this discourse. Not only can we consider Adorno the best-known champion of modernist aesthetic theory, in the center of which stands the category of progress, but he also upheld this theory when faced with trends toward the transgression of the art genres at the end of the 1960s.[2] In this context he actively endeavored to integrate the current developments of the day into his theory to a certain extent. In particular, Adorno's essay "Art and the Arts" ("Die Kunst und die Künste"), first published in 1967, shows all the more clearly at what point and why he draws the line at these developments.[3]

II.

While both Clement Greenberg and Michael Fried, when faced with an increasing number of intermedia productions at the end of the 1960s, insisted that art can only obtain its full meaning within the individual arts,[4] Adorno claimed at the same time that, "Immunity to the zeitgeist is no virtue in itself" (*AA*, 369). For Adorno, the modernist avant-garde is notable for its resistance to the aesthetic expectations that decide what is still art and what is not. Seen in this light, the subdivision of art into the arts would thus seem to be one of the most tenacious conventions, one from which art must liberate itself for the sake of its autonomy. The avant-garde, as Adorno suggests, "took the philistine question 'Is that still . . . ?'" (*AA*, 370) literally and answered it with art that in fact no longer wishes to be art in the sense of the genre-specific categories foreseen for it.

In Adorno's reading, however, the trend toward what he calls the "fraying" of the boundary lines between different art genres does not arise from some sudden generational ignorance of the media specifics of the respective arts. Adorno thus defends a movement that is motivated solely by the developmental logic of the individual arts themselves, and it is a movement that, Adorno suggests, can also be construed as progress. Aesthetic progress for Adorno is confined to the dimension of the aesthetic "material." It bears stating here that the concept of aesthetic material denotes the historically elaborated *principles of construction* that are developed with respect to the artistic media and advanced by the major works of an era. Fully in keeping with this model of progress, according to Adorno, the progressive-critical inquiry of each art into the respective "state of the material" *(Materialstand)* solely legitimates the fraying movement of the arts toward a general idea of art. *Without* an inquiry into the problems of artistic construction that is linked back to the materials, the movement would, Adorno continues, run on empty. However legitimate Adorno may initially find the call for the spiritualization of art as a response to the fetishization of its sensory stimuli, this call becomes problematic for him to the extent that it ignores the fact that artworks nevertheless require a sensory basis if they are to be realized at all. "The more rigorously and ruthlessly [artworks] insist on their spiritualization," he therefore admonishes, "the further they distance themselves from what is supposed to be made spiritual," namely sensory material (*AA*, 373). The consequence, if we follow Adorno's line of argument, is that a "hollow space" finally gapes open between the intended "spirit" and the medium used, and it can only be filled by conventions or by the dubious belief in the immediate symbolic value of colors and tones; in other words by means that involuntarily restore art more closely to the scope of crafts, from which it wished to liberate itself. Adorno avers that the earliest testimony to such a false abstract trend toward spiritualization that results in its opposite, namely spiritless crafts, is Kandinsky's manifesto *Concerning the Spiritual in Art*.[5]

What so discredits Kandinsky's artistic program, namely the false abstraction of the "spiritual" from the material, is by no means merely the subjective problem of an individual "poor" artist. The danger of spiritualization reverting into spiritlessness is, according to Adorno, *the* thorn in the side of the historical development of modern art. For the trend toward "spiritualization," as Adorno suggests, is certainly not merely a contingent trait of modernist art but is embedded in its very essence. Like bourgeois society itself, modernist art obeys the principle of progressive rationalization. Adorno infers that artists cannot resist this development by ideologically declaring their oeuvre a refuge for the irrational in a world dominated by instrumental reason. Artists can instead only resist this trend by critically overcoming their own rationality, by placing the latter in the thrall of the "mimetic impulse," the intrinsic logic of the material. If the non-violent integration of these impulses into aesthetic form (and that is the semblance of reconciliation in art) is not itself to become ideological, then the principle of aesthetic synthesis must also continue to reference the countervailing claim, namely to represent an ipso facto highly unreconciled and antagonistic reality.

According to Adorno, this can only be achieved if the principle of aesthetic synthesis is negated in and through artistic form itself. If this is not achieved, then form frees itself, as it were, of its ties to a socio-critical substance and in so doing elides it. Adorno claims that this happens when the severity of the problem of formal structure is either underestimated from the outset, as with Kandinsky, or is sidestepped altogether, such as in John Cage's aleatory method. However, it also happens if the principles of creating form are rationally permeated to the extent that they are at hand as conventions whose masterful use then becomes the only purpose of artistic production. This consequence is already expressed in the notion of *mastering* material. The construction principle imposes itself over the individual elements, instead of passively following the impulses of the elements in the process of their integration in such a manner that the formal synthesis is just as much the product of these impulses as they must remain necessarily alien to it, moments of objection to it.[6] The intrinsic process that constantly works against itself escapes from the corresponding works, meaning that the "spirit" of the works is transformed into spiritlessness, something that Adorno felt was the case for the merely decorative abstract works that at that time already hung in the top executive offices of major corporations. This insight into the risk that aesthetic rationality can—owing to conventionality—turn into mastery of the material and thus into spiritlessness is the reason for the central status of the notion of progress in Adorno's aesthetic theory.

Progress is only possible via critical inquiry into the respective state of the aesthetic material, and yet for Adorno, such a state evidently only exists with reference to the *individual* arts. Precisely this context is the condition for what he terms the "dual stance of art toward its forms." Art's "dialectical nature," he writes, "consists in the fact that it can carry out its movement toward unity simply and solely by passing through multiplicity. Otherwise, its movement would be abstract and futile" (*AA*, 383). The multiplicity of which he speaks refers to the finite diversity of the arts and not to the infinite diversity of individual works. This is by no means merely because Adorno could not have foreseen the radicalness of the developments whose beginnings he described with respect to the phenomenon of fraying. Rather, this qualifier was part of the central thrust of his (art) critical theory. It may initially seem astounding that Adorno confined his concept of art so emphatically to the traditional arts. For in his view art can precisely not be autonomous by dogmatically defending conventional definitions of distinct art forms. On the contrary, only by negating what is by dint of convention positively termed art can art preserve its authenticity. But although the works do justice to the concept of autonomous art solely through conflict with generic definitions, he goes on to suggest that this conflict may never be completely allayed. On the contrary, precisely the critical focus on the genre-specific tradition is read as constituting the greatest loyalty to that tradition.

Adorno's hypotheses on the fraying of the borders between art genres initially emphasize the historical fact that the arts started to open up to one another precisely at the moment in which they liberated themselves potentially from a representational function and increasingly relied on their *respective* means of representation.[7] The result of these processes of reflection is that this musicalization of music, theatricalization of theater, reflection on the painterly in painting, and so on indeed led to the arts reflexively opening up to one another. And seen in the right light, this opening is an opening only in the sense that it is *implicit* in the reflection on the *specificity* of the means of representation in the respective arts. What is meant by this is easy to establish if we think of the graphic qualities of the printed word as championed by concrete poetry, or the aural aspect of words, such as is encountered in the works of James Joyce or Gertrude Stein, or the sculptural quality of canvas, such as is highlighted in the *Shaped Canvases* of Frank Stella. At any rate, what Adorno had in mind was precisely this emergence of what Martin Seel has termed the *constitutive* intermedial nature *fundamental* to the individual arts.[8] The fact that each art by no means plays the same fundamental role for each of the others reveals that the artistic transgression of the rigid definitions of different aesthetic genres do not at the same time lead to the disappearance of the structural differences between the aesthetic media that correspond to the traditional art genres. Instead they take the stage in a new manner. The transgression of established conventions of form-giving that are valid in the framework of the traditional definitions of the genres evidently does not lead to the abolition of the idea of medium specificity but instead to its liberation from being enveloped by the idea of genre specificity. This is also the case, I believe, with the reflection on the potential of specific aesthetic means of representation that takes as its starting point the issues of an art innately foreign to it, for example the confrontation of different aesthetic media in new hybrid genres or diverse artistic variations on the adage borrowed from McLuhan that the "content" of a more recent medium is always another, older medium.[9]

However, we will not be able to field Adorno to advance this argument, since for him everything depends on the distinction between fundamental or constitutive intermediality on the one hand and the syncretic hybridization of the arts on the other. For Adorno, the fraying of the dividing lines between the art genres is only legitimate if it is intrinsically motivated; that is, by a critical inquiry into the specific problems of *one* particular art, and this is a sine qua non for him, not because art genres need to be preserved per se, but because their differentiation as the *starting point* is an unavoidable fact. This assertion rests first on the assumption that there is an internal relationship between the medial differentiation of the arts and the principle of the division of labor in bourgeois society. Given this assumption Adorno rejects the unification of different aesthetic media, as for example in Wagner's music dramas, as the pretense of a unity that is false, given the reality of the division of labor in bourgeois society. Adorno's critique of the *unitarian ideology* of the *Gesamtkunstwerk* is linked to a critique of the *lack of unity* in its factual structure. For even Adorno's demand that the negation of aesthetic synthesis be the creative principle comes under the primacy of that very synthesis. To repeat, the problem of the construction of aesthetic synthesis can neither be negated abstractly (for example as in Cage's aleatory procedure) nor can it be forced through where medial conditions already contradict the idea of aesthetic synthesis (as in the *Gesamtkunstwerk*). For Adorno, specialization in one aesthetic medium and the related obligation to critically advance the tradition specific to the respective genre is just as much an imperative condition for the production of autonomous art as is the loyalty to the principle of aesthetic synthesis shown by critique. Precisely for this reason, Adorno proves to be absolutely modernist in those instances in which he is open to more recent developments.

The decisive issue for art theory today is whether the possibility of great art need be bound in any manner whatsoever to the artful approach to traditional aesthetic media, as Adorno insists it must. Any reflection on the specifics of the respective media, whether old or new, would then be a possible quality of art, but not its conditio sine qua non. In fact, the trend toward transgression of the dividing lines between the genres already corresponds to an increasing individuation of artworks in modernity that in the final instance is not tied in any way to traditional aesthetic media. The philosophy of art has responded to this among other ways by abandoning traditional theories of art genres, turning instead toward their basis. For it has taken up the *general* concept of art that must systematically be at the bottom of any attempt to classify its actual multiplicity. It is no coincidence that after 1970 this trend became so strong under the influence of the transgression of the arts that we can speak of a veritable paradigm shift. Thus in Germany a large part of the relevant debates in philosophy in recent years has primarily focused on the question of what the practice of *addressing* aesthetic objects — and thus the specific structure of aesthetic *experience* — is.[10] The question of the nature of aesthetic objects was thus *subordinated* to the question of the specific structure of experiencing them. In our context it is significant that this theoretical turn toward the concept of aesthetic experience coincides with the artistic practice of the last three or four decades in the critique of the modernist concept of the artwork. In my opinion, what we see against the backdrop of this coincidence is that the resistance that art of the last thirty or forty years has posited to modernist discourse is by no means the same as a negation of the idea of aesthetic autonomy as such. What the post-1970s works attack is rather only an objectivist misunderstanding of art. I thus believe that when so-called postmodern art dissolves the aesthetic categories that predominated in modernist discourse, this is an act of aesthetic enlightenment or, if you will, progress.[11] This, of course, implies a notion of progress that is different from its modernist understanding and from an objectivist explanation of the historicity of art that goes with it.

In fact, Adorno's justification of aesthetic autonomy on the basis of a theory of progress already becomes porous when confronted with questions of aesthetic reception in the broadest sense. From this vantage point we soon see that the experience of specific artworks by no means coincides with the grasp of the general historico-philosophical frame of reference Adorno believed he had to repeatedly identify in works of modernist art. It is thus no coincidence that Adorno wished works of art to be as non-figurative as possible. Instead, however, the actual artwork constitutes an open horizon of possible linkages and significations for the individual experiencing it, and this horizon may also be saturated by actual socio-political content, as is almost without exception the case in all important art today. Here Adorno's philosophy proves (and this goes against his own intention) to be too general as regards the particular nature of the individual works. For the progress-theoretical hypothesis of the dialectical unity of form and content concentrates only on questions of form-giving that are *as such* imbued with historico-philosophical content. In this way Adorno does justice neither to the particular qualities of the actual works and their respective semantic horizons nor, I suggest, to the concept of their autonomy. For his theory of progress corresponds to what is in the final instance a *technical* (not technological) concept of aesthetic autonomy. This becomes especially clear in its most stringent presentation, namely his *Philosophy of New Music*.[12] In my opinion, precisely a concept of aesthetic autonomy like this, one that refers to the "poetic" (and in this sense "technical") side of the artwork, cannot adequately fulfill the role Adorno primarily envisaged for it: to give an understanding of the incommensurability of the artwork, its autonomy versus the subject, and its reason. For how and in what way art is to progressively avoid its respective definition is decided in advance. And precisely owing to this operation, Adorno cannot, in my view, uphold his basic intuition that art is something that is intangible, namely an enigma. By contrast, his later *Aesthetic Theory* and also his *Parva Aesthetica* are evidently increasingly influenced by an awareness of the difference between aesthetics and technique [*Technik*]. However, in these later works he did not think through the consequences of this far enough. His thinking remained blocked by the attempt to give the autonomy of art technical roots in processes (that are in whatever way true to the material) and forms (that are in whatever way dissonant).

An insight into the fact that the aesthetic quality of a work cannot be reduced to technique or artistic strategies, which is inchoate in Adorno's thought but repeatedly obscured, is now given a radical turn in a theory that makes the insolubility of the enigma of art the decisive point of its definition and function: the aesthetics of experience. The aesthetic phenomenon possesses the "structure of intangibility," says Rüdiger Bubner in his treatise *Ästhetische Erfahrung*.[13] The fact that the object stimulates us to understand and yet, in a strange way, at the same time eludes our acts of understanding in order to provoke them anew—this is the autonomy of art according to a reading informed by the aesthetics of experience. Works therefore become aesthetic by virtue of that which within them cannot be conceptualized or grasped as an idea, a concept, a strategy, or a technique.

Now, from the perspective of a theory of aesthetic experience it is clear that an object's status as art, its autonomy, can be neither a transhistorical value nor one that can be objectively situated in history, as Adorno would claim. Neither can a work secure its status as art by itself—for this status is dependent on the historically changeable experiences that people have—or do not have—vis à vis the work—nor does a work necessarily lose its strength or tension just because of its duration. A logic according to which any artistic strategy will sooner or later be susceptible to a loss in tension that will degrade its once autonomous production to the status of mere decoration reduces the historicity of the individual works to an evolutionary history of artistic strategies: for these are supposed to perform a function that is both historically specific and necessarily constrained by their developmental logic. Even a superficial glance at the reception history of any works at random, however—the highs and lows, the loss of tension, the periods when they exist only latently, and last, but not least, also their renaissances—shows that their historical life cannot be reduced to the role allocated them by *one* specific history of evolution or progress. For experience, which can change over time, might also disclose anew the innovative or critical potential of older, nearly forgotten works. The many rediscoveries of forgotten artists or of artworks by contemporary artists express a relatively new sensibility for this non-teleological sense of (art) history. It is in principle not impossible that, even without ever answering directly, older art may provide answers to future questions. Thus categories such as innovation or even criticality cannot be definitively attached to specific conditions of actual artistic output. In other words, one should limit the critical potential of a work neither to the historical moment of its production nor to the intentions of the artist. Instead, the question whether—and, if yes, in what regard—an artwork can be considered innovative, critical, or progressive, or, complementarily, as boringly decorative or reactionary, has to be reconsidered and constantly re-debated as part of an aesthetic discourse in which experiences of art become publicly manifest.

This is what was shown by the responses to Adorno's value judgments, steeped as they were in a theory of progress. While Adorno essayed to give the category of progress foundations in a philosophy of history in order to define the criteria for art-critical judgments, in terms of an aesthetics of experience "progress" must be construed as an ever recurrent (sub-)problem of art-critical judgment—and not as already providing the solution. At the same time, Adorno's accurate insight into the historicity of aesthetic autonomy should be liberated from its progress-theoretical objectivism and opened up to the historical dimension of experience. Not the sheer fact of duration, but the experiences people have made through the works decide whether and how enduringly they may exist as art.

However, it is indisputable in terms of an aesthetics of experience that we can hardly experience something aesthetically if we believe we have already seen it or something similar several times. This does not automatically give rise to an evolutionary model of progress, but it does indicate the necessity of significant differences between artworks. In light of an aesthetics of experience, these differences again only impact on art criticism because they can be reconstructed in terms of a logic of critical relations, by dint of which the difference that the new artwork shows vis-à-vis older ones can be described as a motivated difference and thus as progress. That such a minimal type of technical progress is required for aesthetic success follows, in terms of an aesthetics of experience, from the *difference* between aesthetics and technique. For the difference between aesthetics and technique is reflected in the artwork as the tension between the general and the particular. While the concept of progress refers to what can be generalized as its concept or idea (that is, as technique), the concept of aesthetic autonomy refers to its particularity, namely that which in the artwork intrinsically refuses to be categorized in terms of such a generalization. Accordingly, in terms of an aesthetics of experience, the aesthetic necessity of technical progress is no longer grounded primarily in the problem that the conventionalization of certain forms comes up against the idea of doing justice to the material, but in the problem that the conventionalization of forms itself stands in the way of the *singularity* of the artwork. One consequence of this shift is that progress no longer unfolds in the framework of an unequivocal logic of progress. Instead, artistic progress today refuses to accept the modernist logic of progress itself, and specifically the strand of it that insists on the identity of the aesthetic and the technical. The modernist emphasis on the technical is rejected by the hybridization of the arts, by the radical opening up of art to non-artistic materials and technologies to the point where traditional artistic media are completely replaced by others, by the destruction of the traditional unity of the work in favor of fragments, and by the suspension of technical skills, for example through aleatory processes. This rejection also entails a critique of the modernist inclination to have aesthetic and technical judgments coincide. These trends can themselves be described as artistic techniques—in fact as progress—yet by not only creating new art forms but also transcending them at the same time, the transgressive works state something about the concept of art per se. They show that, in order to succeed, each work requires not only technical progress but also a trait by dint of which the art work, in its singularity, goes beyond this. In this sense, I think that the trend toward the transgression of artistic genres, in which new digital technologies participate *aesthetically,* is evidence of a kind of meta-progress: a gain in reflection on the difference between aesthetics and technique.

Translation from the German by Jeremy Gaines

Notes

This text is based on arguments first developed in Juliane Rebentisch, *Ästhetik der Installation* (Frankfurt am Main: Suhrkamp, 2003).

[1] See Thomas S. Kuhn, *The Structure of Scientific Revolutions* (Chicago: U of Chicago P, 1970), 88–89.

[2] I will use the term "genre" here to refer to the genres within art, meaning the distinctions between the various arts, and not to refer to poetic or artistic generic distinctions within the individual arts.

[3] Theodor W. Adorno, "Art and the Arts," in *Can One Live after Auschwitz? A Philosophical Reader*, ed. Rolf Tiedemann, trans. Rodney Livingstone (Stanford, CA: Stanford UP, 2003), 368–87. Further references to this work will be given in the text using the abbreviation *AA* and the page number.

[4] See Michael Fried, "Art and Objecthood," *Artforum* 5.10 (1967): 12–23; and Clement Greenberg, "Modernist Painting," in *The Collected Essays and Criticism*, ed. John O'Brian (Chicago: U of Chicago P, 1993), 4:85–93; Clement Greenberg, "Intermedia," in his *Late Writings*, ed. Robert C. Morgan (Minneapolis: U of Minnesota P, 2003), 93–98.

[5] Wassily Kandinsky, *Concerning the Spiritual in Art* (New York: Morgan P, 1972).

[6] "In artworks, spirit has become their principle of construction, although it fulfills its telos only when it emerges from what is to be constructed, from the mimetic impulses, by shaping itself to them rather than allowing itself to be imposed on them by sovereign rule. Form objectivates the particular impulses only when it follows them where they want to go of their own accord. This alone is the methexis of artworks in reconciliation. The rationality of artworks becomes spirit only when it is immersed in its polar opposite." Theodor W. Adorno, *Aesthetic Theory*, ed. Gretel Adorno and Rolf Tiedemann, trans. Robert Hullot-Kentor (Minneapolis: U of Minnesota P, 1997), 118.

[7] A reflection on this linkage is to be found in a decisive form in Romanticism, where it is strongly construed, however, in terms of language (Schlegel, Novalis). The trope of mutual reflection by art forms is of course far older if we think about the debate on art during the Renaissance, when the controversy admittedly focused on the respective representative functions.

[8] Martin Seel, *Ästhetik des Erscheinens* (Munich: Hanser, 2000), 179.

[9] See Marshall McLuhan, *Understanding Media: The Extension of Man* (New York: McGraw-Hill, 1964), 23–24.

[10] To name but a few decisive contributions here: Rüdiger Bubner, *Ästhetische Erfahrung* (Frankfurt am Main: Suhrkamp, 1989); Christel Fricke, *Zeichenprozeß und ästhetische Erfahrung* (Munich: Wilhelm Fink Verlag, 2001); Josef Früchtl, *Ästhetische Erfahrung und moralisches Urteil: Eine Rehabilitierung* (Frankfurt am Main: Suhrkamp, 1996); Hans Robert Jauß, *Ästhetische Erfahrung und literarische Hermeneutik* (Frankfurt am Main: Suhrkamp, 1982); Andrea Kern, *Schöne Lust: Eine Theorie der ästhetischen Erfahrung nach Kant* (Frankfurt am Main: Suhrkamp, 2000); Christoph Menke, *Die Souveränität der Kunst: Ästhetische Erfahrung nach*

Adorno und Derrida (Frankfurt am Main: Athenäum, 1988); Willi Oelmüller, ed., *Ästhetische Erfahrung* (Paderborn: Schöningh, 1981); Martin Seel, *Die Kunst der Entzweiung: Zum Begriff der ästhetischen Rationalität* (Frankfurt am Main: Suhrkamp, 1985); Ruth Sonderegger, *Für eine Ästhetik des Spiels: Hermeneutik, Dekonstruktion und der Eigensinn der Kunst* (Frankfurt am Main: Suhrkamp, 2000); Albrecht Wellmer, "Wahrheit, Schein, Versöhnung: Adornos ästhetische Rettung der Modernität," in *Zur Dialektik von Moderne und Postmoderne. Vernunftkritik nach Adorno* (Frankfurt am Main: Suhrkamp, 1985), 9–47.

[11] See Rebentisch, *Ästhetik der Installation*.

[12] Theodor W. Adorno, *Philosophy of New Music*, trans. and ed. Robert Hullot-Kentor (Minneapolis: U of Minnesota P, 2006).

[13] Bubner, *Ästhetische Erfahrung*, 41.

Part 3: Reworking History

9: Digital Negation and the Fate of Shock after the Avant-Garde

Richard Langston

> *The epoch is over in which an avant-garde would operate with surprises or direct assaults on an unprepared nervous system.*
>
> — Peter Sloterdijk

I.

IF THE HISTORICAL AVANT-GARDE sought to catapult art into life, then the transformation in question was never too far removed from the concerns of physiology and psychology. Even though Peter Bürger refrained from illuminating this relationship between art and medicine explicitly in his seminal 1974 essay on the avant-garde, he did nevertheless allude to its longstanding raison d'être. When he professed that avant-gardes deliver a shock intent on changing the lives of its recipients, he understood this shock to be quite literal.[1] Avant-gardes of the first quarter of the twentieth century shocked human bodies and minds in exactly the same way as did bloody man-made disasters such as trench warfare and train wrecks. Regardless of whether the damage done assumed physiological or psychological proportions, early avant-gardes relied on their imagined ability to violate a presupposed equilibrium between *res cogitans* and *res extensa* as an effective means of actualizing cultural, social, and political change. Upsetting this balance between mind and body through aesthetic acts of violence aimed at the institutions of art was invariably predicated on assumptions about the architecture of the human psyche and its functional threshold. Above all, avant-gardes gravitated toward two fundamental questions: how does the mind protect itself, and to what productive end might an overload of the psyche lead? It was no coincidence, then, that the historical avant-garde's own traumatophilic montage techniques echoed psychiatry's deployment of electric counter-shocks to cure shell shock after the First World War.[2] Yet the usefulness of shock for the avant-garde was doomed to the briefest shelf life. "By its very nature," Bürger wrote, "[shock] is a unique experience."[3] Repeating a shocking stimulus merely conditions humans to ward off further damage. And it invites feigned indignation steeped in ideologies that neutralize an avant-garde's intent on short-circuiting the mind in the name of a better life. In other words, repetition reinstated the dominion of the fortified mind and therewith took the surprise out of everything shocking. For Bürger, the singularity of shocking effects on the mind explained, in part, the historical finitude of the avant-garde. Movements like Dada and surrealism died precisely because they could not sustain the initial force of their own counter-shocks. Similarly, the repetition of shock proved no match for the resilient mind or the logic of capital. A devastating inversion followed the demise of the historical avant-gardes: shocking anti-aesthetics collapsed into a palatable and pandemic aestheticized shock.

At the threshold of the twenty-first century, Bürger's story seems to ring doubly true. For one, shock is purportedly everywhere today, yet its "curative" effects (in the sense of the historical avant-garde) are nowhere to be found. Almost a century after the earliest avant-gardes emerged, our globe has shrunk drastically. Modern geographic space has imploded. Time has accelerated to the speed of light. And the pretense to shock has metastasized to consume a great deal of everyday experience.[4] In the thirty years since pop sociologist Alvin Toffler envisioned it, "future shock"—the state of shattering stress and disorientation cause by rapid technological and social change—has become our present moment.[5] Thanks to modern communication technologies, shock is no longer confined to overstimulation brought about by the fluctuations and discontinuities of urban living that Berlin sociologist Georg Simmel first diagnosed at the fin de siècle and on which avant-gardes later capitalized.[6] The agents to which Simmel in 1903 attributed metropolitan neurasthenia—a precursor of the neurosis that the First World War would later precipitate—have one hundred years later become the standard of production for an entire information society inundated by shock. This saturation is perhaps nowhere better assayed than on television. Whereas cable network news suspends itself in a continuous state of imminent shock with its alarmist ticker tapes, inflated headlines, and suspenseful commercial breaks, prime-time television regularly serves up verisimilitudes in which the pretense of shock predominates both spectacle and narrative. If images, as Guy Debord maintained some forty years ago, mediate social relationships in the society of the spectacle, then today's televisual images, presumably more shocking than those of any historical avant-garde, have advanced as a dominant medium of social experience.[7] A short list of iconic images from recent American television confirms the centrality of aestheticized shock in present-day social relationships: the live television coverage of the terrorist attacks of 11 September 2001, photos of prisoner abuse in Abu Ghraib, coverage of the Iraq War, television footage of bloated bodies floating through New Orleans streets after Hurricane Katrina. And given the spectacle's extended reach via the Internet, anyone with a personal computer, digital camera, or even a cell phone can now tap into and even traffic in the stuff of shock. The novelty lies neither in the quantity nor in the quality of today's images of shock, for humankind has always been busy making images of itself killing and maiming. Rather, the difference very likely lies in the image's total envelopment of shock. The image has not only assumed the previously distinct roles of subject and object of shock but has also advanced the site of shock's mediation as a spectacle in its own right.

Returning to Bürger's treatise, my cursory account of contemporary visual culture as the apotheosis of the spectacle of shock — regardless of whether the shock in question is actually shocking in either the physiological or psychological sense — raises the question of whether shock still is of use in any work of art's attempt to effect social change. Is it possible for socially conscientious art today to gain critical purchase on shock when contemporary affirmative culture is thoroughly inundated by images of it?[8] Or did the death of the historical avant-garde in the interwar period put to rest the utility of shocking aesthetics altogether? To complicate these questions further, it seems that the human body, in general, and the human mind, in particular — the historical avant-garde's primary target — are no longer what they once were. At the very least, two seemingly contradictory arguments seem to advocate this point. On the one hand, it is reasonable to claim that today shock stands no chance of making an impact. From Simmel's vantage point, the success of the historical avant-gardes was directly proportional to their ability to crash through a person's "protective organ," a psychic barrier "metropolitan types" purportedly involuntarily built up against the threat of external disruptions.[9] Assuming that Simmel's foray into psychology was and still remains germane, then any contemporary avant-garde effort would necessarily confront protective barriers of the psyche fortified like never before due to today's apotheosis of shock. One hundred years after he first described the "metropolitan type," Simmel's Newton-like grasp of the etiology of the "protective organ" would very likely hypothesize how the psyche of what we might call today's post-metropolitan "media types" is encrusted with a thick impenetrable skin. (In this respect recent advances in psychopharmacology, for example, do merit further attention with respect to their propensity to soften the blows of the outside world by shocking the brain from the inside.[10]) On the other hand, it is also arguable that the methods of modern medical science have done away with antiquated notions of shock. Grouped under the banner of post-traumatic stress disorder, postmodern theories of trauma have followed on the heels of medical diagnostic imaging to advance a level of positivism in trauma discourse that leaves little room, if any, for matters of the psyche.[11] Consequently the word trauma has slipped its original moorings. Used initially in the nineteenth century to describe physical blows to the head and spine, it now characterizes a remarkably broad spectrum of negative stimuli, from sexual harassment to genocide, all of which purportedly leave their mark on the materiality and functionality of the brain in varying degrees of severity.[12] Given this sweeping span, it appears then that very little in our postmodern world, which is certainly full of shock, is actually shocking. And in spite of their apparent dissimilarity, these two trends—the psychosomatic transformation of the human body and the scientific reification of shock effects—frequently stand in a reciprocal relationship to one another. Assuming that this diversification and mollification do play into the widespread medicalization of trauma, one is left to ponder whether the scions of the historical avant-garde today have accounted for this shift, and if so, how. As will be elucidated in greater detail below, the proliferation and policing of shock so characteristic of this aforementioned psycho-physiological shift has in fact penetrated to the core of the political economy of vanguard image-making.

With so many variables in play, making sense of the fate of shock in twenty-first-century culture is clearly no straightforward matter. In light of my preamble, it seems that science and technology play an overwhelming role in complicating any traditional understanding of shock; contemporary medicine urges us to ponder just how antiquated the sway of psychoanalysis over any culturally critical grasp of shock really is. Medicine not only debunks mentalist concepts like Simmel's "protective organ" but also makes it clear that the human body is only as resilient to shock as it is malleable through, for example, pharmaceutical, surgical, or bioengineered intervention. In a word, the present-day circumstances surrounding shock could be said to arise from an overarching technological paradigm shift that has taken the punch out of everything presumably shocking. In stark contradistinction to these possible lines of argumentation in support of the extirpation of shock along with its effects, this essay advances three interrelated propositions regarding why the architecture of shock is still very much with us today. First, it argues that technical progress has neither mitigated nor magnified the force of shock. Additionally, the human body has, contrary to Peter Sloterdijk's introductory assertions, been neither immunized against nor anesthetized for shock. What, however, our digital age has achieved is a masterful management of the mediation of shock in the form of images. Second, my essay suggests that the critical vocabulary with which a legacy of cultural critique has sought to comprehend shock is deficient. To this end I contend that a longstanding bio-mechanical model of shock espouses a flawed teleology that predicates shock's eventual obsolescence. In contradistinction then to Critical Theory's Freudian conceptualization of shock, to which Bürger also adheres, I petition that we shift our grasp of shock away from models that focus on external causes and internal effects to one in which a third neglected category—the interstitial borders and boundaries that shock stimuli seek to traverse—moves into center stage. In doing so we gain far more penetrating insights into how sites of mediation as well as the essentially digital process of mediation itself have changed both psychologically and phenomenologically, culturally and politically. Third and last, my essay closes by querying how a new register of protective barriers has advanced among the living progeny of the historical avant-garde as primary sites of intervention for those works of art intent on affecting social practice. If the historical avant-garde's positive aim to realize art in life entailed an Hegelian act of sublation rooted in negation *(Aufhebung)*, then the examples that conclude this essay suggest that the negation at work in contemporary avant-garde works of art has changed significantly. Whereas the analogue negation of the historical avant-garde refused, rejected, and disavowed in the sense of Freud's *Verwerfung* and *Verleugnung*, digital negation in contemporary works of art—no longer dialectical—merely confirms like Freud's *Verneinung* the possibility of oppositional distinctions such as off/on, absence/presence, out/in, difference/similarity, and death/life. As will be established, explanations for exactly how these works stage digital negation and to what end they deploy it can only be unearthed if and when we attend to the changing status of boundaries in a society of the digital spectacle.

II.

Revamping shock's theoretical place in the avant-garde will require confronting the apogee of German aesthetic theory from the 1930s. But before doing so, we must first grasp the big picture. What exactly is shock? Did we really become immune to it over the course of the twentieth century? There is no better place to start a diagnostic investigation into contemporary shock than the morgue. In one of America's widely successful homicide television series, *Crime Scene Investigation (CSI)*, the morgues in present-day Las Vegas are the epicenter of high-tech shock management. Interestingly, the head of Las Vegas's fictional crime lab, forensic scientist Gil Grissom, is of the same opinion as Sloterdijk, namely, that shock is a rare commodity these days. Called to investigate an automobile abandoned at the side of a desolate highway, Grissom and his colleagues discuss whether a recent storm compromised their forensic evidence:

> GIL GRISSOM: Has anybody else touched this vehicle?
> POLICE OFFICER: No, sir. And I'm the one who found it.
> CAPTAIN BRASS: Well, just the rain. The evidence on the outside of the vehicle will be compromised.

GIL GRISSOM: Well, maybe there will be some evidence on the inside [Grissom opens the vehicle and a bloodied female corpse falls into his hands.]
GIL GRISSOM: Wow, I haven't felt that in a while.
CAPTAIN BRASS: What's that?
GIL GRISSOM: The element of surprise.[13]

This new corpse is different from all the others that Grissom encounters on a daily basis. Without warning, it literally falls into his hands, crosses a threshold too hard and too fast, and sends his blood racing, as is made particularly evident by the chilling string and piano accompaniment in this scene. Indeed, this surprise is an exception to the rule in *CSI*, for the sheer number of corpses in this television drama usually illustrates exactly how and why nothing is shocking any more.

The scarcity of shock in Las Vegas has little to do with any conditioned indifference on Grissom's part. A further look at Grissom and his in-house pathologist, Dr. Robbins, as they work in the morgue reveals how a composite of televisual apparatus and computer-generated imagery contributes directly to this dearth. In the same episode mentioned above, Grissom and Robbins stand before a deceased middle-aged white male laid out for a postmortem. Slashed hands and a punctured chest divulge clues from the scene of the homicide. Dr. Robbins initially leads Grissom and the spectator through the autopsy, miming the gruesome events as if he were the perpetrator:

GIL GRISSOM: Defensive wounds!
DR. ROBBINS: This guy put up one hell of a fight. Attacked with two weapons.
GIL GRISSOM: Two?
DR. ROBBINS: Two types of stab wounds. First, a long sharp double-edged blade. The blade went in smooth . . .

At this point in the scene, special digital effects take over the reenactment where Dr. Robbins leaves off (fig. 9.1). As if he were the murderer, Dr. Robbins raises his clasped hands over the victim's chest and thrusts downward, at which point digital animation takes the spectator for a plunge into the wound. This gratuitous reenactment of the stabbing—the eye's penetration of the body and its own violent gouging of skin and muscle—is useless for the ongoing forensic investigation. No information is gleaned; no message about the body or crime is conveyed. Particularly salient in this sequence are the acoustics of this reenactment. We hear not only the imagined sounds of human flesh torn asunder, but also the sucking sound of the gaze entering into and withdrawing from the body as if the body were a pressurized vacuum into which the gaze readily enters. Anything but shocking, autopsied bodies like this one afford *CSI* the means with which

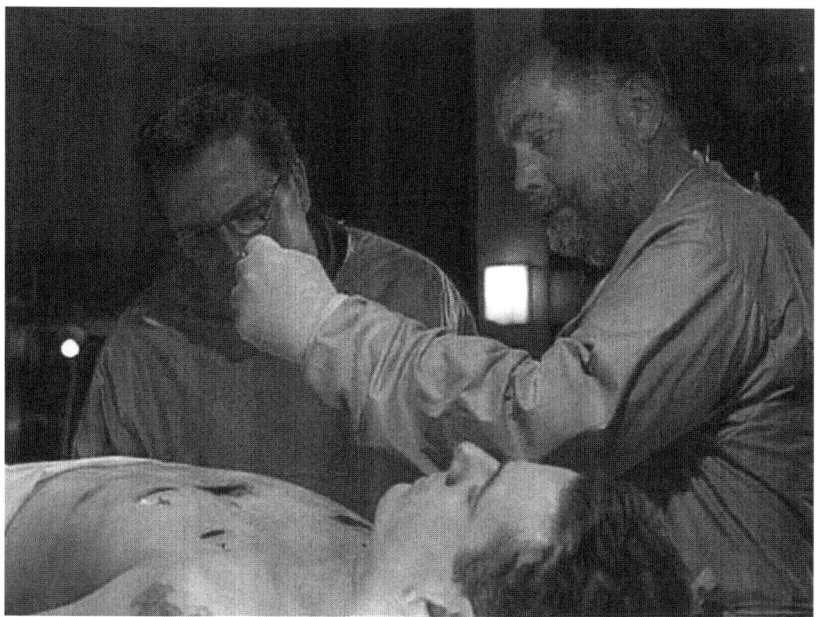

Fig. 9.1. Masters of Shock: Pathologist Dr. Robbins reenacts the murder.
C.S.I.: Crime Scene Investigation, "$35K O.B.O," *29 March 2001.*

to articulate visually and acoustically the relationship between corporeal interiority and the outside world. Grissom masters shock—in other words he mitigates the still very real element of surprise—by suturing together the inside and outside of the body. Only when the spectacle breaches and therewith masters our corporeal thresholds does shock vanish.

The empire of the eye did not always triumph over the gore of the morgue as it does in *CSI*. A leap backward to the beginnings of twentieth-century avant-gardes shows us that those who made autopsies their life's work were susceptible to sensory overload and psychological ruin. Take, for example, Gottfried Benn's semi-fictional pathologist Dr. Werff Rönne. In the first of his eight novellas about Rönne, "Gehirne" (Brains, 1915), readers learn that this young doctor has spent two years performing postmortems on a total of two thousand bodies, "some soft, some hard, all very deliquescent."[14] According to Benn's narrator, the mountain of corpses that passed through his hands "left him exhausted in a strange and unsettled way," suggesting that he arrived at a psychological condition not unlike shell shock. Of all his many symptoms, his feeling of having no borders proved the most debilitating. "I no longer have a barrier behind my eyes," he exclaimed. "The cortex that once carried me has disintegrated."[15] The consequences of this breach of his brain through his eyes affected the most basic of his gross motor skills. Rönne was so debilitated by vertigo that he locked himself in his office in order to erect a makeshift protective barrier around his pulverized cortex. And then suddenly from within this jury-rigged shell he embraced formlessness, substituted aesthetics for medicine (his blue anemone sword), and took off into the ether. Convinced that the world inside the clinic mirrored the world outside the clinic, he accepted the atomization of his forehead and the pulverization of his temples as an immutable condition that necessitated an entirely new post-rationalist view of the world. This new way of seeing is especially prevalent in Benn's autopsy poems of 1912. Consider, for example, his poem "Lovely Childhood," in which the lyrical subject, a pathologist like Rönne and Robbins, gazes inside a corpse:

> The mouth of a girl who had long lain among the reeds
> looked quite gnawed away.
> As the breast was cut open, the gullet was so full of holes.
> Finally in a cavity below the diaphragm
> one found a nest of young rats.
> One little sister lay dead.[16]

Like Rönne, the lyrical voice has gone numb. Whereas the girl's decomposed corpse elicits no affective response, the fate of the scavengers commands his attention and sympathies, as if to suggest that the gore of a breached human body shocks no more. Unlike Grissom's technologically aided mastery over shock, the poem's pathologist is suspended in an interminable state of shock, in which nothing fazes him.

By articulating twenty-first century Las Vegas and early twentieth-century Berlin we can begin to discern definitions and historical trajectories. For one, shock arises when borders are breached too hard, too fast, and without warning. This is certainly the case for both Grissom and Rönne. Second, shock is still conceivable today, yet the forensic apparatus (that is, television) succeeds in mastering it by destabilizing fixed boundaries and borders. Third, the mitigation of shock is technologically inconceivable in Benn's expressionist Berlin; shock is an unavoidable condition of modern life, which positions shell shock as the core of quotidian experience. These unlikely bedfellows, Grissom and Rönne, make it clear that shock has not disappeared in the last ninety years. Instead, our increasingly technologized world has afforded us the tools with which we can ward off the threat of shock. Whereas the missing barrier behind Rönne's eyes threw him into panic, our enhanced vision functions like a sharp blade (or scalpel) capable of destroying any and all boundaries. Nothing seems shocking anymore, but not because we are traumatophiles like Rönne, insouciantly seeing breached borders everywhere. Instead, in our digital age, we no longer see the rigidity of fundamental boundaries between corporeal interiority and exteriority, because technology has effectively eclipsed such divides. In other words, *CSI* stages the destruction of the body as well as the foreclosure of resistance. Measured against basic tenets of German aesthetic theory's engagement with the avant-garde, my juxtaposition of Grissom with Rönne suggests that the actual fate of shock has run counter to predictions first made in the 1930s. For thinkers like Walter Benjamin and Theodor Adorno, avant-garde assaults on the body's borders invariably backfired. Like Simmel, they both eventually espoused a conviction of the tenacity of an adaptive protective organ that protects the mind and body against harmful stimuli. As we shall discover shortly, *CSI* counters all of the implied anatomical assumptions at work in Benjamin's and Adorno's theories of shock. American television has confirmed that no such barrier, were it even to exist, has achieved the level of success that these thinkers once imagined.

III.

In order to illuminate the dominant model of corporeality in Frankfurt School aesthetics, we must borrow language seemingly unfit for describing the body. According to Lacanian cyberneticist Anthony Wilden, the human body is awash with analogue and digital communication. Signals sent within and between cells, tissues, and organs always involve the same switching between analogue and digital forms that is employed by the latest consumer electronics.[17] The complexity of the human body is unquestionably an analogue-iconic system, Wilden notes. Yet for any message to arrive successfully in the body it must cross over innumerable borders and undergo digital translation. A continuously variable analogue message must be broken down into biochemical packets of discrete digital information in order for it to pass through a membrane. Wilden writes, for example, "a digital command [on/off, RL] releases a chemical compound which performs some analogue function . . . , this release or its result is in turn detected by an internal receptor neuron which sends a digital signal . . . , and so on."[18] The continuous amplification of differences that analogue systems use to connote messages must be translated across a threshold into a discrete denotative language, or signifying system, which, in turn, is translated back again into analogue information later down the line. Understood in these terms, shock stimuli, while analogue in nature, invariably induce digital phenomena, since for any stimulus to be shocking it must besiege a barrier. Undoubtedly the most influential thinker for the Frankfurt School's understanding of human anatomy, Sigmund Freud advanced a psycho-neurological theory of consciousness that foreshadowed this structural relationship between the digital and analogue. In *Beyond the Pleasure Principle* (1920) he identified consciousness as a superficial barrier between internal psychic systems and the outer world. This neural system's most important task, Freud explained, involves protecting our internal psychic systems from the intrusion of excessive amounts of energy outside our bodies.[19] Our consciousness achieves this by blocking the outside world while nevertheless gleaning minute manageable samples and sending them safely down the line to deeper and more sensitive psychic systems (that is, the unconscious). To spell this out in Wilden's language of second-wave cybernetics: Freud modeled consciousness as an off/on switch, a cognitive thermostat designed to shut off when an analogue threshold is breached.[20] Like all analogue-to-digital conversions, Freud's consciousness acquired information while mitigating the deadly intensities of the original message.[21]

Freud's analogue-to-digital model of consciousness was enormously influential for Frankfurt School thinking about the biomechanics of the avant-garde. His visualization of consciousness comprised one half of Benjamin's theory of an avant-garde aesthetics of shock. In his first reckonings with surrealism Benjamin suggested, for example, the revolutionary possibility in surrealism's use of technology to thwart the barrier of consciousness.[22] Benjamin saw potential for expanding optical apperception by relentlessly shocking consciousness. Administering shock was to result in sensory overload such that "a vast and unsuspected field of action" (*Spielraum*, as Benjamin calls it in his "Work of Art" essay) would slip past the protective barrier.[23] Benjamin thus insisted on the revolutionary potential of maximizing analogue input and disabling the digital divide of consciousness. Faster cuts, closer shots, time-lapse and slow-motion photography, and other cinematographic techniques, all patently analogue in nature, enabled cinema to take consciousness off-line and therewith deliver images—cinema's precious remainder—directly to the space of the "optical unconscious," a purely analogue realm of experience. Facilitating unfettered analogue perception was inherently revolutionary, thought Benjamin initially, for analogue-to-analogue communication—a communication without barriers—would ensure a far more revolutionary awareness of individual and collective presents, pasts, and futures.[24]

Thanks to Adorno's protestations, Benjamin's original belief in avant-garde shock was short-lived. In a 1936 letter to Benjamin, Adorno confessed: "Despite its shock-like seduction I do not find your theory of distraction convincing."[25] And then, in his 1938 essay on the fetish character in music, Adorno proclaimed, as if it were a matter of common sense, that the machinery of capitalism guaranteed that the shocks of surrealism would degenerate into the cheap amusements of mass culture.[26] As if to trump Adorno's original suspicions of avant-garde shock, a compliant Benjamin later responded with an even more severe formulation, one that reinstated the ineluctability of the digital divide. "Technology," he insisted, "has subjected the human sensorium to a complex kind of training.... In film, perception conditioned by shock was established as a formal principle."[27] As if to champion Benjamin's eventual turn away from the revolutionary power of shock and toward negative dialectics,

Adorno then reiterated in 1951 that in "the mass-society of technical dissemination" shock "becomes really irrelevant" because "sensation... burns out."[28] Five years later Adorno settled the matter once and for all; he wrote that, after the catastrophes of fascism, and especially after the horrors of Auschwitz, no avant-garde could ever muster the force needed to shock.[29] Summing up the debate decades later, Peter Bürger etched Adorno's original protest into stone. The aesthetics of shock was destined to lose its effectiveness over time.[30]

By reiterating the fabled Benjamin-Adorno debate, I wish to direct our attention to the underappreciated importance of Freud's neuroanatomical model of consciousness for the theorization of the historical avant-garde. Ultimately, the common denominator for both Benjamin's theory of shock and Adorno's subsequent correction was their anatomical understanding of the mind. That Benjamin resorted to Freud's morphological representation of the psychic apparatus advanced in *Beyond the Pleasure Principle* is extremely telling in this respect. As historians of neurobiology have recently pointed out, after turning away from his early neurological work as a budding physician in favor of more abstract diagrams of the mind in *The Interpretation of Dreams* (1899), Freud reemployed the law of analogy in order to imbue psychoanalysis with the scientific legitimacy of human anatomy.[31] This was particularly prevalent after the First World War, when he localized consciousness in the cortex. "There's nothing daringly new in these assumptions," Freud wrote of his work on consciousness; "we have merely adopted the views on localization held by cerebral anatomy."[32] Yet, as Freud made clear at the outset of these remarks, his use of metaphor was pure "speculation, ... far-fetched speculation."[33] By 1933 Freud's earlier penchant for visualizing an anatomically correct morphology of psychic structures disappeared entirely.[34] Freud's use of analogy declared itself to be anatomical fact, when in fact it was a rhetorical device intended to challenge those who rebuked psychoanalysis for its apparent positivist deficiencies.

In hindsight, Adorno's insistence that Benjamin adhere to Freud's psychic anatomy raises red flags. First, he and then Benjamin both ascribed to consciousness a behaviorist-like capacity to be conditioned, a propensity that would invariably have led over time to its waxing ability to ward off all stimuli. Mapped onto Freud's neuroanatomical model, the protective barrier of consciousness would have increased in thickness over time to such an extent that internal psychic systems would eventually have retreated to the actual brainstem or its metaphorical equivalent, the unconscious. Furthermore, shock would eventually have to achieve such massive intensity to pierce the barrier that little if anything could coerce the analogue force to switch off the digital divide of consciousness. Yet crime-scene investigator Grissom tells us this cannot be true; the element of surprise, although rare, is still a real possibility today. Second, the unlikely psycho-neurological consequences of Adorno's and Benjamin's adoption of Freud's model does not reinstate Benjamin's initial faith in the revolutionary potential of shock. Were we to backtrack and lend credence to Benjamin's theory of shock, we would soon realize, as with *CSI*, that this has become our twenty-first-century reality; in our society of the digital spectacle, the body's innate digital divide is regularly disabled under the premise of experiencing life more closely than ever before. Third and most fundamental, Freud's temporary model of an anatomically enclosed consciousness, which he fashioned after single-cell organisms, elevated our encased brains to the sole seat of consciousness. The digital divide was therewith enshrined as the unavoidable and vigilant barrier that encases our minds. Whether bodies also contribute to the production or contestation of consciousness remains a question that neither Freud nor the Frankfurt School could effectively answer.

IV.

Marshall McLuhan's concept of new media as extensions of the body is a crucial layover in our query of the fate of shock in the twenty-first century, one that addresses the body problem that Benjamin and Adorno left unresolved. Picking up on Freud's idea of technology as projection and prosthesis in *Civilization and Its Discontents* (1929), McLuhan turned bodily perception inside out and therewith reconfigured the digital-analogue relationship in shock.[35] In the electric age, McLuhan claimed, our "central nervous system did a flip."[36] Because technology has extended our unprotected organs outside our bodies, we experience such an unbridled amplification of stimuli that a switch is tripped.[37] Unlike Freud's earlier model, in which analogue excess from the outside switches off the digital barrier to the inside, thus rendering the psyche defenseless, McLuhan credited external analogue data with turning on a stimulus barrier that inhibits a holistic perception privileging *res extensa* over *res cogitans*. In other words, prosthetic technologies consign us to prolonged states of narcosis. McLuhan's divergent definitions of "off" and "on" have far-reaching implications for our understanding of shock today. For one, McLuhan replaced Freud's idea of the innate digital quality of the human cortex with the assertion that it is the shocking extensions of man that precipitate the development of digital boundaries that leave us feeling numb like Rönne. In a word, McLuhan insisted that technology has reversed the circuitry of the barrier. Second, he argued — well before neurologically informed philosophies advanced models of the "extended mind" — that the seat of consciousness is not restricted to the cortex. Rather, consciousness is a sensory phenomenon that can transpire at various corporeal interfaces: touching, seeing, and hearing.[38] In other words, McLuhan unseated the psyche as the exclusive seat of the digital divide; it may very well reside in the body or even well beyond it. Third, McLuhan illuminated the contradictory nature of dominant spectacles in contemporary visual culture that pierce any and all barriers; while purportedly penetrating the interiority of the human body, forensic spectacles like the ones in *CSI* actually fortify the digital divide of consciousness. The scene in the Las Vegas morgue is a perfect illustration of the technical extension of the eye, which leaves us feeling indifferent to shocking spectacles of the object it lays bare. If indeed the medium is the message, then this message is a shock to our bodies, a shock about which we have no explicit memory or critical knowledge.

As much as McLuhan complicates my initial elucidation of the element of surprise in *CSI*, his are certainly not the final words on shock or the digital divide. While McLuhan does call into question the circuitry of Freud's "protective organ," he refrains from going as far as both *CSI* and contemporary avant-gardes to suggest that the barrier itself has become the object of technological transformation. With respect to the latter, we must therefore ask what aesthetic possibilities exist today with which the work of art can intercede critically in this transformation that simultaneously facilitates the proliferation and mitigation of shock. In this regard, Fredric Jameson gives us occasion to reconsider the value of Adorno's investment in the power of the negative in our third stage of late capitalism, a time when "the final loopholes . . . of individual and collective praxis" have closed up.[39] Accordingly, McLuhan's wish to re-instrumentalize new media aesthetically in the name of finding an antidote to the "narcosis of Narcissus" sounds as exceedingly Brechtian to us as did the early draft of Benjamin's introduction to the *Arcades Project* to Adorno. The overriding problem with both Benjamin's and McLuhan's corporeal models of shock is their starry-eyed belief in the possibility of hijacking shock without the political outcome ever falling prey to co-optation. In our present moment, Adorno's grave reservations about Benjamin's advocacy of shock accrue new significance, for the spectacle's dialectic of shock—its simultaneous production and deactivation—leaves no loopholes for breaking through consciousness, let alone informing any political praxis. In what follows, I present two contemporary works of art that reinvent the avant-garde's legacy for our society of the digital spectacle, examples that occupy opposite ends of a spectrum of possibilities for reviving the avant-garde's longstanding reliance on the power of negation. Each instance calls the historical avant-garde's use of shock entirely into question. No longer the sine qua non separating inside from outside and translating outside for the inside, the digital divide is stripped by these avant-gardes of all its translational properties. In fact, analogue messages no longer cross borders; the digital interface no longer operates as their mediator. The aesthetic of shock that incapacitated Rönne's cortex has become an aesthetic of the stimulus barrier. And whereas Benn's staging of the macabre debilitated the body's borders, these works detach borders from the realm of human consciousness altogether; the barrier of the psyche's "protective organ" has become a constitutive component of the social environment of the work of art. At stake then is no longer the barrier to consciousness but rather the barrier to political praxis and social experience. In spite of this displacement, the human body nevertheless retains a significant role in staging the stimulus barrier in our age of virtual reality. Contemporary avant-gardes now actively enlist bodies in the exhibition of the barrier's otherwise invisible states of total penetrability and impenetrability in order to probe the limits of negating the dialectic of shock.

Often read as an assault on the deficiencies of contemporary Austrian multiculturalism and the rise of right-wing populism, Christoph Schlingensief's action *Foreigners Out!—Please Love Austria* (June 2000) was also an experiment in erecting and piercing phenomenological barriers in our digital age of total access. Intended to simulate the neo-fascist politicization of bare life for all to see, what Schlingensief put on view is in hindsight not so self-explanatory.[40] The architectural space Schlingensief erected alongside Vienna's Staatsoper comprised two layers. The inner core comprised two hundred square feet of livable space inside and outside a set of steel shipping containers. Within this space Schlingensief interned twelve asylum seekers from Africa, Asia, and Eastern Europe for six consecutive days.[41] Around the camp a shrouded construction fence blocked the Viennese public from gazing freely into the spectacle. Yet Schlingensief's peep-show did present its audience with two ocular access points into the inner workings of the container: a narrow slit in the outlying wooden fence and a video feed composed of round-the-clock footage from some six surveillance cameras accessible to outsiders via closed-circuit television or a Web browser. Borrowing the interactivity of the reality television show *Big Brother, Foreigners Out!* invited Austrians to eliminate via phone or Internet all but one of the detained foreigners. Those detainees kicked out of the camp were deported from the country (fig. 9.2). The last remaining contestant won 35,000 schillings and a chance to acquire Austrian citizenship through voluntary marriage.

Although Schlingensief did retain the principle parts of Freud's anatomical model of armor-plated consciousness, he departed radically from this model by displacing, after the fashion of McLuhan, the stimulus barrier from the human mind onto the spectacle itself. Accordingly, Austrians were involuntarily conscripted as environmental stimuli and the barricade around the susceptible foreigners served as a stimulus barrier, a fine filter intended to block the detainees from the Austrian gaze, media publicity, and public outrage. Indeed, by the evening of day five self-proclaimed anti-fascist activists physically assaulted the container, defaced its placard, and liberated (albeit temporarily) the remaining contestants. The shock

Fig. 9.2. Eliminated: another asylum seeker emerges from the digital enclosure. Paul Poet, Foreigners Out! Schlingensief's Container, *2002.*

that this bodily violence meted out to the container's barrier was, however, wholly illusory. The analogue character of the activists' message did not pierce the shell, alter the interiority of the container, redefine the rules of the game, or halt the spectacle altogether. On the morning of day six the container re-emerged unblemished and the business of voting undesirables out and crowning Austria's most likable immigrant was reinstated. Much like reality television, which promises total visibility and unfettered access to the real, the prefabricated portals into the heart of the container were nothing but a ruse. In spite of its formal similarities to reality TV, however, Schlingensief's container project departed crucially from its televisual prototype. Instead of pretending to erase the frame entirely, serving up pure unmediated reality, and surreptitiously confirming the unavoidability of mediation, Schlingensief arrested mediation entirely. According to one astute commentator, the container's impenetrable shell deflected the gaze back at the spectators, regardless of whether they peered through peepholes, closed-circuit monitors, or computer screens.[42]

While Schlingensief fashioned the digital barrier as a deflective shield against which analogue shocks of protest have no impact, playwright René Pollesch reconceptualized the barrier as porous.[43] Like Schlingensief, he,

Fig. 9.3. Domestic floorplan as world-wide interface: Smarthouse inhabitants surf the Net. René Pollesch, Smarthouse ® 1+2, Staatstheater, Stuttgart, 2001.

too, shifted the barrier away from the realm of human anatomy to the technological space that encloses all of modern domestic experience. For Pollesch, the barrier has become our abode. At its core, Pollesch's 2001 theater production *Smarthouse ® 1 + 2* explored the consequences of absolute virtual connectivity (fig. 9.3). Performed only once in the fall of 2001, Pollesch's play introduces the passionate online shopper Frank Olyphant, who lives in a so-called smarthouse, a masterfully networked cocoon of consumer electronics.[44] According to his friends, Frank lives happily in his high-tech home, in which the heating and cooling system is connected to his refrigerator, computer, television, telephone, home security system, and, of course, the Internet. Frank's enthusiasm for his biometric-sensitive home fades, however, at precisely that moment when the voice of conscience kicks in as theoretical jargon. In fact, he and his companions bandy about theoretical vocabulary—the heterosexual means of production, the gendered division of labor, the character of commodities, the fantasy of capital, and everyday subjectivity versus objective reality—in order to expose the pillars of humanism that Frank's home obliterates. In their attempt to make sense of what is missing in Frank's smarthouse, the characters arrive at a point where these keywords no longer militate against what is wrong or missing. Rather, they describe the affirmative conditions under which he lives. Marxism morphs into post-industrial managerial speak. Critique collapses into affirmation. Pain entwines itself with pleasure. Everything outside becomes inside.

Pollesch's play envisions a dystopia in which technology has linked the private sphere and global commerce to create a seamless totality. As a result, all communication has become exclusively digital. Incoming packets of data cross effortlessly into the defenseless smarthouse. As no barrier around this home exists, messages from the outside require no translation. The unimpeded influx of digital information is syntax itself, the discrete organization of inner life within the house according to global capital. In response to this force from without, Frank and his friends project outward their own digital feeds, continually rearranged streams of theoretical signs. However, their recombination of theoretical discourses neither refortifies the threshold in the smarthouse (for none ever existed) nor transforms the intolerable conditions of their post-humanity. What was once the digital divide has become the ineluctable digital enclosure that conjoins inside and outside and private and public seamlessly.

In spite of their divergent conceptualizations of the displaced stimulus barrier, Schlingensief's and Pollesch's works stand on common ground. The digital has become hypertrophic for both, albeit in markedly different ways. For Schlingensief, the barrier is entirely impermeable, so much so that no analogue message can ever pass through regardless of how shocking it is. For Pollesch, our age of ubiquitous digitization has colonized what was traditionally the province of the analogue; both incoming and outgoing messages constitute an untempered and continuous flow of data packets. That these avant-garde instances of externalized stimulus barriers contradict one another confirms (as does the episode in the Las Vegas morgue) the simultaneous permeability and impenetrability of information borders in the age of the digital image. The difference between these two works lies in what they seek to disclose. In *Foreigners Out!* the unyielding containers exposed widespread accountability for the rise of Austrian xenophobic politics that modern technologies not only facilitated but also obscured. In *Smarthouse ® 1+2* the porous digital abode lays bare the intractability of digital technology's infiltration of the private sphere. The two instantiations of digital divides constitute opposing sides of society's critique of the digital spectacle.

Schlingensief's and Pollesch's inversely proportional views on the malleability of the digital divide and the futility of analogue shocks shed much-needed light on the fate of avant-garde at the dawn of the new millennium. In Pollesch's work, the analogue emerges, in part, as a double-edged systemic defect. Too much data into or out of the smarthouse triggers fits of screaming. Actors screech either in protest of the alienation engendered by the smarthouse or because the critical language they employ to expose this alienation overwhelms their powers of speech. In both instances their bodies overheat (as if they were machines), reach a structural limit, and momentarily go offline. Their shrieking and concomitant jerking illuminate, on the one hand, the body as a target of global capital that regularly reaches a threshold where compliance within the digital enclosure becomes unsustainable. On the other hand, they reassert the inherent analogue character of the body's ecosystem, over which no digital stream can ever gain absolute control.[45] In this sense, the screams in Pollesch's play, though analogue in nature, perform a digital function; instead of evincing semantic meaning they merely signify a "no." In other words, screams negate the unbearable state of affairs in the smarthouse by insisting that total digital permeability is not the case; the borders of the analogue body are not reducible to the universalizing push for complete and unfettered connectivity. In contradistinction to Pollesch's digital dystopia, Schlingensief's container insists that the unprecedented mediation digital media promise is, in fact, an illusion. The dream of pure digitality ignores in this instance the fact that natural language is both analogue and digital and must therefore undergo processes of translation that invariably involve traversing a divide. Yet the power of negation fares no better in Schlingensief's work than it does in Pollesch's. Administering shock to the impenetrable digital barrier in the name of its negation merely results in distinctly analogue effects—refusal, rejection, and disavowal—that neither gain purchase on the power of zero nor alter the unsatisfactory relations of reality.[46] In effect, Schlingensief's environment tells us that, in spite of our desire to negate the empire of digital technologies, the ability to access the negativity of a metalinguistic relationship to the real has apparently vanished. Regardless of whether technology renders it entirely permeable or impermeable, the digital divide significantly hampers any avant-garde's critical purchase on enacting protest as social praxis.

If Schlingensief and Pollesch are any indication, the avant-garde use-value of shock has indeed degenerated from once having tried to effect social change to now confirming its inability to alter the borders and boundaries that underlie all communication.[47] Nevertheless, works like Schlingensief's and Pollesch's upstage melancholy declarations about the obsolescence of shock by drawing our attention away from speculations about the effects of technical progress on the power of shock and directing it instead toward the significant ways in which technologies have altered the resilience and function of digital divides through which shock stimuli invariably must pass. To borrow from Jameson once again, it could be said that Schlingensief and Pollesch heed Jameson's call to revive negativity for the postmodern. As postmodernity has enlisted shock for its affirmative objectives, the only remaining recourse against this assimilation is negation. To borrow the words of Jameson in closing, Schlingensief and Pollesch concoct a "corrosive solvent to apply to the surface of 'what is'" no longer shocking in our era of shock.[48]

Notes

I am grateful to those who have pushed me in my thinking about shock; they include Tyler Curtain, Gregg Flaxman, Ken Hillis, John Kirk, and Bill Rasch. The epigraph to this chapter is drawn from "Gespräch zwischen Sloterdijk und Schlingensief zur Wienaktion," http://www.schlingensief.com/downloads/schlinge_sloterdijk_wien.pdf (accessed 25 Jan. 2009). Unless otherwise noted, all translations from the German are my own.

[1] Although he does not elucidate his claim, Bürger does point his readers to the later works of Walter Benjamin, which I shall discuss in the course of my argument. Peter Bürger, *Theory of the Avant-Garde*, trans. Michael Shaw (Minneapolis: U of Minnesota P, 1986), 80, 118–19 n. 35.

[2] See Brigid Doherty, "'See: We Are All Neurasthenics!' or, the Trauma of Dada Montage," *Critical Inquiry* 24 (Autumn 1997): 82–132.

[3] Bürger, *Theory of the Avant-Garde*, 81.

[4] See David Harvey's account of the implosions of postmodernity in: *The Condition of Postmodernity: An Enquiry into the Origins of Cultural Change* (Cambridge, MA: Blackwell, 1989), 291–93.

[5] Alvin Toffler, *Future Shock* (New York: Random House, 1970), 17–18.

[6] Georg Simmel, "The Metropolis and Mental Life," in *On Individuality and Social Forms: Selected Writings*, ed. Donald N. Levine (Chicago and London: U of Chicago P, 1971), 326.

[7] Guy Debord, *The Society of the Spectacle*, trans. Donald Nicholson-Smith (New York: Zone Books, 1994), 12.

[8] Because of the abbreviated nature of my preamble it is impossible to address at length the appropriate signification (post-avant-garde, vanguard, neo-avant-garde, and so on) of any such contemporary work of art that echoes the historical avant-garde's quest to unify art and life. For an extended discussion of my own argument for retaining "avant-garde" for the present, see my *Visions of Violence: German Avant-Gardes after Fascism* (Evanston, IL: Northwestern UP, 2008), 3–22.

[9] As will be elucidated shortly, Simmel appropriated a dominant figure in psychoanalytic thinking that Freud formalizes in writings about trauma. See Simmel, "The Metropolis and Mental Life," 326.

[10] The class of anti-depressants commonly called selective serotonin reuptake inhibitors is especially noteworthy in this respect, insofar as these medications flood nerve cells with an excess of neurotransmitters, thereby resulting in the eventual desensitization of the cells' receptors. Withdrawal from such inhibitors often results in paresthesia, or what is commonly called "electric shock." The excessive introduction of serotonin can also induce a shock of its own that produces anywhere from mild to fatal effects. See Edward W. Boyer and Michael Shannon, "The Serotonin Syndrome," *The New England Journal of Medicine* 352.11 (17 Mar. 2005): 1112–20.

[11] While efforts to marry modern medicine with psychoanalysis exist, the compromises the latter has made with respect to the dictates of the former have disposed of a core element in psychoanalytically informed treatises on shock: the

unconscious. For an exemplary account of the unconscious as insufficient interhemispheric transfer, see Laurence Miller, *Freud's Brain: Neuropsychodynamic Foundations of Psychoanalysis* (New York: Guilford P, 1991), 239–41.

[12] For more on this troubling discursive proliferation of trauma, see Ruth Leys, *Trauma: A Genealogy* (Chicago: U of Chicago P, 2000), 1–2.

[13] "$35K O.B.O.," dir. Roy W. Wagner, perf. William Petersen, Paul Guilfoyle, and Robert David Hall, 29 Mar. 2001, *C.S.I. Crime Scene Investigation—The Complete First Season*, DVD, disc 5, CBS, 2003.

[14] Gottfried Benn, "Gehirne," in *Gesammelte Werke*, ed. Dieter Wellershoff, vol. 2 (Frankfurt am Main: Zweitausendeins, 2003), 1190.

[15] Benn, "Gehirne," 1188.

[16] Gottfried Benn, "Schöne Jugend," in *Gesammelte Werke*, 1:8.

[17] Anthony Wilden, "Analog and Digital Communication: On Negation, Signification, and Meaning," in *System and Structure: Essays in Communication and Exchange* (London: Tavistock Publications, 1977), 157.

[18] Wilden, "Analog and Digital Communication," 158.

[19] Sigmund Freud, *Beyond the Pleasure Principle*, trans. James Strachey (New York: W. W. Norton, 1961), 29–31.

[20] Wilden, "Analog and Digital Communication," 156.

[21] Wilden, "Analog and Digital Communication," 168.

[22] Walter Benjamin, "Surrealism: The Last Snapshot of the European Intelligentsia," in *Selected Writings*, vol. 2: *1927–1934*, ed. Michael W. Jennings, Howard Eiland, and Gary Smith (Cambridge: Belknap P, 2003), 217.

[23] Walter Benjamin, "The Work of Art in the Age of Its Technological Reproducibility," in *Selected Writings*, vol. 4: *1938–1940*, ed. Howard Eiland and Michael Jennings (Cambridge, MA: Harvard UP, 2003), 265.

[24] Walter Benjamin, "On Some Motifs in Baudelaire," 316–17.

[25] Theodor Adorno, letter to Walter Benjamin, trans. Harry Zohn, in *Aesthetics and Politics*, ed. Ernst Bloch, Theodor Adorno, Walter Benjamin, Bertolt Brecht, and Georg Lukács (London: Verso, 1980), 123.

[26] Theodor W. Adorno, "On the Fetish-Character in Music and the Regression of Listening," trans. Maurice Glodbloom, in *The Essential Frankfurt School Reader*, ed. Andrew Arato and Eike Gebhardt (New York: Continuum, 1997), 295.

[27] Benjamin, "On Some Motifs in Baudelaire," 328.

[28] Theodor Adorno, *Minima Moralia: Reflections from Damaged Life*, trans. E. F. N. Jephcott (London: Verso, 1997), 237–38.

[29] Theodor W. Adorno, "Looking Back on Surrealism," in *Notes to Literature*, ed. Shierry Weber Nicholsen, vol. 1 (New York: Columbia UP, 1991), 87. It is important to remember that Adorno's dismissal of shock refers entirely to Benjamin's original idea of avant-garde shock. Adorno did retain the idea of shock in later works such as *Negative Dialectics* (1966) by inscribing it entirely within the domain of a post-metaphysical philosophy.

[30] Bürger, *Theory of the Avant-Garde*, 81.

[31] Cornelius Borck, "Visualizing Nerve Cell and Psychical Mechanisms: The Rhetoric of Freud's Illustrations," in *Freud and the Neurosciences: From Brain Research to the Unconscious,* ed. Giselher Guttmann and Inge Scholz-Strasser (Vienna: Verlag der österreichischen Akademie der Wissenschaften, 1998), 57–58.

[32] Freud, *Beyond the Pleasure Principle,* 26.

[33] Freud, *Beyond the Pleasure Principle,* 27.

[34] Borck, "Visualizing Nerve Cell and Psychical Mechanisms, 84.

[35] McLuhan was especially drawn to Freud's third chapter, in which he designated science and technology as products serving mankind's quest to attain godlike omnipotence. See Sigmund Freud, *Civilization and Its Discontents,* trans. James Strachey (New York: W. W. Norton, 1961), 43–45. See also Richard Cavell, *McLuhan in Space: A Cultural Geography* (Toronto: U of Toronto P, 2002), 81–84.

[36] Marshall McLuhan, *Counter Blast* (New York: Harcourt, Brace & World, 1969), 42.

[37] Marshall McLuhan, *Understanding Media: The Extensions of Man* (Cambridge, MA: MIT Press, 1994), 43. It is worth pointing out at this juncture how McLuhan's attribution of narcosis to technological advances departs significantly from Patrice Petro's own thoughts on the effects of sensory overload. For Petro, the ever more institutionalized shocks typical of interwar political modernism engendered active states of boredom that acted as a bulwark against the illusions of the bourgeois institution of art. Whereas Walter Benjamin's and Siegfried Kracauer's ruminations on what were then new media (e.g., photography and cinema) exemplify for her technologically facilitated modes of agency, these very technologies according to McLuhan, rob the subject of any such empowerment. See Petro's "After Shock: Between Boredom and History," in *Aftershocks of the New: Feminism and Film History* (New Brunswick, NJ: Rutgers UP, 2002), 63–68.

[38] A widely received example of this extended mind model is Andy Clark's book, *Natural-Born Cyborgs: Minds, Technologies, and the Future of Human Intelligence* (New York: Oxford UP, 2003).

[39] Fredric Jameson, *Late Marxism: Adorno, or, The Persistence of the Dialectic* (London: Verso, 1996), 5.

[40] For more detailed readings of Schlingensief's action, see my *Visions of Violence,* 234–44. See also Richard Langston, "Schlingensief's Peep-Show: Post-Cinematic Spectacles and the Public Space of History," in *After the Avant-Garde: Contemporary German and Austrian Experimental Film,* ed. Randall Halle and Reinhild Steingröver (Rochester, NY: Camden House, 2008), 204–23.

[41] Readers interested in assessing the architecture and events of Schlingensief's project can view the documentary film on the action: Paul Poet, dir., *Ausländer raus! Schlingensiefs Container,* Monitorpop Entertainment, 2005.

[42] Cf. Georg Seeßlen, "Der Populist, der Provokateur, der fremde Blick und das eigene Bild, oder die ersten Sätze des letzten Kapitals der Geschichte Österreichs," *Schlingensiefs AUSLÄNDER RAUS,* ed. Matthias Lilienthal and Claus Philipp (Frankfurt am Main: Suhrkamp, 2000), 251.

⁴³ For a more detailed reading of Pollesch's play see my *Visions of Violence*, 244–53.

⁴⁴ In an action indicative of his confrontation with the institution of theater, Pollesch has resisted publishing his plays, personally presides over all performances of his works, and restricts their free circulation. Originally performed in two parts on 23 and 24 November at Stuttgart's Staatstheater, *Smarthouse ® 1 + 2* has never been published. It is, however, largely modeled on a precursor originally performed in November 2000 and available in print: René Pollesch, "world wide web-slums," in *World Wide Web Slums,* ed. Corinna Brocher (Reinbek bei Hamburg: Rowohlt Taschenbuch Verlag, 2003), 103–328.

⁴⁵ Wilden, "Analog and Digital Communication," 160 and 189.

⁴⁶ See Wilden for an explanation of digital negation that applies to both Pollesch's and Schlingensief's works. As established at the close of the first section of this essay, the dialectics of analogue negation (otherwise known as sublation, or *Aufhebung*) negates a negation, whereas digital negation produces denial (*Verneinung*) without ever canceling out the return of the repressed (182).

⁴⁷ Wilden, "Analog and Digital Communication," 186.

⁴⁸ Jameson, *Late Marxism,* 249.

10: Transformations of the Archive

Nora M. Alter

> *There is no archive without a place of consignation, without a technique of repetition, and without a certain exteriority. No archive without outside.*
>
> — Jacques Derrida

> *Archival art is as much preproduction as it is postproduction: concerned less with absolute origins than with obscure traces (perhaps "anarchival impulse" is the more appropriate phrase), these artists are often drawn to unfulfilled beginnings or incomplete projects—in art and in history alike—that might offer points of departure again.*
>
> — Hal Foster

I.

In the past seven years, the artist Mathias Poledna has produced a trilogy of audio-visual work that assumes as its subject three separate moments within popular music: *Actualité* (2001) evokes the post-punk or new-wave movement circa 1979/80; *Western Recording* (2003) references the late 1960s genre of slickly produced pop songs; and both *Version* (2004) and its pendant *Sufferer's Version* (2004) point to Jamaican reggae and ska music of the 1960s and 1970s. With these three pieces Poledna positions his work at the juncture where music and film media meet art. Thus his work participates in the broad phenomenon in the visual arts that fuses popular music and film, but it also brings to light and preserves the largely ephemeral moments it presents in a manner that jibes with the inclination toward the archival process that characterizes much contemporary art.[1]

The concept of the archive as forming traces and functioning as a mnemonic device of shared history is at the root of much of Poledna's work. This has prompted him to produce a body of work that reflects on the complexities and possibilities of the archive (an "archival art," as Hal Foster describes it in my second epigraph) for the present moment. As Poledna explains, he has a "fundamental affinity.... to the whole complex of 'historical materialism,' how it is dealt with, what use it can have, what significance it gains at various points in time, what structures of collection, organization, storage, description, or valuation have been applied or are being developed."[2] By its very nature an archive presents a unique structure that at once contains traces and documents from the past in anticipation of the future.[3] Most archives begin as private collections (or obsessions) that slowly make their way into a space accessible to the public. In their private and public moments alike, archives entail the organization of information; the task of the archivist is to structure and catalogue the chaos that has been accumulated, stored, and assembled. History as collective meaning is determined through the very process not only of processing, but, more importantly, of ordering these residual traces and mnemonic fragments, which function as the very foundation of historical accounts. As Jacques Derrida writes in *Archive Fever* (1995), the very process of "archivization *produces* as much as it records the event" (17). "There is no political power," he continues, "without control of the archive, if not of memory. Effective democratization can always be measured by this essential criterion: the participation in and the access to the archive, its constitution, and its interpretation" (4, n.1).

Archives thus determine history and in their very structure coordinate the historical process. They determine the systems of classification and knowledge in which traces and documents are collected and ordered. However, the importance of those who construct and maintain the archive is usually overlooked. These individuals, who function as "the documents' guardians ... do not only ensure the physical security of what is deposited and of the substrate ... [but] are also accorded the hermeneutic right and competence. They have the power to interpret the archives."[4] The role of contingencies and psychological forces that initiate and preserve an archive, and in particular that of the archivist, who structures and orders the traces of the past and thus produces and shapes knowledge, history, and memory, is often ignored. Derrida goes on to argue that there can be no archive without the concept of an end, an "after" or "outside" moment to that which is archived. As he maintains in the passage in the first epigraph to this essay, archives depend on the notion of an exteriority, an external place, where what is collected and amassed is looked back upon as over, a historical memory. The archivist, in this equation, simultaneously performs the "repetition" that the drive to amass entails, thus performing the destruction of the very thing that she is archiving but also prepares the ground (the "outside," as it were) for the historical memory of that very thing. There is "no archive without outside," writes Derrida.

II.

Poledna's *Fondazione* (1998), a video project that focuses on Italian left-wing politics of the 1970s, details the activities of the publisher Giangiacomo Feltrinelli, who died in 1972 while attempting to paralyze part of Milan by bombing an electrical pylon. What particularly interested Poledna was not the personage of Feltrinelli and the volatility of Italian politics in the 1970s but the "Archive Feltrinelli" that had subsequently been assembled. Thus the artist structured the narrative of *Fondazione* around David Bidussa, the librarian in charge of putting together and cataloguing the Feltrinelli archive. Similarly, a great portion of Poledna's project *Scan* (1997) concerns attempts to track the methods and ways in which the popular culture of punk rock has been recorded for future memory, and includes, for instance, interviews with archivists at the Victoria and Albert Museum in London. For Poledna, the archivist becomes a historical muse who functions to preserve, filter, and disseminate the past; s/he is an important conduit for determining what is and what is not recorded, what are and what are not suitable historical traces. The archivist, in short, is the important intermediary who stands between the historian and the residues and traces of the past, the often overlooked lens through which history is constructed.

Poledna's interest in the archivist and in the archival process rests primarily on his view that archives are the core of the dynamic process of historicization, the basis on which history is written. History and memory have long been central to Poledna's artistic practice. While coordinating the exhibition *The Making Of. . . .* (1998), he set as his starting point "the idea of a historiography in exhibition form."[5] Museum exhibitions have from their first instances aimed to recover the past and construct historical meaning. As sites where citizens construct, reaffirm, and preserve their subjectivity and historical self-consciousness, museum exhibitions have long served as one of the cornerstones of the (bourgeois) public sphere. But Poledna is just as interested in the practice of exhibiting traces and documents (or objects) as he is in analyzing what has been deemed worthy of exhibition. This is what leads him to the figure of the archivist, who is positioned as the one who governs what is said and unsaid, recorded and unrecorded. Thus Poledna assumes the dual roles of artist and philosopher of history.

The now two-decade-long phenomenon of computerized archivization has radically reconfigured the standard operation of an archive. More things are being archived today than at any previous moment in history. Computers have gone from being primarily production tools for the generation of knowledge to functioning as machines for the storage and distribution of digital information.[6] As the amount of data available on the Internet increases everyday with more and more documents, texts, images, and sounds scanned, recorded, and made virtually accessible, the very nature of "research" and the ways in which it is conducted have been transformed. No longer is it necessary to travel great distances to visit and conduct research in many archives; public information is now readily accessible in the private sphere through the Internet.

On the level of technology, advanced digital production has transformed image and sound recording, editing, storage, retrieval, and distribution systems. It is now possible to make a film merely by accessing the ever-expanding digital database of existent audio-visual works. Software programs allow individuals to download music in ever-new configurations, thereby making the customized commercial album a thing of the past. In this way, the digital databank provides the possibility of infinite storage, retrieval, and communication of information without any consideration of original context. Allan Sekula once cautioned against such indiscriminate image use (or abuse) in the traditional archive: "In an archive the possibility of meaning is 'liberated' from the actual contingencies of use. But this liberation is also a loss of context."[7] However, with modern information technology's mechanism of digitization, such a practice has reached an entirely different dimension. Former distinctions between copy and original now become obsolete, and versions become omnipresent.

But there are a number of downsides to the greatly increased access to digital information. For one thing, the mechanism through which the "original" documents, in being converted into bytes of digital information, are democratized in their dissemination, also levels their former uniqueness and singularity. The process of digitization transforms the heterogeneity of disparate and materially distinct media such as text, photographs, sound recordings, films, and the like, into a homogeneous mass of computer data.[8] For another thing, as the actual archive is digitized, the site that houses "special collections" loses its *raison d'être,* rendering obsolete specialists whose task had been to curate, order, and maintain the archive. As Walter Benjamin once observed, with the waning of the role of the archivist comes the decline of the individual character that each archive possesses: "The phenomenon of collecting loses its meaning as it loses its personal owner. . . . Only in extinction is the collector comprehended."[9] The new digital archives are no longer organized by the "personality" of the human "subject" who put the material together in particular constellations; rather her own vision, or version, has been replaced by the cold, impersonal technology of a computer grid.[10] We will return later to the issue of what that shift does to the very nature of an archive. The point I want to emphasize here is that it is precisely at the moment that the traditional role of the archivist is becoming obsolete that Poledna pays tribute to these figures who, in their own idiosyncratic and unpredictable ways, structured and ordered the caches to which they devoted so much time and attention.[11] Furthermore, although in a somewhat more opaque manner than with the former two points, Poledna's project suggests that what is lacking in the transition from the private to the publicly accessible archive is the insight that "the public" has become an increasingly controlled and regulated space and that the insistent, and largely disabling, deflection of the archive onto the domain of public experience itself is part of the effect of that regulatory rerouting.

III.

Each part of Poledna's trilogy performatively recreates and represents a historical period, genre, and technological stage in both film history and popular music.[12] Fredric Jameson has described the nexus between technology, genres, and historical periods as a phenomenon that consists of "a single historical process, whose parts condition each other reciprocally, but also 'reflect' each other in curious aleatory parallel spirals."[13] The title of *Actualité* references the earliest of film productions: fifty-five-second single-take snippets from everyday life by the Lumière brothers at the turn of the twentieth century. Audially and visually however, *Actualité* summons a more topical subject: the post-punk rock band era.[14] The film features a rehearsal session in which no song is played in its entirety. The connecting link between the experiments of the Lumières and the *Actualité* project is the ushering in of a new genre (one cinematic and the other musical). Like the Lumières' films, the post-punk movements were characterized by trial and error experimentation and the full possibility of productive accidents.[15] By contrast, *Western Recording* points to another cinematic moment, namely that of complex studio practice in which all factors are highly controlled and manipulated and nothing is left to chance or error. The film features the solitary figure of a singer singing Harry Nilsson's 1969 song, "City Life," in a fully equipped studio. Here it should also be emphasized that within the world of popular music *Western Recording* interfaces with the celebrated Studio 3 at Western Recorders on Sunset Boulevard, where The Beach Boys, Nancy Sinatra, and many others manufactured highly successful hits. The material body and voice of the singer who is at the center of the film's attention are tightly controlled: his gestures are limited, suggestive of the grand era of studio production that produced an array of classical masterpieces whose artifice and mastery are admirable. Thus if *Actualité* resonates with the first decade of film before the advent of continuity editing (when the medium was still wide open to errors that might lead to advances and new discoveries), *Western Recording* delivers and comments on entirely different manufacturing conditions: the era of the perfect product.[16] From this perspective, one of the filmic references of both *Actualité* and *Western Recording* is Jean-Luc Godard's *One plus One* (1968), which meticulously tracks the often monotonous work that went into the production of The Rolling Stones' hit "Sympathy for the Devil." In all three instances the labor of producing a hit song is emphasized; the slow and tedious process of recording stands in sharp contrast to the visual performance of a live concert, along with the expectations of the effect that the recorded track will have on the viewer. Poledna's objective is to represent change and to create portals that open onto larger discussions of audio-visual production, such as the shift in the 1960s from studio to post-studio production in film and music. As he explains in an early interview, he chooses certain topics for their value as "signs that emblematically express societal change; whether they exist concretely or merely as promises."[17] But unlike Godard, who often intercuts the recording sessions with staged sequences that are full of topicality (as he did with *One plus One* by referencing the Black Panther movement and protests against the Vietnam war), Poledna offers no overt commentary or link. If *Actualité* and *Western Recording* both signal significant moments in the history of film and music production, my interest here is to discern what shifts are marked by the last part of the trilogy: *Version* and *Sufferer's Version*.

On one level, *Version* is about music. But insofar as the work does not advance an explicit message, it does not function as a documentary. Unlike, for example, Dan Graham's video essay *Rock My Religion*, which through its montage, voice-over, found footage, and interviews produces an elaborate thesis built on the parallels between the sounds of religious revival music and rock and roll, the films that comprise Poledna's trilogy offer no narrative. This has not always been the case with Poledna's work; earlier projects presented considerably more information. His interest in music can be traced back to his *Produktion Pop* (1996), which explored British new wave, or to his *Scan*, which, as we saw earlier, consisted of interviews that documented efforts to preserve and narrativize punk rock. However, both of these earlier pieces resembled more traditional information-based documentaries. With *Version*, *Sufferer's Version*, and the other two film installations that constitute his most recent trilogy, something else takes place. Each of the works confronts the viewer with an uncontextualized presentation of music in a studio. In both *Version* and *Sufferer's Version* the cinematic space is limited to a static camera trained on dancers who perform highly choreographed pieces, their movements suspended in a void dislocated in time and place. The critique is not performed through a text or voice-over. Rather, the critical dimension is conducted through the operation of the audio-visual image.[18]

Whereas *Version* is displayed in a film loop as part of a larger sculptural installation, *Sufferer's Version* is designed specifically for one-time screenings in movie theatres.[19] *Sufferer's Version* is based on footage created during the making of *Version* and includes a sound track recorded in the late 1970s and first released in 1983, "Working Hard for the Rent Man," by Jamaican singer Junior Delahaye. The film opens with music and a black screen. After a few bars, three dancers enter the frame and perform a highly choreographed, stylized, and regimented dance number. The trio, consisting of a black woman, a white woman, and a black man, are clothed in simple attire without jewelry or accessories. The camera is static and captures only the top half of their bodies as they move in and out of the frame. Gradually the dancers decrease in number until we are left with only one. The music ends before she finishes dancing. Hence her performance is concluded in complete silence, which renders her movements mechanical and rigid. The routine references both the vernacular movements of modern dance of the 1960s and a highly stylized version of the detached coolness of Jamaican dance of the same period.[20]

In *Sufferer's Version* Poledna interrupts, fragments, and tears apart both visual and audio tracks. The screen is at times empty of figures, leaving only a black void that punctuates the image track. These brief passages do not last more than a few moments, yet they are long enough to draw attention to the limited and framed gaze of the camera and the off-screen space into which the dancers disappear. The artificial nature of the staging is underscored by the black screen against which the dancers are filmed, evoking an absence, a space of non-movement and non-image.

A similar strategy of interruptions is evident in *Actualité* and *Western Recording*. The former audially renders a sampling of post-punk music from bands such as The Gang of Four, the Au Pairs, Wire, and Scritti Politti. Conversations between the actors who perform as musicians break apart the musical interludes and produce an overall fracturing effect. Although the sound track of *Western Recording* follows the production of the song "City Life" in its entirety, a rupture takes place on the audial track. The film begins with the camera trained on the singer/actor who stands alone, wearing headsets, with his hands thrust into his pockets in front of a microphone. There is complete silence on the soundtrack, but the singer listens raptly. The spectator does not hear what the singer hears; that part of the diegesis remains inaccessible. After a couple of minutes the singer begins to sing. But his voice, in a solo without musical accompaniment and back-up, sounds eerily alone, naked, and exposed. Its solitary whine, despite the visual pairing to the singer's body, seems disembodied and disconnected. As the recording progresses, the sounds of the other tracks featuring the music that the singer hears through his headphones fill the room in which he sings. With this, the sound/image become full and both audially and visually complete. The soundtrack then abruptly clicks off, leaving only the voice of the singer. By isolating and extracting the pure qualities of the voice, Poledna underscores the intimate links between sound, music, and a body singing. The voice, minus the other tracks on the soundboard, is disembodied and part of the off-screen world.[21] Unlike image tracks, which generally function as a single layer, sound tracks are extremely complex and involve a number of different layers that need to be mixed. By disentangling the parts from the whole, Poledna points to the invisible complexity that is conventionally held together by an intricate system of overlaying and stitching.

Version is shot on 16mm black-and-white film with the same static camera angle and mid-level shot employed in *Sufferer's Version*. But the film is entirely silent. Bodies move in and out of the film rectangle. Sometimes, when the clothes of the dancers are near the camera, they tend to blur. The figures dance, not in an obviously choreographed manner, as in *Sufferer's Version,* but in a more spontaneous, natural way. Their movements are rhythmic and the texture of their swaying clothes creates strong tonal contrasts of dark and light. The bodies in movement come to resemble the abstract shapes that flitter across the screen in Hans Richter's early *Rhythmus* film series. Even when the camera eventually pans upward to focus on the faces of the dancers, the latter remain mute and expressionless, devoid of emotion. The human subject in motion becomes a mere object. The silence is striking and renders what appears on the screen abstract and purely visual.

The silence surrounding the dancer renders her movements strange and disembodied. As with the end of *Sufferer's Version,* the absence of a soundtrack functions as a blank—a space devoid of signification, like the black screen, waiting to be filled. In the installation of *Version,* the silence is all the more resounding, and it is entirely up to the spectator to imagine and fill in the accompanying music to which the silent bodies are in motion. Recall that *Version* is meant to be screened in an exhibition gallery and the work is constituted as much by the installation as by the projected image on the screen. With the projection of the film in the darkened gallery emanating from behind the entrance, the shadows of the spectators in the room become part of the image. Because of this the stationary observational stances of the viewers contrast sharply with the filmed moving figures. Moreover, the resounding silence of Poledna's mute film underscores the visual arts' traditional resistance to sound. During the late 1920s and early 1930s, when sound was first introduced, it was a common adage among filmmakers that "silence meant art."[22]

One way to fill the void is to trace the significance of the music one does hear. *Sufferer's Version* references a rich history of diasporic music of resistance. It signals what Dick Hebdige has identified as the beginnings of "a 'cultural revolution,' . . . a generalized shift in patterns of industrial as well as ideological development away from Europe and America towards Cuba and the Third World."[23] The word "sufferer" refers to a type of song produced in Jamaica by the disenfranchised, who occupy the lowest position in the society. The songs allude to the tragedies of everyday life and are related to "sufferation," which in West Indian folk culture refers to the abuses endured because of colonial and economic exploitation. "Sufferer's Songs" made their way into popular music through the Rastafarian movement, which proposed a solution to the destitute material conditions by advocating both a literal and a symbolic return to "Africa."[24] The musical expression of this ideology initially emerged as reggae and ska, was later transformed into dub, and more recently has taken the forms of rap and hip-hop. Its condition is further complicated because the resulting cultural production is hybrid or syncretic, combining strains from first-world countries with the indigenous music. Thus songs by James Brown or Elvis Presley are transported to the West Indies, changed, and then returned to the United States and Britain in an altered, hybrid form or *version*.

IV.

The term "version" is crucial for understanding reggae, for it refers to the process whereby a "reggae record is released and literally hundreds of different versions of the same rhythm or melody will follow in its wake."[25] Every time a version is released, the original tune will be slightly modified. "Versioning" is at the heart not only of reggae but also of most (if not all) Afro-American and Caribbean music, including jazz, blues, rap, rhythm and blues, calypso, soca, salsa, Afro-Cuban, and so on."[26] This key term explains the dual structure of Poledna's *Version* and *Sufferer's Version*. The two pieces are directly related to one another. The formal structure that drives these two film installation projects thus performs the musical dynamic of "versioning." The two parts, silent film and sound film, as much as the intermedial fusion of installation and film, speak to one another in a relational exchange. The complex dual structure also has a musical reference, namely that of early "singles," 45-rpm records on which the "A-side" would feature the title song with vocals and the "B-side" would consist of just the music track. But as Poledna demonstrates with the mute celluloid part of *Version*, it is the music, the sounds, that make the images legible. Without sound *Version* is but an abstract study in motion and rhythm. The highly charged socio-political content of *Sufferer's Version* is simply not present in the silent *Version*.

Version is supplemented with a vitrine, placed outside the darkened projection theatre, in which samples of album covers from the label "Folkways" are displayed. The "Folkways" label was active from 1948 to 1986 and produced more than 2000 sound recordings ranging from traditional ethnic music, spoken word, and folk music by artists such as Leadbelly, Woodie Guthrie, and Pete Seeger, to scientific and documentary field recordings with titles like "Ionosphere (High Altitude Sounds)," or "Sounds of North American Frogs." Folkways also featured jazz, classical, and spoken-word recordings, sound effects, Comanche flute music by Doc Tate Nevaquaya, and the Festival of Japanese Music in Hawaii. The label's aim, according to its founder, Moses Asch, was to produce an encyclopedic catalogue of the "entire world of sounds." Asch, an impassioned collector who was determined never to allow a recording to go out of print, saw "Folkways" as a library of sound. His mission was to document rare or threatened traditions and to provide resources for future scholars. Asch was at once both a commercial record producer and a dedicated collector. But by classifying, recording, and putting into order the sounds of the world for the future, he also functioned as an archivist, and "Folkways" operated as an archive. One significant and striking aspect about Moses Asch's archive (in contrast to Poledna's earlier projects involving archives) is its audial component. Some, including Derrida, argue that the archive is fundamentally a repository of written documents—that it is ontologically graphic—and therefore silent. Archives are often quiet places and the process of archiving and conducting research in archives is primarily a solitary activity. But Asch has created an archive organized along the principles of sound by collecting and classifying world sounds and making the aural dimension of sound historically accessible. To that extent, Asch's enterprise resonates with Godard's *Histoire(s) du cinéma* (1988–98), which the filmmaker distributed not only as videotape (and now DVD) but also in CD form as a separate soundtrack, rendering the sonic the principle conduit of history and memory.[27] Although the idea of an archive based on sound seems unusual and extraordinary, nothing could be more unnatural than total silence.

In new media-speak, the term "version" refers to the countless different variations and versions that can be automatically generated by modern information technology.[28] To that extent, the computer program becomes the contemporary *coup de dés*, or throw of the dice, with the difference that chance is now digitally manufactured. Dub versioning thus corresponds technologically to the digital revolution and in particular to cultural production in the age of new media. But, as we have seen, Poledna also points to the "B-side" or version of the digital phenomenon, suggesting that the prospect of endless layering and accretion is accompanied by the possibility that data be decreased in order to enable an increase of perception.

Seen from this perspective, *Version* is characterized by a *subtraction* of information bytes, with its negative moments and silences pointing to movement and to dance. If slow-motion photography allows us to see that which was invisible, then the subtraction of visual information allows us to hear previously inaudible tracks. As noted earlier, each part of Poledna's trilogy restages a particular historical moment in recent music history that is charged with insight: post-punk, pop, and dub. These moments are presented as historical reenactments, as audio-visual snapshots of a precise time and place that resonate with complexity and meaning.[29] Each part of the trilogy addresses a different cinematic and musical period, bringing them together in a constellation: pre-modern, modern, and postmodern, or, in terms of production, pre-industrial, Fordist, and digital post-Fordist. Poledna's works thus seek to trace a history of both popular sound and popular image, linking the two tracks across time and space.

Projects such as *Actualité*, *Western Recording*, and *Version* and *Sufferers' Version* foreground the temporal discontinuities in the development from silent early moving-image technology to advanced computer-generated graphics. The trilogy compresses a century of film history into two decades of music production. The latter thereby testifies to the increasing speed and velocity of technological developments and their impact on culture. However, Poledna's work also indicates that, through this process and this rush to embrace the ever new, something crucial is lost. Each part of the trilogy can be read as a marker, a material memory of something that has become obsolete and of a past type of production. But on another level, the trilogy pays tribute to the archive, both visual and audial, and to the archivist. The three projects recall the individual characteristics of documents, photographs, records, or image sequences, before the *noise* has been eliminated and they have been transformed into data. These are data that can now be indiscriminately accessed. But they are also data that are no longer mediated by a human archivist, with her own psychological doubts about the excessive investment of labor in what will perhaps be a useless cache, and her own idiosyncratic logic of collecting and ordering patterns. At the very moment of the displacement of the material archivist by new technology, a critical flash of recognition of the important role with which this figure was once charged is released. It is this thought, or flash, that runs as an undercurrent to Poledna's trilogy.

And yet, with modern technology's digitization of all residual traces and documents, a new "noise," namely sound, has found its place in the once-silent archive. The translation of all material into "information bytes" has leveled previous hierarchies of archival material, especially the former predominance of the visual over the aural. In the digital age the archive exists as a truly dynamic and democratic audiovisual space—one in which history can be produced, stored, and retrieved not only as a legible trace or visual document but as an audible pronouncement. Perhaps, then, the "outside" of the traditional archive is a significantly richer mode of historical memory and knowledge production, with cognition drawing on more than just the visual for the production of meaning and understanding.

Notes

The epigraphs to this chapter are drawn from Jacques Derrida, *Archive Fever: A Freudian Impression*, trans. Eric Prenowitz (Chicago: U of Chicago P, 1995), 11, and Hal Foster, "An Archival Impulse," *October* 110 (Fall 2004): 5.

[1] On the significance of the archive for contemporary art see Charles Mereweather, ed., *The Archive* (London: Whitechapel, 2006; and Cambridge, MA:

MIT Press, 2006), as well as the essays in *Interarchive* (Cologne: Walther König, 2002), *Lost in the Archives* (Toronto: Alphabet City, 2002), and *Deep Storage* (New York: Prestel, 1998).

[2] Mathias Poledna, *The Making Of...* (Vienna: The Generali Foundation, 1998), 228.

[3] Derrida, *Archive Fever: A Freudian Impression,* trans. Eric Prenowitz (Chicago: U of Chicago P, 1995), 33–34.

[4] Derrida, *Archive Fever,* 2.

[5] Poledna, *The Making Of...*, 165.

[6] Lev Manovich, *The Language of New Media* (Cambridge, MA: MIT Press, 2002), 4.

[7] Allan Sekula, "Reading an Archive: Photography," in *Blasted Allegories,* ed. Brian Wallis and Marcia Tucker (Cambridge, MA: MIT Press, 1987), 114–28, here 116.

[8] As Manovich observes: "Modern technologies ... allow the storage of images, image sequences, sounds and text using different material forms—photographic plates, film stocks, gramophone records etc. ... the translation of all existing media into numerical data accessible through computers. The result is new media—graphics, moving images, sounds, shapes, spaces, and texts that have become computable; that is, they comprise simply another set of computer data" (*The Language of New Media,* 20).

[9] Walter Benjamin, "Unpacking My Library: A Talk about Book Collecting," in *Illuminations,* ed Hannah Arendt, trans. Harry Zohn (New York: Schocken Books, 1968), 59–67, here 67.

[10] Again Manovich: "Whose vision is it? It is the vision of a computer, a cyborg, an automatic missile. It is a realistic representation of human vision in the future, when it will be augmented by computer graphics and cleansed from noise. It is the vision of a digital grid" (*The Language of New Media,* xxiii).

[11] Questions now arise: who or what will produce systems of knowledge and, further, if everything can be digitized, what are the implications for cultural production more generally? As Hal Foster observes, particular objects and entire media are being transformed into information pixels within the electronic archives; so too is the human subject ("An Archival Impulse," 98).

[12] For a link between a specific historical period and Poledna's work, see Sabeth Buchman, "Das Jahr 1979 findet noch statt," *Starship* 5 (Spring 2002): 71–72.

[13] Fredric Jameson, "The Existence of Italy," in *Signatures of the Visible* (New York: Routledge, 1992), 155–229, here 182.

[14] See Pamela M. Lee, "*Actualité;* or Mathias Poledna's 'Regressive Seeing," in *Mathias Poledna: Actualité,* ed. Grazer Kunstverein (Frankfurt am Main: Revolver—Archiv für aktuelle Kunst, 2002), 16–26.

[15] As Diedrich Diederichsen notes, it "attempts to get as close as possible to the moment where youthful destructive demolition and reduction develop into deconstruction (which however, had not yet found its own new, accessible forms for purposes, political or otherwise." Diedrich Diederichsen, "Modules of the

Eternal Song," in Grazer Kunstverein, ed., *Mathias Poledna Actualité*, 88–106, here 99.

[16] Perhaps as a means to pay tribute to that era, Poledna insisted on filming inside the real Western Studio, as if to capture the "aura" of that original space.

[17] Poledna, *The Making Of* . . . , 227.

[18] Fredric Jameson asks us to reflect anew on Francis Ponge's question of how to "escape from the image by means of the image," though he now directs that question to an age dominated by mass media. See Jameson, "The Existence of Italy," 162. It would be useful here to extend this question to pop music: how can we rethink pop music by using it as a form of self-reflexive interrogation?

[19] It should be noted that both *Actualité* and *Western Recording* take the form of installations, but the filmic component in both installation and theater is identical, whereas in *Version* and *Sufferer's Version* it is different.

[20] See Juliane Rebentisch on the importance of dance and the haunting quality of 1960s art in Poledna's work: "Deconfigurations of Community: Matthias Poledna's *Version*," in *Mathias Poledna: Version* (Cologne: Galerie Daniel Buchholz, forthcoming). The dance referenced probably is that of the Judson dance group comprising Yvonne Rainer and Robert Morris. A further reference may be to the dance/work movements of Bruce Naumann.

[21] The separation between body and voice that occurs during the process of synchronization leads to what Mary Anne Doane has called the fantasmatic body—a "body reconstituted by the technology and practices of cinema." Mary Ann Doane, "The Voice in the Cinema: The Articulation of Body and Space," in *Film Sound: Theory and Practice*, ed. Elisabeth Weiss and John Belton (New York: Columbia UP, 1985), 162–76, here 163.

[22] Alberto Cavalcanti, "Sound in Films," in Weiss and Belton, *Film Sound: Theory and Practice*, 98–111; here 101.

[23] Dick Hebdige, *Subculture: The Meaning of Style* (London: Routledge, 1988).

[24] Hebdige, *Subculture*, 34.

[25] The term "version" refers to both the metamorphosis, change, incarnation, and generation of new texts without an original and to a system of "quotation" and the indiscriminate citing from texts and musical compositions prevalent in dub music. "The original version takes on a new life and a new meaning in a fresh context. Just like a rhythm or a melody which is brought in from another source in a record or in the live performance of a piece of music. They're just different *kinds* of quotation." Dick Hebdige, *Cut 'n' Mix: Culture, Identity and Caribbean Music* (London: Methuen, 1987), 14.

[26] Hebdige, *Cut 'n' Mix*, 12.

[27] Jean-Luc Godard, "Introduction à une véritable histoire de cinéma," *Camera Obscura* 8–10 (1980): 75–88, esp. 78.

[28] As Manovich explains in relation to the term variability and its uses in new media: "Instead of identical copies, a new media object typically gives rise to many different versions. And rather than being created by a human author, these versions are often in part assembled by a computer. . . . Thus the principle of variation is closely

connected to automation" (*The Language of New Media*, 36). The possibility of a computer's generating images and sequences is the basis for Stan Douglas's DVD loop *Win Place or Show* (1999), in which a software program produced countless versions of the same basic scenario.

29 Here it may be useful to recall Poledna's final statement in an interview from 1998: "My interests, however, always go beyond the factographical," a statement that resonates with Benjamin's observation about principles guiding a collector: "Dates, place names, formats, previous owners, bindings, and the like: all these details must tell him something—not as dry, isolated facts, but as a harmonious whole" (Benjamin, "Unpacking My Library," 63–64).

11: The City in the Ages of New Media: From Ruttmann's *Berlin: Die Sinfonie der Großstadt* to Hypermedia Berlin

Todd Samuel Presner

I.

THE CO-CONSTITUTIVE RELATIONSHIP between the metropolis and new media—photography, photomontage, film, and radio—has long been recognized as a familiar and significant part of the history of modernism.[1] To the extent that the modern urban experience was characterized by unprecedented mobility and speed, the fragmentation and dissolution of subjectivity, the multiplicity of experience and the abstraction of individuality, the ascendancy of the masses and the shock of new nervous stimulations, the circulation of money and the rise of a mass industrial society, new media embodied these qualities in their formal innovations and representational practices. Citing the observations of Baudelaire and Poe on the movements of the masses and the shock of the urban experience vis-à-vis the media of photography and film, Benjamin explains:

> Of the countless movements of switching, inserting, pressing, and the like, the "snapping" of the photographer has had the greatest consequences. A touch of the finger now sufficed to fix an event for an unlimited period of time. The camera gave the moment a posthumous shock, as it were. Haptic experiences of this kind were joined by optic ones, such as are supplied by the advertising pages of a newspaper or the traffic of a big city. Moving through this traffic involves the individual in a series of shocks and collisions. At dangerous intersections, nervous impulses flow through him in rapid succession, like the energy from a battery. . . . In a film, perception in the form of shocks was established as a formal principle. That which determines the rhythm of production on a conveyor belt is the basis of the rhythm of reception in the film.[2]

The new media of photography and film capture, in their formal principles, the shock of the city, the danger of urban modernity, and the persistent dialectic of continuity and discontinuity found in industrial, capitalist production. A few years earlier, Benjamin had already articulated the "formula in which the dialectical structure of film" finds its expression using much of the same language. Referencing "the assembly line" on the one hand and "the staccato bits of movement" on the other, he described the dialectic with this pithy statement: "Discontinuous images replace one another in a continuous sequence."[3] The filmstrip is homologous to the modern, capitalist mode of production (the linearity of the assembly line), yet its discontinuous juxtaposition of images is betrayed by the "jerky" gestures of the body (epitomized, in his example, by Charlie Chaplin films). Continuity and discontinuity not only characterized the experience of urban modernity but also the formal structuring principles of new media.

Beyond this structural homology, other contemporaneous critics, especially those involved in the so-called "Kino-Debatte" (film debate) of the early twentieth century, noted additional points of overlap between urbanity and new media.[4] Hermann Kienzl, for example, argued in 1911 that "[the] psychology of the cinematographic triumph is metropolitan psychology" and even conflated the "metropolitan soul" with the "cinematographic soul."[5] But it was the theorization of the phenomenon of the masses, I would suggest, that solidified the relationship between new media and the modern urban experience. One need only recall the synchronic convergence in 1895 of the birth of cinema and the theory of the masses: the Lumière brothers screened the famous first film of an approaching train in 1895, the same year in which Gustave le Bon published his immensely popular *Psychologie des foules,* where he declared his age to be "the era of crowds" characterized by "the power of the masses."[6] Years later, writing under the pressures of fascism, Benjamin argued that "the most powerful agent" of "contemporary mass movements" is film.[7] Cinema is not only a mass medium but is, more ominously, a way of bringing "the masses . . . face to face with themselves."[8] With Leni Riefenstahl's *Triumph of the Will* (1934) clearly in mind, Benjamin connected "mass reproduction" (in photography, film, and newsreels) with "the reproduction of masses."[9]

But it would be Joseph Goebbels, in his incarnation as media theorist for the Third Reich, who would articulate the closest connection between new media and the masses. In a speech given in August 1933 at the opening of the tenth German Radio Exhibition, which commemorated the anniversary of the broadcast of the first German radio program in 1923, Goebbels argued that, if Napoleon was right to consider the press the seventh wonder of the world, radio would have to count as the eighth.[10] He argued that one cannot imagine the historic events of the nineteenth century without considering the role of journalism, the press, and the newspaper. Analogously, in 1933 it was the radio that had gained "truly revolutionary significance" (197) by reaching all of the masses and bringing the nation together. As Goebbels explained, "We live in the age of the masses; the masses rightly demand that they participate in the great events of the day. The radio is the most influential and important intermediary between a spiritual movement and the nation, between the idea and the people" (200). The radio—as a mass medium—produces, mediates, extends, and unites the masses.

When Hitler's disembodied voice entered the household of every German family through the *Volksempfänger,* an epistemological break also took place: distance had been overcome; the human voice was detached from the speaking subject; and the private, domestic space of the home was exploded by the transmission of public, political discourse.[11] Of course, this is an epistemological-perceptual break that applies to other new media and technologies as well.[12] As Benjamin explained with regard to film, our phenomenological experiences of space and time changed with the advent of new media:

> Our taverns and our metropolitan streets, our offices and furnished rooms, our railroad stations and our factories appeared to have us locked up hopelessly. Then came the film and burst this prison-world asunder by the dynamite of the tenth of a second, so that now, in the midst of its far-flung ruins and debris, we calmly and adventurously go traveling. With the close-up, space expands; with slow motion, movement is extended.[13]

The experience of the nineteenth-century flâneur made famous by the likes of Baudelaire or Poe—the dandy or the man of the crowd, an individual subject who apprehends and enters the city as an embodied spectator—was displaced by the non-contiguous, disembodied experience of the city that is now seen or heard from a distance, at varying tempos, and in a new sequence. The age of new media not only meant mass reproduction and the reproduction of the masses but also a new orientation of time, space, and subjectivity.

In an essay entitled "Malerei mit Zeit" (Painting with Time), composed seven years before he produced his 1927 landmark film, *Berlin: Die Sinfonie der Großstadt* (Berlin: Symphony of a Great City), Walter Ruttmann remarks that the "tempo of our time" has radically changed because of the media in which information is produced and disseminated.[14] He cites the telegraph, express trains, stenography, photography, and the news press for their role in contributing to the "acceleration" of time and explains, "Because of the speed by which information is made available, the single individual is flooded by a constant stream of material in which the old methods of communication break down."[15] Cinematography, Ruttmann argues, is ideally suited to respond to this information flood because it uniquely embodies the temporal and optical exigencies of modernity. Employing what N. Katherine Hayles would later call "media-specific analysis,"[16] Ruttmann pointed out, after the completion of *Berlin: Die Sinfonie der Großstadt*, that film must "strive to emancipate itself from theater" as well as from the "photo book" (*Bilderbuch*).[17] Insofar as film mimicked the techniques of theater, it was, according to Ruttmann, still indebted to the paradigms of realism and naturalistic mimesis, reproducing the structuring logic, spatial organization, and temporal rhythms of the stage. And insofar as he sought to differentiate film from the photo book—a specifically Weimar media tradition practiced across the political spectrum by the likes of Ernst Jünger, Ernst Friedrich, Kurt Tucholsky, and John Heartfield[18]—Ruttmann was expressing his distrust of the materiality of the book, not to mention its fixedness, for conveying the experience of urban modernity. The linear and sequential strictures of the book inevitably simplify the complexity that Ruttmann sees film as unlocking. As he indicated with respect to the editing, cutting, and final organization of the shots that he took in Berlin, "The structure [of the film follows that] of a complicated machine that can only gain momentum if every one of the tiniest parts connects with the others with the most exacting precision."[19] This is essentially an incipient theory of complexity, which would later become crystallized in network and hypertext theory.[20]

Two things are worth highlighting here: first, Ruttmann considered his film to be a complicated, machine-like narrative produced from what we would now call a database of images. Not unlike the "database cinema" of directors such as Dziga Vertov and Peter Greenaway, Ruttmann employs the logic of the database to capture and catalogue the widest selection of images from the modern city, ranging from images of transportation networks, processing machines, and phone operators to the salaried masses, schoolchildren, and cabaret performers.[21] As Lev Manovich argues with respect to Vertov's city film, *The Man with the Movie Camera*, an argument that may just as well apply to Ruttmann: "Records drawn from a database and arranged in a particular order become a picture of modern life—but simultaneously an argument about this life, an interpretation of what these images, which we encounter every day, every second, actually mean."[22] Second, Ruttmann considered the medium of film less an embodiment of the dialectic of continuity and discontinuity (à la Benjamin) and more a medium for producing and examining machine-like complexity wherein every part (or shot) can be connected to a multiplicity of other parts (or shots). Even though the shots are finally arranged in continuous succession, the spatial logic motivating the "narrative" approximates that of a network or web. In effect, the film produces a new space, one that takes the contiguities of the "real" Berlin, disaggregates them, and reassembles them into something that might be called the contiguity of the non-contiguous.

As we will see, Ruttmann's Berlin film and his theories of cinema anticipate many of the contemporaneous debates in the field of new media studies, or perhaps more precisely put: new media studies—with its emphasis on complexity, database narrative, hypertextuality, network theory, contingency, and navigation—remediates many of Ruttmann's ideas and media practices.[23] The purpose of this essay, then, is twofold: first, I examine what happens to the metropolis in our contemporary age of new media. If film and photography were centrally connected to the perception, experience, and representation of the modern urban space, what happens to the metropolis in an age of deep-linked information webs, hypermedia, social networking, and remixable software culture? What happens to the "metropolitan soul" of the modernist imaginary when cinema is no longer the determinate medium? And second, in what ways have the media-specific innovations of cinema been taken up and remediated today? In other words, how might we characterize and historicize the relationship between the city and these two ages of new media? To answer these questions, I will focus on two concrete examples: Ruttmann's 1927 film, *Berlin: Die Sinfonie der Großstadt*, and a digital, Web-based mapping project called "Hypermedia Berlin" (http://www.hypercities.com), which I founded and direct at UCLA.[24] Building on and inspired by the broad insights of Lev Manovich, particularly his discussion of Vertov's *Man with the Movie Camera* vis-à-vis the language of new media, I juxtapose Ruttmann's film with Hypermedia Berlin in order to investigate what the remediation of the city means. I begin by introducing Hypermedia Berlin, and from there, I examine three elements of new media and their remediation: first, network theory and contingency; second, embodiment and navigation; and third, participatory platforms and remix culture.

II.

Great cities like Berlin are almost inconceivably complex and multilayered. Over its nearly eight centuries, Berlin emerged from a backwater mercantile town built on sand to become the capital of a unified Germany under Bismarck and the site of Hitler's dream for a world-dominant Germania. It was devastated by the Thirty Years War, occupied by Napoleon in 1805, rebuilt numerous times throughout the eighteenth and nineteenth centuries, destroyed in the Second World War, divided by the Berlin Wall for twenty-eight years, and put back together again in 1990. Poised on the border between Western and Eastern Europe, this cosmopolitan city has variously welcomed and persecuted its minorities: Huguenots, Jews, Poles, Russians, Turks, and others. It doubled in size in less than a quarter of a century between 1890 and the outbreak of the First World War, reaching a size of four million people; another quarter of a century later, it lost almost half of its population and nearly all of its Jewish population in the Second World War and the Holocaust. Berlin, like other great cities, comprises densely layered architectural, social, political, and cultural palimpsests. The motivating question for Hypermedia Berlin is this: How can one make sense of this complexity in terms of both synchrony (spatial simultaneity) and diachrony (the transformation of space over time)?

Although geographers are often credited with developing the first non-print Geographic Information Sciences (GIS) tools in the 1970s and 80s, Benjamin, not unlike Ruttmann, realized nearly eighty years ago that the medium of the printed page could not possibly articulate the cultural complexity and historical layers of a city space. His *Arcades Project* (1927–40) sought to analyze the cultural geography of nineteenth-century Paris by "[carrying] over the principle of montage into history."[25] By rejecting the strictures of linear print in favor of the spatiality of montage, Benjamin attempted to create a new critical methodology for imagining cultural history. Although he does not fully articulate a media-specific analysis, the montage principle is both a recognition of the limitations of print and a meditation on the normative medium of the discipline of history.[26] I believe that Benjamin would have found the tools of new media, specifically the rhizomic techniques of hypertext and the hypermedia possibilities of the Web, especially well suited for "giving dates their physiognomy" (*AP,* 476) and realizing what he once called "the Copernican revolution in historical perception" (*AP,* 883).

Tracing its historical genealogy back to both Ruttmann's *Berlin: Die Sinfonie der Großstadt* and Benjamin's *Arcades Project,* the goal of Hypermedia Berlin is to construct an interactive, Web-based research platform for representing and studying the cultural, urban, and architectural history of a city space. Hypermedia Berlin is organized according to "Zeitschichten," or time-layers, in which the uneven spatial and temporal coordinates of Berlin's cultural and architectural histories can be apprehended.[27] Unlike traditional models of cultural history, which proceed chronologically and take the linearity of temporality as their structuring principle, Hypermedia Berlin is a digital spatial network that uses a geo-temporal database to probe Berlin's time-layers. Hypermedia Berlin is connected together by interlinking "hotspots" at thousands of key regions, structures, and streets on scores of richly detailed, collaboratively annotated, and geo-referenced historical maps stretching back to 1237, when the city was founded, and extending up to the present using Google's hybrid map-satellite imagery. The result is a spatialization of historical practice into urban palimpsests, transforming cultural history into a kind of database of cultural geography.[28] Using the graphical interface with its geo-temporal navigation and search tools, users decide how to proceed through the nearly 800 years of Berlin's history.

Compared to Hypermedia Berlin, Ruttmann's film, of course, is significantly more condensed in terms of duration as well as historical and spatial representation. This is partly because Hypermedia Berlin was created as a participatory platform, while *Berlin: Die Sinfonie der Großstadt* is a "one-off" historical-artistic work. In the film, which runs just over an hour in length, Ruttmann sought to make the Berlin of 1927 the protagonist. He explains that he shot far more footage of the city than he could have possibly included in the film and decided to "cut out many of the most beautiful shots" in order to prevent the film from becoming a "*Bilderbuch*" of Berlin.[29] The result is a kind of spatial-temporal narrative of a single-day-in-the-life of Berlin that is derived from an extensive database of imagery. The film's five acts, structured as a chronological time narrative stretching from early morning to night, celebrate Berlin's modernity in all its technological innovation.[30] Within each act the film moves synchronically by way of temporal montage, a technique that Manovich succinctly defines as "separate realities [forming] consecutive moments in time."[31] The result is a bursting apart of the "prison-world" of the city and the reassembly of its constituent parts in a new sequence. Not only does this process embrace Bloch's historiographic concept of the "simultaneity of the non-simultaneous" [*Gleichzeitigkeit des Ungleichzeitigen*][32] insofar as images collected over days and months are rendered synchronic with one another but, perhaps more radically, the urban space itself is reconfigured through what I would call the "contiguity of the non-contiguous" [*Gleichräumigkeit des Ungleichräumigen*]. Objects, buildings, streetcars, train stations, factories, theaters, and even entire regions of Berlin are remapped through cinema and placed side-by-side *as if* contiguous. The result is that the new-media flâneur can experience the city in a way that was simply not possible for Poe's man of the crowd or Baudelaire's dandy, both of whom had to physically enter into the built space of the city. Now a viewer of Ruttmann's film can travel through and experience Berlin synchronically: a single night, at scores of non-contiguous locations rendered consecutive, contiguous, and virtually simultaneous—precisely the way a traditional flâneur could never perceive or experience the city.

To understand the significance of new media and the specific ways in which Hypermedia Berlin remediates some of the principles of Ruttmann's film, I would like to now turn to three defining features of new media. I will begin with network theory and contingency, follow with embodiment and navigation, and conclude with a brief discussion of participatory platforms and remix culture.

Although a number of cultural critics have recently celebrated the "death of distance" and "the collapse of space and time" with the rise of the Internet, the World Wide Web, and other telecommunications technologies,[33] it is worth remembering that technology networks are hardly new, let alone neutral.[34] One need only cast a cursory glance at the history of the networked world to see how it has always operated and expanded unevenly in terms of social and economic power. Indeed, many of the advances associated with modernity—the collapse of space and time, interconnection, speed, acceleration, contingency—found their first, decidedly uneven expressions at the beginning of the nineteenth century. Here, we see, for example, the conceptualization of a worldwide postal system and a world postal institute (1811); the building and spread of passenger trains across the European continent beginning in 1825; the development and refinement of the electric telegraph (1836); the conceptualization and the first stages of implementation of a transnational network of trains linking newly opened canals and ports in the Netherlands and along the Rhine to France, to the Germanic states, and eventually to Russia (beginning in 1835); the systematization of world standard time, first imagined and implemented in England between 1840 and 1842 to coordinate railways and postal deliveries; the heyday of colonization and the worldwide exploitation of both the natural world and the working class with the rise of transnational finance and technology aggregates; and finally the invention and popularization of the automobile as well as the construction of highways and the necessary infrastructure to support motorcar traffic. The death of distance, the reconfiguration of time and space, and the imbalances of the networked, globalized world began long before the Internet Age.

While each of these developments deserves attention in the history of a networked world, I will focus here on the railway, arguably one of the emblematic technologies of what might be called the dialectic of modernity, the progressive hopes invested in and catastrophes created by mobility and networking. In the nineteenth and early part of the twentieth century, the railway system transformed much of the world into a horizontally differentiated network, one in which every part is connected with multiple other parts through the proliferation of stations, links, nodes, and hubs. Not only did the railway literally stitch together nations (Germany, Russia, Italy, and the United States) and transform the globe into a networked whole through the standardization of time, but the train became seen as the engine of modernity. It was the iconic symbol of progress, modernization, industrialization, speed, and capitalist exchange, a symbol that, as we all know, had a dialectical underbelly marked by nationalism, border-control, technological warfare, and deportations.[35] It is not by accident that Ruttmann would choose the speeding train rushing north toward Berlin as the opening figure for his film. Beginning with an abstract montage that morphs into a traffic crossing, the opening sequence is intercut with a multiplicity of quick shots spliced together in rapid succession, consisting of the side of the train, the front of the train, the passing landscape, electricity lines, the railway tracks, and the train's wheels. A couple of minutes later, when the train arrives at Berlin's Anhalter Bahnhof—the greatest and arguably most famous railway station in all of Europe—the viewer is treated to several bird's eye views of Berlin that evoke a quiet city on the edge of a new day. Interestingly, this is the only time Ruttmann will provide a semblance of a transcendental view from above, as if both to remind us of a time when transcendental views were possible and perhaps to anticipate the return (not to mention pleasures) of transcendental viewing with Google Earth.[36]

Ruttmann does not simply epitomize Berlin's modernity in the figure of the train or in the recurrent images of transportation networks and streetcars; instead he uses the complex logic of a network to organize the temporal-spatial logic of the film and articulate some of its consequences for the dissolution of subjectivity. The modernist space is predicated on the idea that anything may, in one way or another, be linked together in a system, but the system can no longer be surveyed in its totality or disaggregated in its complexity.[37] There is no privileged position of spectatorship or external view of the system. Moreover, this space (whether built space or cinematic space) is a space of contingency, wherein everything could be otherwise. Contingency—that which is neither necessary nor impossible—is one of the defining attributes of Ruttmann's modernity.[38] Once one enters into the modernist space of Berlin—built, cinematic, and narrative[39]—virtually anything is possible, but nothing has to happen out of necessity. The narrative that Ruttmann created is one possibility, selected from myriad possibilities, shots, and sequences from a database of Berlin imagery. In this regard, new media and the experience of the modern urban space go hand in hand: both are structured by the complex, horizontally differentiated logic of a system that cannot be viewed in its totality (the railway grid, the database, the network) and the contingency of narrative (choosing a path, selecting material, sequencing shots). The result is a non-linear, non-contiguous experience of the urban space rendered in a continuous temporal montage by the filmstrip itself.

It is no coincidence, then, that the two principles that form the very basis of the Internet—the theory of the distributed network and the idea of packet switching, both of which were developed in the mid-1960s by Paul Baran and his team at the RAND Corporation—follow the same logic of the railway system. Baran sought to design what he called a "distributed network" in which every node is connected to several others, thus rendering it "survivable" in the case of an enemy attack. In a famous brief from 1964, Baran demonstrates that the redundancy level—"the link-to-node ratio in an infinite size array of stations"—can be relatively low, yet the network will still survive most attacks.[40] The principle of a decentralized, distributed network with a moderate level of redundancy would form the backbone of the Internet. Baran essentially remediated the logic of a railway system, one in which a part of the system can be destroyed but the network continues to function because a sufficient number of alternative stations and pathways are still available for communication.

Fig. 11.1. From top: Layers of geo-referenced historical maps form the centerpiece of HyperCities. Users search and annotate by "drilling down" through time at particular locations. Users can upload and download media content through mobile devices, and all objects in HyperCities are "time-space" tagged, thus fostering diachronic and synchronic movement through the layers of urban history. Screenshot of HyperCities 2.0, showing user-created media objects, including a "counter-factual" overlay of contemporary Wilhelmstrasse on an 1805 map of Berlin.

This remediation of the railway system, as found in both Ruttmann's film and Baran's theorization of the Internet, also informs the structuring logic behind Hypermedia Berlin (fig. 11.1). Viewers navigate interlinked maps of Berlin, traveling by space or time through a non-linear network of digital assets. All of the media objects found in Hypermedia Berlin are connected together by various levels of nodes and links. The objects are time-space tagged, so that there is no free-floating, decontextualized archive of material. Every object—whether a photograph, text document, audio or video file, micro-annotation, or multimedia article—is time-space stamped, appearing or disappearing as a function of the proximity and duration selected by the viewer. A visit to Potsdamer Platz may begin in the Berlin of the present, jump back to 1811, when the area was a city gate, and, then, move diachronically through the nineteenth century. As the user proceeds—that is, navigates and, hence, narrates—the database sifts out the irrelevant material, leaving only the digital assets associated with Potsdamer Platz that fall within the selected temporal span.

Analogous to the process of archaeological coring, the data searches are bound by place (proximity) and time (duration), not simply a keyword: a user might encircle a larger region extending, for example, fifteen city blocks south of Potsdamer Platz over the years 1920 to 1962. The data objects displayed in the results field are a function of the time-space coordinates determined by the user; this essentially amounts to a contingent narrative told from the database of possible elements. In this regard, Hypermedia Berlin, not unlike Ruttmann's film, responds to Manovich's challenge to consider the recursive nature of database and narrative: "How can a narrative take into account the fact that its elements are organized in a database? *How can our new abilities to store vast amounts of data, to automatically classify, index, link, search, and instantly retrieve it, lead to new kinds of narratives?*"[41] For the new media flâneur navigating through Berlin, a unique hypermedia narrative is produced with each iteration, track, or pathway through the time-space database of the city.

While the new media flâneur (of cinema) stares at the light projected onto a rectangular screen when watching Ruttmann's film, the new media flâneur (of the Web) not only stares at but also interacts with the rectangular, pixilated screen of the computer window. In both cases, the screen or window—the fundamental media metaphor and epistemological configuration of media studies—is denaturalized and remediated. But far from offering up a transparent, immediate, or realistic view of the world "out there," the window betrays the contingency, enframement, embodiment, and mediation of any viewing.[42] Just as there is no transparent or neutral interface, there can be no surrogate spectator observing the immediacy of the city through a window or on the screen. And just as Ruttmann remediates the "window paradigm" by exploding temporal succession and spatial contiguity (two of the presuppositions of realist representation), Hypermedia Berlin never gets at the "real" Berlin; rather, it offers up mediation on top of mediation, map after map, representation after representation.[43] While all the historical maps are geo-referenced with latitude and longitude in order to perform spatial queries (such as mapping census data or performing *longue durée* comparisons), every map is preserved in its integrity as an epistemological record of the way in which Berlin was perceived, organized, and represented at a given time. Unlike the ambition of mimetic geo-browsers such as Google Earth, the window or screen can never become a portal of clarity, realism, or truth.

When viewing both *Berlin: Die Sinfonie der Großstadt* and Hypermedia Berlin, vision is extended and transformed because the phenomenological experience of spectatorship in an urban space has been replaced by a new kind of perception (the contiguity of the non-contiguous, the simultaneity of the non-simultaneous). No individual subject or spectator on the ground could possibly have experienced or apprehended Berlin in such a manner in a single night. A new kind of flâneur has emerged, one who has, as Manovich points out, transformed yet again into the figure of the "data dandy" or "Net surfer": "The Net is to the electronic dandy what the metropolitan street was for the historical dandy."[44] Through the graphical user interface for Hypermedia Berlin, the data dandy explores Berlin by zooming in and out of the maps, scrolling—in any order—through some 800 years of time, and clicking on various regions, neighborhoods, blocks, buildings, streets, and addresses. As the navigation is refined, both spatially and temporally, the database populates the search results with relevant media objects, which can then be viewed, selected, sorted, and recombined.

But far from an information silo or "read-only" site, Hypermedia Berlin is constructed as a participatory platform with an elaborate authorship component and a community annotation feature for generating content and data sets. Users can create collections in which they add and curate media objects as well as select material for courses and individual research projects. They can also author and publish vetted multimedia articles using the resources of Hypermedia Berlin. Moreover, users of Hypermedia Berlin are able to add micro-annotations by geo-tagging points, lines, and polygons, such as Motzstrasse 48 in the year 2003, or the northwest corner of Leipzigerstrasse and Wilhelmstrasse from 1920 to 1945. These micro-annotations are community-generated, in any language, and added to Hypermedia Berlin in real-time. The rationale is that micro-annotations contribute to the creation of a "people's history" of the city, leveraging the democratizing possibilities of the Web to create, display, and distribute information. To add an entry such as "My grandmother lived here from 1903 to 1937" is to participate in the creation of a commemorative spatial memory, recreating what Dolores Hayden has eloquently called "the power of place."[45] These annotations function as "folksonomies" that complement, but do not displace, the academically generated taxonomies or content, which is still peer-reviewed and authenticated. In this respect, Hypermedia Berlin makes use of the Wikipedia model of multiple authorship and "writerly" content, while also maintaining a tiered authorship platform for evaluating and reviewing research submissions. Because the micro-annotations are space-time stamped, they, too, can be searched, culled, and cross-sectioned, thereby generating new research possibilities as well as location and time-sensitive social networks for users. Viewers interested in other kinds of content can decide to turn off "micro-annotations," toggle the hot-spots on or off, and select (or de-select) particular kinds of media objects using the view control features of Hypermedia Berlin.

Finally, Hypermedia Berlin leverages some of the new possibilities of the geo-spatial web by interfacing between the digital world and the physical environment. Because every object within Hypermedia Berlin is geo-referenced, a person equipped with a hand-held GPS device or a GPS-enabled phone can both download and upload geo-specific historical information about his or her precise location. Through such location awareness technologies, a user standing in front of the Brandenburg Gate today will be able to automatically query Hypermedia Berlin for a 1962 picture of the Brandenburg Gate behind the Berlin Wall or view a map of the same location from 1811. The objective is to endow the Berlin of the present with its missing (or invisible) historical dimension. In this regard, the modern metropolis and new media begin to re-interface through a deep-linking dialectic: the metropolis changes new media, and new media change the metropolis. The line separating media and the metropolis becomes blurred as Hypermedia Berlin is built on top, out of, inside, and throughout the physical space of the city: what we have created is a kind of "augmented reality" (or, depending on which side one favors, an "augmented virtuality") where the agent of augmentation is new media. In the present age of new media, the digital representational platform cannot be separated from the physical, geographic referent. Unlike photography or cinema, it allows the city to merge permanently with the new media.

These "new" new media thus move significantly beyond first-generation Web applications and content providers by combining a geo-temporal database with locative technologies, a participatory platform for community-generated data, an interface between the digital and the built environment, and robust content created by extending and remixing publicly available interfaces (APIs). Hypermedia Berlin uses the Google Maps API for the satellite images of present-day Berlin as well as for its KML-based file structure to organize and annotate geo-referenced historical maps and objects. But these technologies and images of Berlin are not simply accepted at face value or considered to be objective representations; instead, they are historicized, contextualized, and remixed vis-à-vis centuries of representations of city spaces in a multiplicity of media forms. In this regard, remixability has become the order of the day for Web 2.0 content and technologies.[46] This is because, as Manovich points out, what makes new media new is the fact that "new properties (i.e. new software techniques) can always be easily added to it."[47] Plug-ins, mash-ups, creative commons, and folksonomies are all characterized by the reuse, re-purposing, and re-presentation of content, interfaces, and applications. Hypermedia Berlin is "new" new media in this sense.

When the "new" new-media flâneur returns to the built environment with his or her GPS-enabled Web-device, the window, the screen, and the city are blended together and fundamentally interfaced. For this reason, the "metropolitan soul" is no longer "cinematographic" today; it is hypermedial and melds the physical with the digital, the built with the virtual. Indeed, le Bon and Benjamin were not wrong: their age of new media (cinema, radio, photomontage) was born of the era of crowds and functioned by representing the masses to themselves. Today we are in another age of new media (Web 2.0) that at first glance seems strangely devoid of those images of crowds and urban masses found throughout the first decades of cinema. But in an age marked by PageRank, blogging, Wikipedia, Facebook, and endless social networking, the power of the masses has returned—perhaps somewhat more subtly but arguably just as powerfully—through "the wisdom of crowds."[48] The geo-spatial Web is the venue of the masses today. Hypermedia Berlin is one of its participatory platforms.

Notes

[1] As Anton Kaes writes, for example, "Cinema and the metropolis are equally products of late capitalism and the technical-industrial revolution." Kaes, "The Debate about Cinema: Charting a Controversy (1909–1929)," *New German Critique* 40 (Winter 1987): 7–33, here 10. Also see the fascinating study by Mary Ann Doane, *The Emergence of Cinematic Time: Modernity, Contingency, the Archive* (Cambridge, MA: Harvard UP, 2002); Patrice Petro, *Joyless Streets: Women and Melodramatic Representation in Weimar Germany* (Princeton: Princeton UP, 1989); and Sabine Hake, *The Cinema's Third Machine: Writing on Film in Germany, 1907–1933* (Lincoln: U of Nebraska P, 1993).

[2] Walter Benjamin, "On Some Motifs in Baudelaire," in Benjamin, *Illuminations*, ed. Hannah Arendt, trans. Harry Zohn (New York: Schocken Books, 1968), 174–75.

[3] Walter Benjamin, "The Formula in Which the Dialectical Structure of Film Finds Expression" (1935), trans. Edmund Jephcott, in *Walter Benjamin: Selected Writings*, vol. 3: 1935–1938, ed. Marcus Bullock and Michael W. Jennings (Cambridge, MA: Harvard UP, 2002), 94.

[4] Cf. Anton Kaes, ed, *Kino-Debatte: Texte zum Verhältnis von Literatur und Film, 1909–1929* (Tübingen: Max Niemeyer Verlag, 1978).

⁵ Hermann Kienzl, "Theater und Kinematograph," *Der Strom* 1 (1911/12). Qtd. in Kaes, "The Debate about Cinema," 12.

⁶ Gustave le Bon, *The Crowd*, introduction by Robert Nye (New Brunswick, NJ: Transaction, 1995), 34, 35. For a discussion of the origins of cinema, see Friedrich Kittler, *Gramophone, Film, Typewriter*, trans. Geoffrey Winthrop-Young and Michael Wutz (Stanford, CA: Stanford UP, 1999) and Mary Ann Doane, *The Emergence of Cinematic Time*.

⁷ Benjamin, *Illuminations*, 221.

⁸ Benjamin, *Illuminations*, 251.

⁹ Benjamin, *Illuminations*, 251.

¹⁰ Joseph Goebbels, "Der Rundfunk als achte Großmacht," *Signale der neuen Zeit: 25 ausgewählte Reden von Dr. Joseph Goebbels* (Munich: Zentralverlag der NSDAP, 1934), 197–207. Further citations are documented parenthetically. All translations in this essay are my own.

¹¹ While Hitler was not the first German leader to make use of the radio, he did achieve an unprecedented level of penetration. Radio extended the limited human faculty of hearing in all directions, across all of Germany, to the ear of potentially each and every citizen. In Marshall McLuhan's apposite words: "Radio is provided with its cloak of invisibility . . . It is really a subliminal echo chamber of magical power to touch remote and forgotten chords. All technological extensions of ourselves must be numb and subliminal, else we could not endure the leverage exerted upon us by such extension. Even more than telephone or telegraph, radio is that extension of the central nervous system that is matched only by human speech itself." McLuhan, "Radio: The Tribal Drum," in *Understanding Media: The Extensions of Man* (Cambridge: MIT Press, 2002), 302.

¹² Before the age of global telecommunications and air travel, the railway reconfigured both distance and duration, especially after the introduction of world standard time in the late nineteenth century. See Stephen Kern, *The Culture of Time and Space, 1880–1918* (Cambridge, MA: Harvard UP, 1983); Wolfgang Schivelbusch, *The Railway Journey: The Industrialization of Time and Space in the 19th Century* (Berkeley: U of California P, 1977); Andrew Thacker, *Moving Through Modernity: Space and Geography in Modernism* (Manchester: Manchester UP, 2003); and Todd Presner, *Mobile Modernity: Germans, Jews, Trains* (New York: Columbia UP, 2007).

¹³ Benjamin, *Illuminations*, 236.

¹⁴ Walter Ruttmann, "Malerei mit Zeit" (1920), in *Walter Ruttmann: Eine Dokumentation*, ed. Jeanpaul Goergen (Berlin: Freunde der deutschen Kinemathek, 1989), 73–74.

¹⁵ Walter Ruttmann, "Malerei mit Zeit," 74. Reinhart Koselleck argues that "modernity" or *Neuzeit* is characterized by a new temporality marked by progress, the openness of the future, the non-simultaneity of many simultaneous histories, and, most of all, by the experience of acceleration. See his essay, "The Eighteenth Century as the Beginning of Modernity," in *The Practice of Conceptual History: Timing History, Spacing Concepts*, trans. Todd Presner (Stanford, CA: Stanford UP, 2002), 154–69.

[16] Cf. N. Katherine Hayles, *Writing Machines* (Cambridge, MA: MIT Press, 2002). Media-specific analysis pays attention to the specificity and significance of the "material apparatus producing . . . the physical artifact" (29).

[17] The first quote comes from an article called "Der neue Film" (1927) and the second from "Wie ich meinen Berlin-Film drehte" (1927). Both are reproduced in Goergen, ed., *Walter Ruttmann: Eine Dokumentation*, 80.

[18] For a history of the origins and development of the genre of the photo book in Weimar, see Michael Jennings, "Agriculture, Industry, and the Birth of the Photo-Essay in the late-Weimar Republic," *October* 93 (Summer 2000): 23–56. As a sequence of photographs arranged as a political argument, one might mention Jünger's *Das Antlitz des Weltkrieges: Fronterlebnisse deutscher Soldaten* (The Face of World War: Front Experiences of German Soldiers, 1930); *Hier spricht der Feind: Kriegerlebnisse unserer Gegner* (The Enemy Speaks Here: War Experiences of Our Opponents, 1931); *Der gefährliche Augenblick* (The Dangerous Moment, 1931); *Die veränderte Welt: Eine Bilderfibel unserer Zeit* (The Transformed World: A Picture Guide to Our Time, 1933); and *Luftfahrt ist Not* (Flying is Necessary, 1933). On the other side of the political spectrum one could mention Ernst Friedrich's anti-war photo book, *Krieg dem Kriege* (War against War, 1924), and Tucholsky and Heartfield's satirical *Deutschland, Deutschland über Alles* (Germany, Germany, above All Else, 1929). For a discussion of Jünger's photo books, see my article, "The End of Sex and the Last Man: On the Weimar Utopia of Ernst Jünger's 'Worker,'" *Qui Parle* 13.1 (Fall/Winter 2001): 103–36.

[19] Ruttmann, "Wie ich meinen Berlin-Film drehte," 80.

[20] Cf. Mark C. Taylor, *The Moment of Complexity: Emerging Network Culture* (Chicago: U of Chicago P, 2001); George Landow, *Hypertext 3.0* (Baltimore, MD: Johns Hopkins UP, 2006).

[21] The term "database cinema" comes from Lev Manovich's discussion of Vertov in *The Language of New Media* (Cambridge, MA: MIT Press, 2001), 237. Here, unlike some of the arguments made by Siegfried Kracauer or Sabine Hake, which emphasize the differences between Vertov and Ruttmann, I want to stress a point of overlap in their filmic practice.

[22] Manovich, *The Language of New Media*, 240.

[23] The simplest definition of "remediation" is "the representation of one medium in another." Jay David Bolter and Richard Grusin, *Remediation: Understanding New Media* (Cambridge, MA: MIT Press, 2001), 45.

[24] Hypermedia Berlin was originally incubated at the Stanford Humanities Laboratory and has been funded by the American Council of Learned Societies (2006–7), the UCLA Center for Digital Humanities, the UCLA Office of Instructional Development, and the UCLA Academic Senate Faculty Grants Program. Since 2008, Hypermedia Berlin has become part of a broader digital cultural mapping initiative called HyperCities, which I direct at UCLA. The collaborative project was recently awarded one of the first "digital media and learning" prizes by the MacArthur Foundation/HASTAC and currently includes Los Angeles, New York, Lima, Rome, and Tel Aviv in addition to Berlin, with more cities coming soon.

25 Walter Benjamin, *The Arcades Project*, trans. Howard Eiland and Kevin McLaughlin (Cambridge, MA: Harvard UP, 1999), 461. Further citations will be documented parenthetically using the abbreviation *AP* followed by the page number.

26 I have discussed this in more detail in my article "'Hypermedia Berlin': German Cultural Studies and New Media," *German Politics and Society* 74.1 (2005): 171–88.

27 The term "Zeitschichten" comes from Reinhart Koselleck, who argues that "the advantage of a theory [of history attuned to] time-layers consists in the fact that different speeds can be measured, accelerations or decelerations, thus making various phases of change visible, which demonstrate significant temporal complexity." Koselleck, *Zeitschichten: Studien zur Historik* (Frankfurt am Main: Suhrkamp, 2000), 22.

28 This notion of the city as a "palimpsest" accords with Andreas Huyssen's *Present Pasts: Urban Palimpsests and the Politics of Memory* (Stanford, CA: Stanford UP, 2003).

29 Ruttmann, "Wie ich meinen Berlin-Film drehte" (1927), 80.

30 For more on this, see Sabine Hake, "Urban Spectacle in Walter Ruttmann's *Berlin, Symphony of the Big City*," in *Dancing on the Volcano: Essays on the Culture of the Weimar Republic,* ed. Thomas W. Kniesche and Stephen Brockmann (Columbia, SC: Camden House, 1994), 127–37; and Carsten Strathausen, "Cyborgian Visions, Uncanny Spaces: The City in Ruttmann and Vertov," in *Screening the City,* ed. Mark Shiel and Tony Fitzmaurice (London: Verso P, 2003).

31 Manovich, *The Language of New Media*, 148.

32 Cf. Ernst Bloch, *Erbschaft dieser Zeit*, vol. 4 of *Gesamtausgabe* (Frankfurt am Main: Suhrkamp, 1977).

33 Among others, see Frances Cairncross, *The Death of Distance: How the Communications Revolution Is Changing Our Lives* (Boston: Harvard Business School Publications, 2001); Stanley D. Brunn and Thomas R. Leinbach, eds., *Collapsing Space and Time: Geographic Aspects of Communication and Information* (London: HarperCollins, 1991); and Nicolas Negroponte, *Being Digital* (New York: Knopf, 1995).

34 For a cogent (and relatively early) critical analysis of technology and the various forces of imbalance in globalization, see Jean-Marie Guéhenno, *The End of the Nation-State*, trans. Victoria Elliot (Minneapolis: U of Minnesota P, 1995); also, Saskia Sassen, *The Global City: New York, London, Tokyo* (Princeton, NJ: Princeton UP, 2001), and the volume edited by Saskia Sassen, *Global Networks, Linked Cities* (New York: Routledge, 2002). For a popular cultural history of networks, see Albert-László Barabási, *Linked: How Everything Is Connected to Everything Else and What It Means for Business, Science, and Everyday Life* (New York: Plume Books/Penguin, 2002).

35 For a thorough discussion of the railway and fantasies of (German/Jewish) modernity, see my *Mobile Modernity: Germans, Jews, Trains*. See also Benjamin's *The Arcades Project*, Convolute U, "Saint-Simon, Railroads," 571–602.

36 One is also reminded of the opening scenes of Robert Musil's seminal modernist novel, *Der Mann ohne Eigenschaften,* which begins with a transcendental bird's eye view of the city before rushing downward into the highly coordinated, synchronized city below. The victims of an untoward traffic accident are quickly tended to, while the "sense of incessant movement" carries everyone else along: "Air trains, ground trains, underground trains, people mailed through tubes special delivery, and chains of cars race along horizontally while express elevators pump masses of people vertically from one traffic level to another." Musil, *The Man Without Qualities,* trans. Sophie Wilkins (New York: Vintage Books, 1996), 27.

37 For a theorization of complexity, see Niklas Luhmann, *Social Systems,* trans. John Bednarz, Jr. with Dirk Baecker (Stanford, CA: Stanford UP, 1995).

38 This is Aristotle's definition of contingency. For further discussion, see Niklas Luhmann, *Observations on Modernity,* trans. William Whobrey (Stanford, CA: Stanford UP, 1998).

39 Alfred Döblin's *Berlin Alexanderplatz* (1928) is the modernist novel's counterpart to Ruttmann's cinematic space of contingency.

40 Paul Baran, *On Distributed Communications: Introduction to Distributed Communication Networks* (Santa Monica, CA: RAND Corporation, 1964), 3, 8. For a good overview of the history of the Internet and World Wide Web, see James Gillies and Robert Cailliau, *How the Web Was Born: The Story of the World Wide Web* (Oxford: Oxford UP, 2000).

41 Manovich, *The Language of New Media,* 237 (italics in original).

42 For a discussion of the history of the window vis-à-vis Western modes of seeing, see Anne Friedberg, *The Virtual Window: From Alberti to Microsoft* (Cambridge, MA: MIT Press, 2006); Martin Jay, *Downcast Eyes: The Denigration of Vision in Twentieth-Century French Thought* (Berkeley: U of California P, 1993); and Lutz Koepnick, *Framing Attention: Windows on Modern German Culture* (Baltimore, MD: Johns Hopkins UP, 2007). For more on the window paradigm and the dreams of realist representation, see my article "'Hypermedia Berlin': German Cultural Studies and New Media." Bolter and Grusin also provide a brief overview, saddling Alberti—perhaps unfairly—as the key figure in developing "the logic of transparent immediacy" (*Remediation,* 21–31).

43 To illustrate the idea of never arriving at the "real" Berlin, I sometimes call upon a story conveyed by the ethnologist Clifford Geertz: "There is an Indian story—at least I heard it as an Indian story—about an Englishman who, having been told that the world rested on a platform which rested on the back of an elephant which rested in turn on the back of a turtle, . . . asked what did the turtle rest on? Another turtle. And that turtle? 'Ah, Sahib, after that it is turtles all the way down.'" Clifford Geertz, *The Interpretation of Cultures: Selected Essays* (New York: Basic Books, 1973), 28–29. Hypermedia Berlin is representation all the way down.

44 Adilkno, *The Media Archive* (Brooklyn, New York: Autonomedia, 1998), 99. Qtd. in Manovich, *The Language of New Media,* 270.

45 Cf. Dolores Hayden, *The Power of Place: Urban Landscapes as Public History* (Cambridge, MA: MIT Press, 1997). For a fascinating Web-based project on New

Orleans and the Gulf Coast that binds personal stories of loss and destruction with place, see the Hurricane Digital Memory Bank: http://hurricanearchive.org (accessed 25 Jan. 2009).

[46] As Tim O'Reilly argues, open platforms, not closed applications, are the future of Web 2.0. The ability to collect, manage, tag, annotate, and recombine data (not just publish it once and for all) is what is at stake. As he maintains: *"The value of the software is proportional to the scale and dynamism of the data it helps to manage"* (1). For an overview of Web 2.0, see O'Reilly, "What Is Web 2.0: Design Patterns and Business Models for the Next Generation of Software" (30 Sept. 2005), http://www.oreillynet.com/pub/a/oreilly/tim/news/2005/09/30/what-is-web-20.html (accessed 25 Jan. 2009).

[47] Lev Manovich, "Alan Kay's Universal Media Machine" (unpublished manuscript), 13. Also see his chapter, "Remixability," in this volume.

[48] James Surowiecki, *The Wisdom of Crowds* (New York: Random House, 2004).

12: Fragging Fascism

Margit Grieb

> *Our analysis of interactive media must . . .
> go beyond theories of representation in images.
> The image is just the target, the surface.*
> —Simon Penny

PRODUCTIVE CONTEMPORARY MEDIA SCHOLARSHIP has distilled a definition for new media that is not particularly concerned with explaining and isolating the newness in various digital technologies, whether it be in appearance, capability, or comparison to analogue technology that came before it. Instead, this definition focuses on new media's ability to erase the distinctiveness and independence of individual digital technologies. It is new media's capability for remediation (in the sense of Bolter and Grusin[1]) that affords them the label "new." As the editors of this volume point out in the introduction, these media scholars have developed "persuasive criteria for what we may label as new in the first place and how this newness alters our relation to the old." This latter concern informs my essay on recurring and persistent cultural appropriations of twentieth-century iconography of evil. As a point of departure, I will reexamine Susan Sontag's seminal essay on the particulars of a fascist aesthetic in order to delineate whether her insights into analogue manifestations of fascist aesthetics are still meaningful when these are transposed and translated into digital technologies. Specifically, I will look at the video game with its various genres and sub-genres in order to trace the re-fashioning and reframing of Nazi iconography in the realm of the digital. As I will show, attempts to understand the popularity of Nazi imagery and themes in video games must take into account the genre specificity with which themes and imagery appear in games. Video-game representations of fascism are neither homogeneous nor straightforward; they are nuanced and complex, as they are in other media. In order to interpret the re-embodiment and transformation of fascist aesthetics in the digital age, it is instructive to revisit the reception of such manifestations prior to their digital mutations.

Susan Sontag's seminal essay "Fascinating Fascism," published in the mid-1970s, aimed at exposing Leni Riefenstahl's publication *The Last of the Nuba,* a collection of photographs depicting the tribes of the African Nuba Mountain region, as a continuation of the filmmaker's earlier fascist aesthetic; it is Sontag's reaction to the book's attempt to rehabilitate Riefenstahl's career. However, in her essay the author did not confine herself to condemning the comeback of the filmmaker as an ostensibly innocuous photographer of "everything that is beautiful" (Riefenstahl cited in Sontag).[2] In the second part of her essay Sontag tackles a more contemporary and problematic issue: the public's resurgent fascination with fascism's erotic allure, as evidenced by sexualized representations of fascism in popular as well as "high culture" international texts.

Sontag's polemic sought to serve as a deterrent, a warning against a continuing trend that would increasingly obscure the underlying historical foundations and realities of fascism and replace them with a more general and mythical attraction, but "fascinating fascism" is as prevalent today as it was when Sontag wrote her treatise more than thirty years ago. One of its mutations, updated to fit comfortably into the parameters of mass consumer culture, now wears the label "Nazi Chic";[3] replete with many of the components that Sontag evokes in her description of a fascist aesthetic, it seeps, compliant as the underlying ideology to which it is tied, into nearly every crevice of popular culture.[4] It has been spotted on fashion runways and catapulted a British royal heir, as well as the chief of grand prix motor racing, into the spotlight of the paparazzi.[5] Nazi Chic has appeared on television as well as in Hollywood films and in the contemporary music scene. It is not only a fashionable look that adorns "real" bodies, but it also defines imagery and themes found in graphic novels, political cartoons, and video games.[6]

Although what Sontag characterized as an aesthetic with significant ideological underpinnings has, in its popular culture metamorphosis to Nazi Chic, aligned itself more closely with fashion and style than politics and hence remained in the domain of the superficial, what she characterized as the erotic appeal of fascist aesthetics is nonetheless still omnipresent. As she comments in "Fascinating Fascism," "the sexual lure of fascism seems impervious to deflation by irony or over-familiarity" (101). This is not to say that fascism has completely lost its ideologically grounded appeal in contemporary Western society. A case in point is cable television's History Channel, dubbed by some "The Hitler Channel"; the popularity of its seemingly endless broadcasting of documentaries about the Third Reich is a testament to the American public's continued fascination with charismatic, mythical leaders. Several recent films also fit into this category, for example, the German box-office hit *Downfall,* which was also relatively popular in the United States. Nazi Chic, as a social phenomenon, nevertheless aligns itself more closely with the familiar and universal territory of eroticism and, as the name implies, with fashion. Its erotic appeal, in particular, has found fertile ground in the subculture of hard-core gaming, where sexual imagery is as ubiquitous as simulated violence; in fact, they often appear within the same context.

In *Sex Drives: Fantasies of Fascism in Literary Modernism*, Laura Frost examines this alignment of fascism with eroticism (and by extension sexual deviance) within the context of modernist literary figures such as D. H. Lawrence and Sylvia Plath.[7] I will use some of her observations here to describe the historical background against which Nazi Chic has developed its particular appearance. Frost argues that, in addition to the sexualized imagery and language used by fascists themselves, erotic fascist imagery has also evolved as a product of Allied anti-fascist rhetoric from before and after the Second World War. Britain, France, and the United States, self-proclaimed pillars of democracy, perceived conventional "heterosexuality, founded on equality, respect, and nonviolence . . . as a reflection of democratic national ideals, while sexualities that did not fall into line with this norm were designated 'fascist'" (6–7). Frost explains that "fascism, therefore, with its institutions of oppression and domination became the sadomasochistic politics par excellence" (7). Such characterizations cultivated by an alliance of heterogeneous states were instrumental in establishing a common and unified vision of the totalitarian enemy. Furthermore, Frost argues that the image of a sexualized German enemy is not tied exclusively to fascism but goes back further in history and informed the European propaganda effort of the First World War. Popular perceptions of the Prussian tradition as permeated by "rigid hierarchy, discipline, masculine domination, and ritualized violence" allowed the British and French to paint a picture of the German adversary as an uncivilized, sexually deviant barbarian (19).

Frost suggests that the return of Germany as enemy during the Second World War precipitated a deployment of powerful political imagery in which Germans were again associated with aberrant sexualities such as sadomasochism. Images of whip-toting Germans in stances of sexual dominance infused representations of fascism with erotic appeal. Popular post–Second World War historical narratives, such as Shirer's *Rise and Fall of the Third Reich*, continued this rhetoric by characterizing high-ranking SA and SS officers as men with "unnatural sexual inclinations" in order to construct a general psychological profile of the Nazi, who is associated with a homosexuality pathologized as and conflated with sadomasochism.[8]

Sontag likewise highlights the eroticization of violence, specifically sadomasochism, as an integral part of the fascist aesthetic:

> Fascist aesthetics include but go far beyond the rather special celebration of the primitive to be found in *The Last of the Nuba*. More generally, they flow from (and justify) a preoccupation with situations of control, submissive behavior, extravagant effort, and the

endurance of pain; they endorse two seemingly opposite states, egomania and servitude. The relations of domination and enslavement take the form of a characteristic pageantry . . . fascist dramaturgy centers on the orgiastic transactions between mighty forces and their puppets, uniformly garbed and shown in ever swelling numbers. Its choreography alternates between ceaseless motion and a congealed, static, "virile" posing. (91)

She even goes so far as to proclaim: "Between sadomasochism and fascism there is a natural link" (103). George "Mosse's argument that modern national identity is constructed around a contrast between abnormal and respectable sexuality"[9] underpins the political investment inherent in such portrayals. It is not surprising that the pre–and post–First World War political discourse, preoccupied with tying national identity and the democratic form of government to hetero-normativity, is not confined to the first half of the twentieth century but still resonates in the current political landscape of the United States, where heterosexual relationships informed by prescribed moral and religious values are virtually synonymous with the highly regarded institutions of marriage and family and perceived as essential to democracy.

However, as Frost points out, the First and Second World Wars spawned predominantly gender-specific images in which German males are shown as barbarian aggressors. One might ask, then, why contemporary representations that link sadomasochism with fascism depict not just men as sadists but also women in the role of the dominatrix. Although Frost notes that this inversion of gender roles belongs predominantly to the postwar era and has been disseminated by the popular press, she does not address in detail what prompted this reversal except to say that female sexual violence is "a gendered extension [of earlier fascist male sadism] since female violence and sexual violence are even more culturally aberrant than male sadism" (154). I will not dissect this phenomenon within a *broader* cultural context here; rather, I will confine my comments to one particular sector of popular entertainment, the video game. Video games have their own historically and culturally motivated reason for the crossover from the sadistic Nazi male to a female counterpart. In order to show how and why the female Nazi dominatrix (together with the sexually-charged Nazi male) appears within the genre of video games known as first-person shooters (FPS) and adventure games, I will turn to the history of video games in general as well as discuss specifically the games *Return to Castle Wolfenstein* and *BloodRayne*.[10]

Some scholars in feminist media studies have attributed the proliferation of female protagonists and foes in action video games with warlike settings to the close cooperation that exists between game manufacturers and the US Department of Defense, serving the latter's interest during a time of soldier shortage. Claudia Herbst, for example, points out that the virtual female soldier is designed to make a woman in uniform, depicted as conquering hero as well as victim of war, more palatable to a public still uncomfortable with the idea of women in such roles.[11] However, action heroines in shooter games as well as other video-game genres also have a history independent of present-day US military engagements.[12] They not only predate the war in Iraq but have appeared in steady numbers in other media, such as films and graphic novels of the 1990s and before.

One of the first female action heroines to grace the video game landscape was Lara Croft in the popular game *Tomb Raider* in 1996. At that time the use of a female protagonist in an action-themed video game was far from common, but the design team working on *Tomb Raider* claimed, when they created Lara Croft, to be less interested in gender-bending the genre than in avoiding possible copyright infringements. *Tomb Raider*'s female lead was intended to preempt any complaints concerning the game's astonishing similarity to the film franchise *Indiana Jones*.[13] Lara's commercial success paved the way for female principal characters in a number of other games as developers realized that male gamers (the target audience of action-themed, and especially FPS games) did not reject female stand-ins but instead were eager to embrace these highly sexualized Lara-like heroines.

The representation of female game characters as eroticized vixens also found fertile ground in many video games with a Nazi theme. However, Nazi Chic refashions Lara's rugged all-purpose eroticism into a female Nazi adversary with sadomasochistic appeal. Activision's *Return to Castle Wolfenstein* is an excellent example of this, as it is littered with Nazi fembots that ooze taboo sexuality. Although a plethora of stereotypical male Nazis with stylish uniforms, muscular physiques, and angular faces—characters so prominent in Riefenstahl's *Triumph of the Will* and *Olympia*—offer a multitude of potential enemy targets in this game, the most visceral attention of gamers is commanded by the female characters, whose ample breasts, ultra-thin waists, oversized lips, and revealing outfits have become trademarks of the virtual Nazi femme fatale (fig. 12.1b). In order to accentuate the erotic otherness of these female killing machines, they are often cast in opposition to innocent, virginal civilian girls with stereotypical German features and dress, virtual Heidiesque counterparts who appear devoid of sexual connotation (fig. 12.1a).[14]

Although a juxtaposition such as this reinforces the equation of Nazism with sex, other video games blur these connections by purposefully mixing their metaphors. In the Nazi vampire adventure game *BloodRayne*, for example, the protagonist, a female vampire Nazi hunter, embodies many of the erotic characteristics present in *Wolfenstein*'s Nazi femmes fatales. Although the title character in *BloodRayne* is not a Nazi but a Nazi hunter and is therefore not decked out in Nazi regalia, she still

Fig. 12.1. Clockwise from top left: (a) civilian in Return to Castle Wolfenstein; *(b) female adversary in* Return to Castle Wolfenstein; *(c) Nazi hunter in* BloodRayne; *(d) Über-soldier in* Return to Castle Wolfenstein.

evokes the sadomasochistic association through her attire and hyper-sexual physique. This invocation of transgressive eroticism is further reinforced by some of the action sequences in which the player can engage, such as sucking blood out of Nazi adversaries' necks while straddling them in a stance suggestive of sexual intercourse.[15] Rather than deriving its eroticism exclusively from fascist imaginary, video games such as *Wolfenstein* and *BloodRayne* style the image of woman as sex object in a general sense, presumably to appeal to what continues to be a predominantly male gaming community (fig. 12.1c). Scantily clad buxom blondes and brunettes abound in the video game landscape, reminiscent of the predecessor for such female characterizations, Lara Croft. To be sure, genre conventions play an even more important role in the appearance of Nazi Chic in FPS and adventure video games than does the popular appeal of fascist aesthetics described by Sontag and Frost.[16]

The erotic glamour of Nazi Chic is also at home within the aesthetic and spatial architecture of video games and is not only confined to the action sequences that unfold during the game play. Females with gravity-defying physiques and male figures displaying the kind of physical perfection that would have fared well in Nazi propaganda posters not only function as interactive elements but are also an integral addition to the mise-en-scène of the video game. In lieu of narrative exposition, with which we are familiar from other entertainment media and which is severely limited in first-person shooters, game developers draw in the player by focusing on creating atmosphere through music and paying close attention to detail in settings. Because the Nazi S/M connection is so indelibly etched into the popular imaginary, it also serves to authenticate the setting. In *Wolfenstein*, the simulated Nazi landscape is additionally accessorized with elements that often surprise us with their precise historical references; the location itself, castle Wolfenstein, is an obvious allusion to Himmler's occult castle Wewelsburg. Furthermore, the game's many levels and locations are littered with SS regalia, and the uniforms of the adversaries show the kind of details that Sontag describes as "the units of a particularly powerful and widespread sexual fantasy" (95). This culminates in the final stages of the game with the introduction of a character the game refers to as the *Über*-soldier (fig. 12.1d). All this is done with the purpose of reinventing the Third Reich for a consumer who likely has very little historical knowledge of this period and thus conceptualizes it mainly through popular cultural representations from other mass media. But because the game's artificial, compact, and heavily accessorized space serves only to provide a trajectory for the player, as well as to keep him or her interested in the game, the representation of the Third Reich remains a preoccupation with surfaces, which is exactly where Nazi Chic is most at ease.

How this Nazi imagery presumably affects players depends not only on how it is specifically infused into the game design, for example, as setting, or the fact that this "young" medium has already established its own conventions. An analysis of the possible effects must also take into consideration the degree to which the appearance and function of this imagery emerge in the game "narrative" and how this fits into the category of Nazi Chic. Looking at games individually and from a genre-based perspective allows for some distinctions to be made and effects to be isolated. FPS genre games like *Return to Castle Wolfenstein* as well as adventure action games such as *BloodRayne*, both part of a sub-genre that includes non-networked, singular players[17] and a non-realistic premise, predominantly engage players less with the appeal of enacting or revealing a narrative, and more with procedural quests to solve puzzles, collect treasure (ammunition, life, keys, and so on), move through different territories (often with varying vehicles), and engage in combat to eliminate the enemy.[18] There may be a simple plot, or even a back-drop story, established through cut-scenes, but essentially *Wolfenstein* and *BloodRayne* appeal to gamers through non-stop action and movement.

Much contention exists between video-game theorists who challenge the existence or the importance of narrative (in the traditional sense) in video games and others who insist that distinct diegetic elements exist. Ludologists—digital game theorists, such as Espen Aarseth, who see video games as cultural forms in their own right that need not necessarily be approached from the viewpoints of established scholarly criticisms—represent one end of this critical spectrum and are in conflict with scholars on the other end, who see games as a storytelling medium. This latter group of scholars, the narratologists (sometimes called neo-Aristotelians, for example, Janet Murray), believe that humanity has a universal and enduring need for narrative, and they classify video games as a medium that finds new ways of conveying it. A video-game scholar more comfortable on middle ground, Henry Jenkins, maintains in "Game Design as Narrative Architecture" that both sides add important arguments to the discourse of game analysis under the aegis of the nascent discipline of video-game scholarship.[19] The ludologists contend that game-specific mechanics need to be brought to the foreground, while the narratologists believe—indeed hope—that games clearly utilize diegetic exposition during play. To this discourse Jenkins adds a third conceptual model, which he calls narrative architecture, that explores a consideration of both sides of the argument. It allows for the surveying of narrative embedded in games that, at first glance, appear to be highly limited in their "story-value," at least in the traditional—literary or filmic—sense. Jenkins' narrative model of environmental storytelling privileges "spatial exploration over plot development" and defines stories as "held together by broadly defined goals and conflicts and pushed forward by the character's movement across the map" (124) replete with a narrative resolution in the form of winning. In my opinion, his mapping of narrative in video games is also useful to the analysis and differentiation of individual games and a game genre's inherent narrative possibilities. The question of narrative, and hence Jenkins's model, is important to my analysis of digital games, because my interpretive focus highlights the importance of considering genre conventions when "reading" a video game. I contend that Nazi Chic is not synonymous with Sontag's "fascinating fascism," as it appears in different types of games and through varying types of narrative and exposes the gamer to different levels of ideological directives through diegetic elements, dependent on and reinforced by genre-specific conventions.

In his model of video-game narrative architecture, Jenkins distinguishes between "embedded" and "emergent" narratives.[20] Embedded narratives in video games are stories that players assemble from cues, clues, and artifacts contained in the game's mise-en-scène. Emergent narratives are not preprogrammed into the game but are the result of unstructured game play and interaction with the mise-en-scène or other characters; these narratives are contained in the performative action and individual expression of gamers in the course of game play. In *Castle Wolfenstein* meaningful information, and hence narrative, is presented mainly within the spatial configuration and through the artifacts in the game; player movement and story space are closely linked. For example, an abundance of Nazi flags in various rooms of the castle denotes Nazi control over these spaces, but, when players shoot and destroy these flags (which curiously does not add any game points or reveal any hidden spaces), they symbolically take control of the spaces, ultimately the goal of the game, through several of what Jenkins refers to as micro-narratives.[21] *Wolfenstein*, as a single-player FPS, utilizes predominantly embedded stories in its narrative architecture. This narrative, albeit defined by a Nazi theme, never allows ideological elements of fascist ideology to penetrate any further than its façade, the embedded story space. Although *Wolfenstein* simulates a Nazi setting with accessories that contain historical references, these elements are defused, if not neutralized, through exaggeration, irony, and artificiality.

In contrast to the superficial and mostly innocuous stylizations used in shooters such as *Wolfenstein* to tell a story, other video-game genres, especially flight simulators, attract players by utilizing a much more ideologically grounded narrative, in the form of embedded as well as emergent stories. Whereas *Wolfenstein* privileges conceptual abstractions and exaggerated, indeed chimerical, elements in its representation of the Third Reich, games such as *Secret Weapons of the Luftwaffe* (one of the first flight simulators), *IL-2 Sturmovic*, and, one of the most popular of all Second World War flight simulators, Microsoft's *Combat Flight Simulator WWII*, all offer players a chance to fly realistic and historically accurate aircraft of either the Allied or *Luftwaffe* forces.[22] Flight simulators aim for a close approximation of actual airplane models in terms of look as well as technological capabilities. This genre is particularly invested in attracting players through its representational realism. This realism, embedded in the available aircraft and weaponry, and hence the representations of Third Reich military power, along with the earnest, true-life combat scenarios, lead the game into ideological territory not necessarily germane to Nazi Chic. In *Secret Weapons,* for example, players who decide to fly missions as Allied pilots can choose from common Second World War planes, such as the US fighters P51 Mustang and P47 Thunderbolt and, on the British side, the Spitfire, Hurricane, and Typhoon; players who choose to fly missions as German World War II pilots have the choice of a much more exotic selection of planes. While the British and US planes are more or less historically accurate common fighters, the German planes are represented by such exotic specimens as the DO 335, aka "The Arrow," of which only eleven were made (and none was deployed in combat), as well as the Horton Gotha 229 and several Messerschmitt models (none of which was a common German fighter plane during the Second World War). What the German planes all have in common is their superior design, advanced technology, and pure, unadulterated power.

These exotic fighters are presumably much more appealing to most gamers than the run-of-the-mill Allied machines. Gamers are seduced by the superior technology of the Third Reich, or in other words, by perfect fighting machines. Whereas in *Return to Castle Wolfenstein* gamers must overcome the absurd Nazi *Über*-soldier to win, these Second World War flight simulators use an appeal far more subtle and nuanced. The flight simulators suggest that if gamers want to be assured of a victory they had better side with the Nazis, who have the most advanced and powerful toys. This is not to say that game developers use clandestine techniques to try and convince young male adults to subscribe to right-wing politics. After all, there is potentially just as much dubious narrative contained in the enacted stories as there is in the preprogrammed embedded stories. Rather, I suggest that some game developers, consciously or otherwise, create games that, through embedded and emergent narratives, fetishize Nazi technology and consequently contribute to a fetishization of the culture that produced it. Even in most simulator games that don't use exotic and superior German machinery but allow playing on either the Axis or Allied side, there is no incentive, moral or otherwise, to motivate players to side with the Allies, nor is there a clear directive that indicates one side as the better choice. On the contrary, in order to assure that there will be "bodies" on both sides, at least in the online versions, the games reduce the Second World War to a conflict of vague origins that was fought without reasonable objectives.

Although *Wolfenstein* does little to go beyond Nazi Chic in its representation of the Third Reich, it does explore aspects of Nazi ideology by integrating into its narrative backdrop National Socialism's preoccupation with myth and supernatural lore.[23] Concomitantly, however, these abstractions are ridiculed when they come to life in the form of *Über*-soldiers and monsters. In *BloodRayne* as well, occult Nazi artifacts grant supernatural abilities and are used by Jurgen Wulff, the antagonist, to try to bring Hitler into power, but they can just as well fall in the wrong—or, better, right—hands in the course of the game. Elements of the horror genre, the supernatural, and mythology are popular themes in FPS and other adventure games. Since these elements were also part and parcel of the Third Reich's fascination with the occult, this theme readily lends itself to video-game adaptation. However, whereas Nazi occultist practices and beliefs derived much of their intrigue from the fact that the supernatural was confined to the imaginary or infused into staged spectacle, video games such as *Wolfenstein* and *BloodRayne* allow these tendencies to take physical shape. They appear reified as monsters and fantastic killing machines, thus removing them from the mythical realm (the noncorporeal) by placing these creatures alongside the Nazi antagonists. In an ironic twist, some of the monsters and un-dead creatures in *Wolfenstein* turn against the Nazis and eliminate them whenever and wherever they can. Similarly, in *BloodRayne,* the Nazi hunter is a vampire with an insatiable appetite for Aryan blood. In both cases, the irony and humor embedded within these narrative scenarios should not be ignored: monsters turn on their creators, Nazis get caught in supernatural traps, vampires and zombies kill Nazis for nourishment, and so on.[24] In the genre of flight simulators, such irony and hyperbole is missing altogether. There combat scenarios strive to project verisimilitude whenever possible.

In order to heighten the realism of flight simulators and expand playing time and scope, many of these video games include an online multiplayer mode in which scenarios involving entire fleets of aircraft, each controlled by an individual networked player, can be played out in real time. These so-called massively multiplayer online games (MMOGs) are virtual worlds in which potentially thousands of players can interact with each other over the Internet. In contrast, many popular FPS games, such as *Grand Theft Auto, 25 to Life,* and *Max Payne,* tap into the mythology of the adventurous American loner made popular by Westerns and Film Noir—one man "with nothing to lose" trying to tame a hostile environment—and employ this as their base narrative strategy and means for character identification.[25] Flight simulators, on the other hand, employ a different approach in structuring their embedded narrative context and emergent interaction. Of the flight simulators already mentioned, all but one have versions that can be played as MMPOGs. Others have no single-player mode at all. Games such as *Battleground Europe* (a combination of simulator, FPS, role-playing game, and strategy game) only exist in networked space. Flight simulators and other Second World War–themed action games use popular mythologies that revolve around the Second World War as their basis for appeal and emphasize the exact opposite of the lone-man, everything-goes scenarios stressed in many FPS games. Second World War scenarios evoke an implicit understanding of the historical significance of the "Last Great War," and draw on countless cultural representations that have reshaped, reinterpreted, and highlighted selective aspects of this historical event. Game designers fabricate a narrative and performative backdrop in which community, cooperation, and ritual play an important role in constructing the players' identities within the game. Emergent narratives serve an important role here as the basis for fun in game play. As I previously pointed out, Second World War games strive for historical accuracy, especially with regard to weapons, military craft, and terrain, while at the same time stripping historical events of all moral and political ambiguity and context. As Barry Atkins notes in *More Than a Game,* "the grand sweep of historical narrative becomes comprehensible in miniature, and the individual is presented as being able to 'make a difference' in circumstances [i.e. battles] where the outcome was uncertain and not already decided by sheer weight of numbers or an imbalance in available *materiel*."[26] The emphasis here is not on "why we fight wars" but "how we fight them" (and that we win); to quote a promotional video for *Battleground Europe*: "Choose a side, report for duty, and rewrite history."[27]

MMOGs construct an alternate reality for players in which they can, through performativity inherent in emergent story space, reenact and restage a war that has not been "tainted" by ambiguous representations in popular media (as is the case for the Vietnam conflict, for example). The expression "Axis of evil," a term that has informed US political discourse in the years since September 11, 2001, specifically evokes the term "Axis" to draw parallels to the Second World War, where, in general public opinion, the United States played an unequivocally virtuous role as liberator of states under German and Japanese occupation, not to mention concentration camps. In the game *Battleground Europe*, players can virtually perform and reenact the role that Allied forces played in the Second World War, an experience that gains meaning as it connects to the players' own political and historical context.[28] In order to attract players to these sites of reenactment, game developers have built an immersive context into their online games. For example, *Battleground Europe* includes real-time updates on troop deployment and loss, frequently updated newsletters describing the goings-on in this simulated Second World War universe, bulletin boards that encourage interaction between players and groups, and periodic conventions where players get to meet other players in the flesh. While there are sites and moments in game play that allow participants to build unimpeded social bonds through communication and actions, albeit "in character," *Battleground Europe*'s Web site is highly prescriptive with regard to how the game should be used.[29] Newsletters, game statistics, and announcements on the web page, the portal to the game, are written and updated regularly by game staff rather than by people playing the game. As is the case for most video games involving role-playing, out-of-character interaction is discouraged and hence the opportunity for emergent narratives to unfold enhanced. *Battleground Europe* offers a multitude of opportunities for players to uncover emergent narratives, all of which are designed to gloss over the fact that the Second World War is long over and that they are only participating in a virtual reenactment of a reinvented war. Embedded narrative also plays a role in this game, because both sides of the combat staged in *Battleground Europe* need "bodies." Apart from the prestructured Web-portal, players are also enticed to join the German side through access to weaponry, uniforms, and equipment that in many cases are ostensibly superior in power and more seductive in style to those of the Allied powers.

Jenkins argues that the degree to which emergent narratives are made possible in games depends on the richness of narrative potential infused into game spaces, which, in turn, enables the player to participate in diegetic experiences of varying intensity through his or her activities and actions. The spatial layout of *Battlefield Europe*, part of a video-game genre that includes networked space, is rife with potential emergent stories, as the predominant part of game play takes place in this relatively unstructured space and on one of the largest virtual battlegrounds in any MMOG. The vast amount of virtual space, as well as the large number of players, allows for a multitude of situations that hold narrative potential. The stories that play out on this networked battlefield through real-time engagement are also embedded narratives, as already mentioned, as the game includes a detailed web portal and variety of *materiel* that is available to players. But, unlike the playful, larger-than-life artifacts and adversaries in *Castle Wolfenstein*, the emergent and embedded narratives here are ultra-realistic and therefore afford no critical distance to the player. If the player is part of the Axis forces he or she will not likely question the representation of Nazi Germany within the game. On the contrary, as part of a unified force during war, the player is encouraged to identify with and feel pride for the German side. As a status update on the web site ensures players on the Axis side: "The German forces are fighting day and night along the front with the best men and the best equipment available to the Wehrmacht."[30]

As is well known, video games are among the fastest-growing, most profitable business ventures in the entertainment world. In order to reach such astronomical sales, the gaming industry must operate on a global scale in order to appeal to potential customers all over the world. It is therefore not surprising that the Nazi Chic aesthetic and its popular culture manifestations in games such as *Wolfenstein* are conspicuously devoid of specific historical underpinnings. The Nazi "bad guy" in these video games does not offend in the global marketplace; he or she represents the kind of adversary that almost anyone can enjoy killing. Following this logic, Nazis are an extinct breed reincarnated by popular culture; they once existed but have long since departed the geopolitical landscape and therefore represent the perfect template for styling the universally appealing video-game opponent. Whereas an evil Russian or Japanese adversary would encounter resistance in certain parts of the world, the Nazi is universally accepted and recognized as malevolent and beyond the reach of cultural reproach. Anton Kaes has noted the following in a discussion of fascist imagery in films:

> ... colorful red swastika flags, tight-fitting SS uniforms, shaven necks, black leather belts and boots, intimidating corridors, and wide marble stairways. These stereotypical signs do nothing more than provide a dramatic backdrop, ... Fascism ... is reduced to a colorful setting ... it is trivialized and co-opted by the entertainment industry as mere mise en scene. The Hitler period as a referent for countless historical films has by now been so often recycled that is

has become automatized. It can no longer provoke reactions, trigger memories, or yield an experience.[31]

To a large degree this characterization of filmic Nazi iconography and public consciousness applies to the video-game context as well; the defusing of reactions to images of Nazi Germany owes much to prior and adjacent cultural media representations, for example, films. However, unlike films, *Castle Wolfenstein* does not claim to provide more than a mise-en-scène for the player; it readily acknowledges that other visual media, such as television and films, have trivialized this particular iconography and, instead, uses this fact to its advantage. The figure of the Nazi in contemporary popular culture has lost its historical and geopolitical specificity and morphed into a universal archetype. This is evident not only in video games but also in graphic novels and films such as *Hellboy* and *Bulletproof Monk,* where Nazis occur in an anachronistic and geographically vague setting, and thus represent innocuous, albeit ultra-cool, bad guys (and girls).

In *Battlefield Europe*, in comparison, it is not the Nazi, as a ready-to-frag popular culture icon, that serves as the basis for game play, but a reimagined, virtual version of a physical historical event that provides the context for narrative exposition. This simulation is dependent on another type of narrative potential inherent in video-game design, located in what Jenkins terms "evocative space." Evocative spaces either "remediate a preexisting story . . . or draw upon a broadly shared genre tradition" (123). Rather than retelling a story that is already known, such as the film narrative of *Star Wars*, evocative space allows for video games to "[convey] new narrative experiences through its creative manipulation of environmental details . . . to give concrete shape to our memories and imaginings of the storyworld, creating an immersive environment we can wander through and interact with" (124). In other words, effective game design will not try to adapt faithfully a story that originated in another medium to the video-game medium in terms of narrative. Instead, game designers will use players' preexisting knowledge of stories, events, characters, and so on, from other media sources to sculpt immersive spaces and add to, reshape, and update the cultural significance and narrative potential of the originals. This is not only the case for fictional stories, such as *Star Wars*, but also for events in history, such as world wars, that have been molded and retold by several different media in a variety of ways and from a multitude of perspectives and have become "open source" themes for remediation. In *Battleground Europe* as well as in non-networked flight simulators, game designers have adopted the Second World War and its cross-media representations to the video-game medium in such a way that everything but the actual conflict and the stereotypical representations of the opposing sides has been erased.

FPS games have received much attention from the popular press and child psychologists as they have evolved into giants of the popular entertainment media world. *Wolfenstein 3D* (the prequel to *Return to Castle Wolfenstein*) as well as *Doom*, for example, became household names in 1999, when they were cited in connection with high-school shootings. *Wolfenstein 3D* became notorious as one of the favorite games of Eric Harris and Dylan Klebold, the teenage boys who killed fifteen and wounded twenty-three people in suburban Denver. Newspaper and television news reports were quick to postulate a direct correlation between violence in video games, especially those belonging to the FPS genre, and the violent actions that unfolded at Columbine. Although the *Wolfenstein/Doom* controversy centered on the violence in which young adults engage in video games (in other words the emergent spaces of video-game narrative[32]), the embedded story space (details regarding the themes and involving the Nazi Germany setting) never featured prominently on either side of the debate about video games and teen violence, although embedded narrative space is much more developed in first-person shooters than is emergent space. Juveniles' interaction with Nazis as eroticized adversaries and a simulated fascist Germany as the backdrop for aggression had already amassed a decades-long legacy in popular media such as film and television and hence were not perceived as significant to the discussion at hand.

The failure of the news media and general public to recognize a Nazi-themed narrative as dubious teen entertainment, or even worse, as a potential ideological tool in shaping the consciousness of young male adults, attests to the superficial impact Nazi Chic has on its subject matter as well as on consumers. Because the emphasis in flight simulators is on historical accuracy and realistic competition rather than on exaggerated gore, neither the narrative elements that allow for the quasi-heroic and morally unambiguous aggression of the Axis forces nor any other detail allow it to enter into the limelight of the video game and violent media spectacle. In her essay "Fascinating Fascism," Susan Sontag appealed to contemporary society's institutions of art and culture to banish the fascist aesthetic from all forms of expression in order to eradicate the ideological trappings enveloped in this aesthetic. But, when dressed up in the fashion of Nazi Chic, fascinating fascism's ideological components are defused without the conscious effort of cultural agency; they are banished by consumer culture to the innocuous realm of surface appeal. This is especially evident in video games like *Return to Castle Wolfenstein*. The elements of fascinating fascism embedded in other types of games, however, are a different matter altogether.

In light of the rapid innovations in hardware and software, as well as commercial viability of themes, that drive the development of video-game design, the original versions of *Castle Wolfenstein* and *BloodRayne* are already dusty relics in the annals of video-game history. It is not surprising to find that Nazi Chic in video games was a manifestation as ephemeral as a season's fashion, one that reached its peak appeal in the late 1990s and in the early years of the twenty-first century. In the sequel to *BloodRayne*, released just a couple of years later, Nazi characters still play a role in the initial backstory, but the ensuing primary storyline and story space centers on a new kind of evil—Kagan, a vampiric cult—in a contemporary, post-twentieth-century setting. In the last several years, representations of Nazis appear mainly confined to realistic Second World War adventure games and shooters, as well as flight simulators; gone are erotic Nazi vixens and fantastic *Über*-monsters.[33] But, as Susan Sontag predicted even thirty years ago, eradicating, or in video-game jargon, "fragging," fascinating fascism is not that easy a task; it "fascinates in a way other iconography . . . does not" (101). Instead, like a *Star Trek* Borg, it has adapted and become assimilated and thus has fortified its position in the contemporary video-game landscape.

Notes

The epigraph to this chapter is drawn from Simon Penny, "Representation, Enaction, and the Ethics of Simulation," in *First Person: New Media as Story, Performance, and Game*, ed. Noah Wardrip-Fruin and Pat Harrigan (Cambridge, MA: MIT Press, 2004), 73–84.

[1] Jay David Bolter and Richard Grusin, *Remediation: Understanding New Media* (Cambridge, MA: MIT Press, 2000).

[2] Susan Sontag, "Fascinating Fascism," in *Under the Sign of Saturn: Essays* (New York: Picador, 1980), 73–105, here 85.

[3] The term Nazi Chic is also part of the title of Irene Guenther's book, *Nazi Chic? Fashioning Women in the Third Reich* (Oxford: Berg, 2004), which examines female fashion during the Third Reich. Rather than using the term in a contemporary context, Guenther employs it as a play on words to describe how much fashion was a part of Nazi ideology and politics.

[4] In a special issue of the *Journal of Contemporary History*, Jeffrey Schnapp argues that "fascism never possessed a philosophical system of its own . . . nor did it actively seek such philosophical underpinnings. . . . Rather, fascism was determined to remain a paradoxical creature: part doctrinal beast descended from the anarcho-syndicalist wing of anti-materialist Marxism and part chameleon." Schnapp goes on to say that due to this lack of ideological fetter to a philosophical treatise, "fascism often sought answers to its identity crisis in the domain of culture." Jeffrey T. Schnapp, "Fascinating Fascism," *Journal of Contemporary History* 31.2 (Apr. 1996): 235–44, here 237–38.

[5] In January 2005 Prince Henry (Harry) appeared on the front page of the British newspaper *The Sun* wearing a swastika armband on a uniform. He later apologized, saying the outfit was a badly chosen costume for a friend's costume party. Likewise, Max Mosley, the overseer of grand-prix racing, made tabloid news in April 2008 when a video showing him at a Nazi-themed sex orgy was made public

in Britain. An article in the *New York Times* in 2000 details how fashion has incorporated the fascist aesthetic into designs and hair styles on runways in New York and elsewhere. Ruth La Ferla, "The Latest Look: Unforgiving," *New York Times*, 12 Nov. 2000.

[6] Right-wing pundit Ann Coulter appears in several cartoons and photomontages in Nazi regalia on the Web. Most of them include a visual reference to her sex appeal, such as bare breasts and fishnet stockings.

[7] Laura Frost, *Sex Drives: Fantasies of Fascism in Literary Modernism* (Ithaca, NY: Cornell UP, 2002).

[8] Jennifer Craik also cites the transgressive nature of sexuality exhibited by Nazis themselves specifically as contributing to the erotic appeal of Nazi uniforms: "A number of leading Nazis were camp and engaged in transgressive sexual practices . . . Nazi uniforms became fetishized . . ." (39–40). *Uniforms Exposed: From Conformity to Transgression* (Oxford: Berg, 2005).

[9] Frost, *Sex Drives*, 22.

[10] Although interesting arguments tied to the issue of perspective in video games exist, they are not relevant to my discussion here. Therefore I will use the abbreviation "FPS" to refer to all games that fit into the genre of "shooters."

[11] Claudia Herbst, "Shock and Awe: Virtual Females and the Sexing of War," *Feminist Media Studies* 5.3 (Nov. 2005): 311–24.

[12] Herbst acknowledges that virtual female heroines such as Lara Croft appeared in the 1990s but sees these developments as early milestones in the ongoing effort to paint "women as apt and capable soldiers" and believes that "[the virtual heroine] caters to present US military interests" (311).

[13] Steven Poole, *Trigger Happy: Videogames and the Entertainment Revolution* (New York: Arcade Publishing, 2000), 153.

[14] Game designers have adapted another German stereotype, the maiden from the *Heimat* genre, to serve as a template for these characters.

[15] *BloodRayne* also features female Nazi characters dressed in scant, often blood-stained, transgressively sensuous Nazi uniforms.

[16] It could also be argued that transformations in the appearance of male characters in many video games, Nazi or not, go hand in hand with developments in the action-figure toy industry—although the two industries are so closely linked that it makes any independent analysis impossible. Many action figures, male and female, have undergone an astonishing makeover in last few decades, a trend that is mirrored in video-game design. To highlight this development, the artists Andrea Robbins and Max Becher have documented action-figure evolution in a series of photographs. Robbins and Becher's work juxtaposes recent editions of action figures and their original release counterparts from the 1970s and shows that there exists a cultural preoccupation with increasingly action-oriented, muscular body types. These body transmutations inform the design of video-game avatars as well. For images of Robbins and Becher's photography, see Walter Robinson, "Weekend Update," *Artnet Magazine*, http://www.artnet.com/Magazine/reviews/robinson/robinson6-4-02.asp (accessed 25 Jan. 2009).

17 A multi-player *Wolfenstein* and *Bloodrayne* version also exists, as well as a spin-off, online-only version entitled *Wolfenstein: Enemy Territory*.

18 Second World War–themed games, such as *Call of Duty* or *Metal of Honor*, belong to another sub-genre of the FPS genre that feature Nazi Germany. I am not including them here, because it would go beyond the scope of this chapter to analyze what kind of "hook" game designers have built into these games to attract players.

19 Henry Jenkins, "Game Design as Narrative Architecture," in *First Person: New Media as Story, Performance, and Game* (Cambridge, MA: MIT Press), 118–29.

20 He also isolates the categories of "enacting story" and "evocative spaces," the latter of which I will turn to later in my argument.

21 In his explanation of how narrative can be embedded in space, Jenkins convincingly analyzes the role of space in melodramas in telling a story. Furthermore, Jenkins uses Hitchcock's *Rebecca* as an example to show how artifacts can play an important role in film — in the case of *Rebecca* they conjure up and give information about the very important title character, who is absent throughout the film.

22 Patrick Grogan discusses Microsoft's Second World War simulator and the question of narrative in detail in "Gametime: History, Narrative, and Temporality in *Combat Flight Simulator 2*," in *The Video Game Theory Reader*, ed. Mark J. P. Wolf and Bernard Perron (New York: Routledge, 2003), 275–301.

23 See Nicholas Goodrick-Clarke, *The Occult Roots of Nazism: Secret Aryan Cults and Their Influence on Nazi Ideology* (New York: New York UP, 1993).

24 In the Third Reich Jews were often imagined and portrayed by the Nazi propaganda machine as bloodsuckers, literally and figuratively; hence, intentional or not, the vampire Nazi hunter in *BloodRayne* represents yet another ironic twist on history. Nazis as vampires have also become a sporadic trope in video games, for example, *Operation Darkness* and *Call of Duty: World at War*.

25 The frontier narrative, familiar in countless Hollywood Westerns, also finds expression in a variety of other video-game genres, where it is often adapted to fit the context of the conquest of alien worlds or historical and imagined spaces, or used straightforwardly in actual Wild West reenactments. One of the reasons that frontier narratives lend themselves to video-game adaptation is that conflict and violence are integral parts of historical westward expansion in the United States and feature prominently in popular cultural representations with narratives centered around this theme (for example, the Western). For more on the frontier motive in twentieth-century cultural productions see Richard Slotkin, *Gunfighter Nation: The Myth of the Frontier in Twentieth-Century America* (New York: Atheneum, 1992).

26 Barry Atkins, *More Than a Game: The Computer Game as Fictional Form* (Manchester and New York: Manchester UP, 2003), 93.

27 YouTube: *Battleground Europe World War II Online*, http://www.youtube.com/watch?v=I0XacXFZROc (accessed 25 Jan. 2009).

28 It should be noted that *Battleground Europe*, as of now, does not include US forces in its make-up of the Second World War Allies. However, this is not detrimental to US players' identification with the soldiers of the Allied side. Specific

nationalities do not play a significant role, as the game sets up an oversimplified conflict of two sides—Allies vs. Axis.

[29] *Battleground Europe*, http://www.playnet.com/scripts/wwiionline/index.jsp (accessed 25 Jan. 2009).

[30] *Battleground Europe*, http://www.battlegroundeurope.com/index.php/campaign-community/axis-command (accessed 25 Jan. 2009).

[31] Anton Kaes, "History and Film: Public Memory in the Age of Electronic Dissemination," in *Framing the Past: The Historiography of German Cinema and Television*, ed. Bruce A. Murray and Christopher J. Wickham (Carbondale: Southern Illinois UP, 1992), 308–23, here 315–16.

[32] By highlighting the violence presented in FPS the media also centered on "enacted stories," Jenkins's fourth category of narrative in video games. Enacted stories gather meaning from the goals and/or conflicts that define particular games as well as the "localized incidents" (124) such as isolated combat action.

[33] Although in 2006 Activision released *Return to Castle Wolfenstein: Operation Resurrection*, it is merely an expansion of the original game. Similarly, the Nazi vampires in the fifth installment of the popular game series *Call of Duty* (released in 2008) do not represent a significant narrative element but are part of an embedded mini-game in the multi-player version of the game.

Contributors

NORA M. ALTER is Professor of English, Film and Media Studies, and German at the University of Florida. She is the author of *Vietnam Protest Theatre: The Television War on Stage* (1996), *Projecting History: Non-Fiction German Film* (2002), and *Chris Marker* (2006), and co-editor with Lutz Koepnick of *Sound Matters: Essays on the Acoustics of Modern German Culture* (2004). She has been awarded year-long research fellowships from the National Endowment for the Humanities, the Howard Foundation and the Alexander von Humboldt Foundation. She is currently completing a new book on the international essay film.

MICHEL CHAOULI is Associate Professor of German, Adjunct Professor of Comparative Literature and of Cognitive Science, and Director for the Institute of German Studies at Indiana University. His fields of interest include eighteenth-, nineteenth- and twentieth-century German literature and culture, embodied cognition and aesthetic imagination, and literature in the digital media. He is the author of *The Laboratory of Poetry: Chemistry and Poetics in the Work of Friedrich Schlegel* (2002) and numerous articles and book chapters. His current book project is entitled *Touch and Taste: Embodied Cognition and the Emergence of Aesthetics*.

DIEDRICH DIEDERICHSEN is a cultural critic, journalist and Professor of Theory, Practice and Communication of Contemporary Arts at the Academy of Fine Arts in Vienna. His recent publications include *Musikzimmer: Avantgarde und Alltag* (2005), *Personas en loop* (2006), *Golden Years: Materialien und Positionen zu queerer Subkultur zwischen 1959 und 1974* (2006), *Argument son: Critique electroacoustique de la societe* (2007), *Über den Mehrwert (in der Kunst)* (2008), *Kritik des Auges: Texte zur Kunst* (2008) and *Eigenblutdoping: Selbstverwertung, Künstlerromantik, Partizipation* (2008).

SABINE ECKMANN is Director and Chief Curator of the Mildred Lane Kemper Art Museum at Washington University in St. Louis. She is a specialist in twentieth- and twenty-first-century European art and visual culture. Recent projects include *The Art of Two Germanys: Cold War Cultures* (2009, with Stephanie Barron), *Thaddeus Strode: Absolutes and Nothings* (2008, with Meredith Malone), *Reality Bites: Making Avant-garde Art in Post-Wall Germany* (2007), *Caught by Politics: Hitler Exiles and American*

Visual Culture (2007, with Lutz Koepnick), *Window | Interface* (2007, with Lutz Koepnick) and *Grid < > Matrix* (2006, with Lutz Koepnick).

MARGIT GRIEB is Assistant Professor of German and Director of the Film Studies Certificate Program at the University of South Florida. Her research interests include videogames and twentieth-century German film and theater. She is currently completing a book manuscript entitled *Transformation: German Film in the Wake of New Media*. She has published articles in *Screenplay: Cinema/Videogames/Interfaces*, *European Cinemas in the Age of Television* and *European Avant Garde Critical Studies*.

BORIS GROYS is Professor of Fine Arts, Philosophy and Media Theory at the Academy of Design in Karlsruhe, Germany and Global Distinguished Professor of Russian and Slavic Studies at New York University. He is perhaps best known for his monograph *The Total Art of Stalinism* (1992). Recent publications include *Unter Verdacht: Eine Phänomenologie der Medien* (2000), *Ilya Kabakov: The Man Who Flew into Space from his Apartment* (2006), *Art Power* (2008) and *Thinking in Loop: Three Videos on Iconoclasm, Ritual and Immortality* (2008).

LUTZ KOEPNICK is Professor of German, Film and Media Studies at Washington University in St. Louis. He has written widely on German film, visual culture, and literature, on media arts and aesthetics, and on critical theory and cultural politics. Book publications include: *Framing Attention: Windows on Modern German Culture* (2007); *The Dark Mirror: German Cinema between Hitler and Hollywood* (2002); *Walter Benjamin and the Aesthetics of Power* (1999); and *Nothungs Modernität: Wagners Ring und die Poesie der Politik im neunzehnten Jahrhundert* (1994). Co-edited or co-authored volumes include: *Window | Interface* (2007); *The Cosmopolitan Screen: German Cinema and the Global Imaginary, 1945 to the Present* (2007); *Caught by Politics: Hitler Exiles and American Visual Culture* (2007); and *Sound Matters: Essays on the Acoustics of German Culture* (2004).

JULIET KOSS is Associate Professor and Chair of Art History at Scripps College and Coordinator of the Joint Program in Art History at the Claremont Colleges. She is the author of *Modernism After Wagner* (2010), which received the Millard Meiss Award from the College Art Association. Her work has appeared in numerous journals and edited volumes and has been supported by the American Association of University Women, the Getty Research Institute, the National Endowment for the Humanities, the Humboldt Research Foundation, the Mellon Foundation, the Canadian Centre for Architecture, and the American Academy in Berlin.

CONTRIBUTORS ♦ 207

RICHARD LANGSTON is Associate Professor in the Department of German Languages and Literatures at the University of North Carolina Chapel Hill. His research focuses on the intersections of aesthetics, social change, and the body. He is the author of *Visions of Violence: German Avant-Gardes after Fascism* (2008) and articles in *Germanic Review, Gegenwartsliteratur, modernity/modernism, Women in German Yearbook, German Quarterly, Proverbium* and numerous edited volumes. His current project examines the role of fantasy in the political philosophy of Negt and Kluge.

LEV MANOVICH is Professor of Visual Arts at the University of California San Diego and directs the Software Studies Initiative at the California Institute for Telecommunications and Information Technology. He is the author of *Software Takes Command* (2008), *Black Box—White Cube* (2005), *Soft Cinema* (2005), *The Language of New Media* (2001) and *Tekstura: Russian Essays on Visual Culture* (1993). He has been the recipient of a Guggenheim Fellowship (2002–3), a Digital Cultures Fellowship from UC Santa Barbara (2002), a fellowship from the Zentrum für Literaturforschung (2002), a Mellon Fellowship from Cal Arts (1995) and a Humanities High Performance Computing Program grant (2008).

ERIN MCGLOTHLIN is Associate Professor of German and Jewish Studies at Washington University in St. Louis. Her main research interests are in the areas of German-Jewish literature, the literature of the Holocaust, narrative theory, the graphic novel and autobiography. She is the author of *Second Generation Holocaust Literature: Legacies of Survival and Perpetration* (2006) and articles on Ruth Klüger, Art Spiegelman, Bernhard Schlink, Martin Amis, Maxim Biller, Edgar Hilsenrath and Jane Campion. She has received research fellowships from the Washington University Center for the Humanities, the U.S. Holocaust Memorial Musuem's Center for Advanced Holocaust Studies and the Fulbright Commission.

TODD SAMUEL PRESNER is Associate Professor of German and Jewish Studies at the University of California, Los Angeles. His research interests include German-Jewish literature, culture, and intellectual history; visual vulture, media studies, and art history; and digital humanities and new media. He is the author of *Mobile Modernity: Germans, Jews, Trains* (2007) and *Muscular Judaism: The Jewish Body and the Politics of Regeneration* (2007) and the founder and director of two digital mapping projects that examine the layered cultural histories of city spaces: Hypermedia Berlin and HyperCities.

JULIANE REBENTISCH teaches philosophy at the Johann Wolfgang Goethe University in Frankfurt am Main, where she is also a Research Associate at the Cluster of Excellence "The Formation of Normative Orders."

Her research focuses on the intersections of aesthetics, ethics and politics. Recent publications include: *Ästhetik der Installation* (2003, 3rd ed. 2009) and *Kunst—Fortschritt—Geschichte* (ed. with Christoph Menke 2006). She spent 2008–9 as the Heuss Lecturer at the New School for Social Research in New York.

CARSTEN STRATHAUSEN is Associate Professor of German and English at the University of Missouri at Columbia. His current research interests focus on the emerging aesthetics of digital technology in the context of contemporary political philosophy. He is the author of *The Look of Things: Poetry and Vision Around 1900* (2003) and the editor of *A Leftist Ontology* (2009). His current project is entitled *Aesthetics of New Media: Art and Politics in the Digital Age*. He was the recipient of an Alexander von Humboldt Fellowship in 2006.

Index

Aarseth, Espen, 193, 99n2
Addelman, Ben, 115n18
Adjaye, David, 78, 79
Adorno, Theodor Wiesengrund, 6, 7, 10–12, 13, 14, 16, 18, 35, 36, 49, 50, 51n10, 58, 59, 74–75, 76, 119–25, 127n6, 139, 140–41, 142 143, 150n29
Adorno, Theodor Wiesengrund, works by: *Aesthetic Theory,* 124, 127n6; "Art and the Arts," 119–21; "Culture Industry" from *Dialectic of Enlightenment,* 11, 36, 49; "Culture Industry Reconsidered," 50, 51n10; *Dialectic of Enlightenment,* 11, 36; "Looking Back on Surrealism," 150n29; *Negative Dialectics,* 150n29; "On the Fetish Character in Music and the Regression of Listening," 10, 140; *Parva Aesthetica,* 124; *Philosophy of New Music,* 124
aesthetic autonomy, 9–11, 14, 16, 118, 123–26
Agamben, Giorgio, works by: *Profanations,* 23
Alberti, Leon Battista, 184n42
Amerika, Mark, works by: "Grammatron," 88
archive, 12, 16–17, 55, 92–97, 153–57, 162–63, 164n11, 177; E-mail as, 93, 94–97, 99n10
Aristotle, 59, 184n38
Asch, Moses, 161–62
Assmann, Aleida, and Jan Assmann, 92, 93
Atkins, Barry, works by: *More Than a Game: The Computer Game as Fictional Form,* 196

attendance, aesthetics of, 102–3, 113
aura, the auratic, 10, 13, 15, 16, 26, 69, 70, 73–76, 78, 80, 84, 85–86, 90, 99n7, 121, 165n16
avant-garde, 17, 28, 36, 37, 38, 53, 63n10, 88, 119, 131–35, 137, 139, 140–41, 143–44, 147–48, 149n8, 150n29

Barabási, László, 183n34
Baran, Paul, 175, 177
Barthes, Roland, 25, 72, 97
Batchen, Geoffrey, 56
Battleground Europe, 196–98, 199, 203n28
Baudelaire, Charles, 167, 169, 173
Baudrillard, Jean, 53, 103
Baumgärtel, Tilman, 81
Bazin, André, 6
Bell, Alexander Graham, 107, 113n1, 115n14
Bell Laboratories, 110
Bell Telephone, 107
Benjamin, Walter, 3, 6, 7, 9–10, 11, 12, 13, 14, 15, 16, 18, 26, 36, 40, 73–74, 75, 76, 89, 90, 97, 99n3, 139, 140, 141, 142, 143, 149n1, 150n29, 151n37, 156, 166n29, 167–68, 169, 170, 172, 180, 183n35
Benjamin, Walter, works by: *The Arcades Project,* 143, 172, 183n35; "The Formula in Which the Dialectical Structure of Film Finds Expression," 168; "The Work of Art in the Age of Mechanical Reproduction," 26, 73
Benn, Gottfried, 137–38, 143–44

Benn, Gottfried, works by: "Gehirne," 137–38, 143–44; "Lovely Childhood," 138
Berthier, Denis, works by: *Méditations sur le Réel et le Virtuel,* 71
Bidussa, David, 155
Birnbaum, Daniel, 81
Bishop, Claire, 116n25
Bismarck, Otto von, 171
Bismuth, Pierre, 112, 116n27
Bloch, Ernst, 173
BloodRayne, 189, 190–91, 192, 195, 196, 200, 201, 202n15, 203n17, 203n24
Boellstorff, Tom, 65n23
Bolter, Jay David, 19n5, 53, 54, 183n23, 184n42, 186
Bolz, Norbert, 71
le Bon, Gustave, 180
le Bon, Gustave, works by: *Psychologie des foules* (*The Crowd*), 168
Boom, Holger van den, 86n1
Borck, Cornelius, 151n31
Bourriaud, Nicolas, 76, 84–85
Boyer, Edward W., 149n10
Brecht, Bertolt, 36, 104; Brechtian, 80, 143
Bredekamp, Horst, 105
Broodthaers, Marcel, 29–30
Brown, James, 161
Brunn, Stanley D., 183n33
Bubner, Rüdiger, works by: *Ästhetische Erfahrung,* 124, 127n10
Buchman, Sabeth, 164n12
Bürger, Peter, works by: *Theory of the Avant-Garde,* 131–32, 133, 134, 141, 149n1

Cage, John, 120, 122
Cailliau, Robert, 184n40
Cairncross, Frances, 183n33
Caldwell, John Thornton, 58
Call of Duty, 204n33
Camille, Michael, 72
Cavalcanti, Alberto, 165n22
Cavell, Richard, 151n35
Chun, Wendy Hui Kyong, 18n1, 62n1
Clark, Andy, 151n38
Craik, Jennifer, 202n8

Crary, Jonathan, 114n3
critical theory, 12–14, 19n12, 104, 121, 134
curator, curatorial practice, 23–26, 28, 30

Dada, 132
Davis, Whitney, 115n13
Debord, Guy, 132
deconstruction, 96, 164n15
Delahaye, Junior, 158
Delany, Paul, 99n4
Deleuze, Gilles, 57, 60, 72, 89
Derrida, Jacques, 27
Derrida, Jacques, works by: *Archive Fever: A Freudian Impression,* 93–96, 153, 154, 162
Diederichsen, Diedrich, 164n15
différance, 93
Dilly, Heinrich, 105
Dixon, Steve, 64n18
Doane, Mary Ann, 165n21, 180n1, 181n6
Döblin, Alfred, works by: *Berlin Alexanderplatz,* 184n39
Doherty, Brigid, 149n2
Druckrey, Timothy, 63n10, 64n19
Duchamp, Marcel, 118
Duguet, Anne-Marie, 87n21
Dybwad, Barb, 43

Eco, Umberto, 75
Einfühlung, 102, 103–4, 110
Eliasson, Olafur, 16, 60, 77–81, 85–86
Eliasson, Olafur, works by: *Weather Project,* 60; *Your Black Horizon,* 77–81
Elsaesser, Thomas, 18n2, 55
E-mail, 12, 43, 44, 93, 94–98, 99n10, 100n20, 101, 103
Enzensberger, Hans Magnus, 58–59
experience, aesthetics of, 118, 124, 125–26

fascism, aesthetics of, 10, 186–89, 191, 193, 198, 200–201, 210n3, 201n4, 201n5, 201n8
Feltrinelli, Giangiacomo, 155
film studies, 2, 17, 18

Finkel, Jori, 115n21
flâneur, 169, 173, 177–78, 180
Flaubert, Gustave, 89
Flavin, Dan, 75
"Folkways" music label, 161–62
Foster, Hal, 153, 154, 164n11
Foucault, Michel, 57–58, 61, 72
Foucault, Michel, works by: *The Archaeology of Knowledge,* 58, 65n25; "The Hermeneutics of the Subject," 58
Fraser, Andrea, 114n11
fraying, of borders between artforms (Adorno term), 119, 121–22
Freud, Sigmund, 93, 104, 108, 114n9, 134, 135, 139–44, 149n9
Freud, Sigmund, works by: *Beyond the Pleasure Principle,* 139–40, 141; *Civilization and Its Discontents,* 142, 151n35; *The Interpretation of Dreams,* 141; "Notiz über den Wunderblock," 100n21
Fricke, Christel, 127n10
Fried, Michael, 114n3, 119
Friedberg, Anne, 184n42
Friedrich, Ernst, 170
Friedrich, Ernst, works by: *Krieg dem Kriege,* 182n18
Frost, Laura, works by: *Sex Drives: Fantasies of Fascism in Literary Modernism,* 188, 189, 191
Früchtl, Josef, 127n10

Gadamer, Hans-Georg, 100n18
Geertz, Clifford, 184n43
Gere, Charlie, 66n36
Gesamtkunstwerk (universal artwork), 122
Gianetti, Claudia, 59, 62
Gillies, James, 184n40
Glass, Philip, 110
Godard, Jean-Luc, works by: *Histoire(s) du cinéma,* 162; *One plus One,* 157–58
Goebbels, Joseph, 168–69
Goodman, Brenda, 116n24
Goodrick-Clarke, Nicholas, 203n23
Graham, Dan, works by: *Rock My Religion,* 158

Grau, Oliver, 63n10
Greenaway, Peter, 170
Greenberg, Clement, 35, 83, 119
Greene, Rachel, works by: *Internet Art,* 63n10
Grogan, Patrick, 203n22
Grusin, Richard, 19n5, 53, 54, 183n23, 184n42, 186
Guattari, Félix, 72
Guéhenno, Jean-Marie, 183n34
Guenther, Irene, 201n3
Gursky, Andreas, 110
Guthrie, Woody, 161

Hacking, Ian, 62
Hake, Sabine, 180n1, 182n21, 183n30
Hansen, Mark, works by: *Listening Post,* 109–10
Hansen, Mark B. N., 19n13, 64n18, 66n38
haptic experience, 15, 16, 101, 102–3, 106, 108, 167
Hardenberg, Friedrich von (Novalis), 127n7
Harvey, David, 149n4
Hayden, Dolores, 178
Hayles, N. Katherine, 66n38, 170
Heartfield, John, 170
Heartfield, John, works by: *Deutschland, Deutschland Über Alles,* 182n18
Hebdige, Dick, 160, 163n25
Hediger, Vinzenz, 116n27
Heidegger, Martin, 15, 32, 60, 116n22
Heidegger, Martin, works by: "The Origin of the Work of Art," 31
Heimer, Mel, 114n1
Herbst, Claudia, 190, 202n12
Hitler, Adolf, 169, 171, 181n11, 187, 195, 198
Hölderlin, Friedrich, 91
Holzer, Jenny, 110
Horkheimer, Max, 12
Horkheimer, Max, works by: "Culture Industry" from *Dialectic of Enlightenment,* 49
Huhtamo, Erkki, 54, 58
Huygue, Pierre, 112, 113
Huyssen, Andreas, 183n28

Hypermedia Berlin, 17, 171, 172–73, 177–80, 182n24, 184n43
hypomnesis, 100n18

iconoclasm, 27–30
Ikonomou, Eleftherios, 114n9
illusionism, 35–36, 38, 73; anti-illusionism, 35
Invisible, the, 26, 27, 29, 30

Jameson, Fredric, 58, 143, 148, 157, 165n18
Jauß, Hans Robert, 127n10
Jay, Martin, 184n42
Jenkins, Henry, 54, 58
Jenkins, Henry, works by: "Game Design as Narrative Architecture," 193, 194, 197, 199, 203n21, 204n32
Jennings, Michael, 182n18
Jones, Caroline A. 19n13
Jordan, Chris, 110–11
Joyce, James, 122
Joyce, James, works by: *Ulysses,* 91
Judd, Donald, 75, 110
Jünger, Ernst, 170
Jünger, Ernst, works by: *Das Antlitz des Weltkrieges: Fronterlebnisse deutscher Soldaten,* 182n18; *Der gefährliche Augenblick,* 182n18; *Hier spricht der Feind: Kriegserlebnisse unserer Gegner,* 182n18; *Luftfahrt ist Not,* 182n18; *Die veränderte Welt: Eine Bilderfibel unserer Zeit,* 182n18

Kaes, Anton, 180n1, 180n4, 198
Kandinsky, Wassily, works by: *Concerning the Spiritual in Art,* 120
Kern, Andrea, 127n10
Kern, Stephen, 181n12
Kienzl, Hermann, 168
Kino-Debatte, 168
Kittler, Friedrich, 32, 54, 55, 60–61, 62, 64n18, 93
Klotz, Heinrich, 87n21
Klüver, Billy, 110
Knappen, Mary, 115n16
Knappen, Ron, 115n16
Koepnick, Lutz, 184n42

Koselleck, Reinhart, 181n15, 183n27
Koss, Juliet, 114n8, 115n15
Kracauer, Siegfried, 6, 7–9, 10, 11, 12, 13, 14, 15, 18, 25, 32, 102, 105–6, 113, 116n28, 151n37, 182n21
Kracauer, Siegfried, works by: The Mass Ornament," 7–9
Krahberger, Franz, 86n7
Kraynak, Janet, 112
Kuhn, Thomas S., 127n1
Kurzweil, Ray, 53, 63n4
Kwon, Miwon, 110

La Ferla, Ruth, 202n5
Laclau, Ernesto, 64–65n20
Landow, George, 99n4, 182n20
Langston, Richard, 149n8, 151n40
Latour, Bruno, 65n22
Latour, Bruno, works by: *Reassembling the Social,* 56–57
Lawrence, D. H., 188
Leadbelly, 161
Lee, Pamela M., 112, 113, 164n14
Leinbach, Thomas R., 183n33
Leys, Ruth, 150n12
Lockheart, Sharon, 110
Lovink, Geert, 58
Luhmann, Niklas, 100n16, 184n37, 184n38
Lumière, Auguste and Louis, 157, 168

MacManus, Richard, 46
Magritte, René, 29
Majerus, Michel, 16, 77, 81–86
Majerus, Michel, works by: *bring the next line up,* 82–84; *donkey kong,* 82; *if we are dead so it is,* 84–85; *it's cool man,* 82; *yet sometimes what is read successfully, stops us with its meaning, no. 2,* 81
Mall, Samir, 115n18
Mallgrave, Harry Francis, 114n9, 114n10
Manovich, Lev, 3–5, 53–54, 55, 59, 61, 64n18, 164n6, 164n8, 164n10, 165n28, 170, 171, 173, 177, 178, 180
Manovich, Lev, works by: *The Language of New Media,* 3–5, 53–54

Manzoni, Piero, 37
Marks, Laura U., 19n13
Marxism, 35, 57–58, 146
mass culture, 10, 11, 13, 34, 49–50, 81, 140
mass media, 7, 10, 11, 12, 26, 165n18, 192
mass production, 48–49
Matta-Clark, Gordon, 112, 113
McLuhan, Marshall, 54, 93, 96, 122, 142–43, 144, 151n35, 151n37, 181n11
media archaeology, 54–58, 62, 64n19
media specificity, 5, 118
Menke, Christoph, 127n10
Mereweather, Charles, 164n1
Merrill, A. W., 115n16
Mersch, Dieter, 75, 76
Miller, Laurence, 150n11
modernism, 5, 6, 7, 11, 13, 14, 17, 34, 48, 74, 117–19, 120, 123, 126, 151, 168, 171, 175, 184n36, 184n39, 188
modernity, 8, 38, 117, 123, 167–68, 170, 173, 174–75, 181n15, 183n35
modularity, 4, 15, 43–50
montage, 5, 14, 34, 50, 112, 131, 158, 167, 172, 173, 174, 175, 180, 202n6
Moravec, Hans, 53, 63n4
Morris, Robert, 75
Mosse, George, 189
Mouffe, Chantal, 64–65n20
Munster, Anna, 19n13
Münsterberg, Hugo, 6
Murray, Janet, 99n2, 193
music: hip-hop, 33, 39, 40–42, 161; pop, 15, 37–38, 40, 153, 157, 160, 162, 165n18; punk and post-punk, 38, 153, 155, 157, 158, 159, 162; sampling, 15, 16, 32, 33–34, 35, 39–41, 45, 47, 50, 159; simulation, 34, 38–39, 41
Musil, Robert, 184n36
mutability, of texts and words, 16, 90–92, 97, 98

Nake, Frieder, 70
Negroponte, Nicolas, 183n33
Nevaquaya, Doc Tate, 161

new media, 1–6, 13–16, 18, 19n5, 38, 41, 42, 52–55, 57–62, 62n1, 63n2, 63n10, 64n18, 96, 118, 142, 143, 151n37, 164n8, 162, 165n28, 167–69, 171, 172, 173, 175, 177, 179–80, 186
Nilsson, Harry, 157
Novalis. *See* Hardenberg, Friedrich von

O'Connor, Flannery, 89
O'Donnell, James, 92
Oelmüller, Willi, 128n10
Ong, Walter, 92
O'Reilly, Tim, 185n46

Pamuk, Orhan, works by: *My Name is Red,* 28–29
Parnet, Claire, 66n36
Penny, Simon, 186
Pensky, Max, 11
Petro, Patrice, 151n37, 180n1
pharmakon, 27
Plath, Sylvia, 188
Plato, 72, 87n14, 92
Poe, Edgar Allan, 167, 169, 173
Poet, Paul, 145, 151n41
Poledna, Mathias, 17, 153–66
Poledna, Mathias, works by: *Actualité,* 153, 157–58, 159, 163, 165n19; *The Making Of . . . ,* 155; *Sufferer's Version,* 153, 158–59, 160–61, 163, 165n19; *Version,* 153, 158, 160, 161, 162, 163, 165n19; *Western Recording,* 153, 157–58, 159, 163, 165n19
Pollesch, René, 17, 145–48, 152n44, 152n46
Pollesch, René, works by: "Smarthouse ® 1+ 2," 146–48, 152n44
Pollock, Jackson, 110
Poole, Steven, 202n13
pop art, 36–27, 50, 63n10
popular culture, 11, 13, 15, 37, 153, 155, 157, 160, 163, 183n34, 187, 189, 192, 197, 198, 199, 200, 203n25
Porter, Joshua, 46
Poshardt, Ulf, works by: *DJ Culture,* 44–45
postmodernism, 39, 118, 148, 149n4

Presley, Elvis, 161
Presner, Todd Samuel, 181n12, 181n15, 182n18, 183n26, 183n35, 184n42
Preziosi, Donald, 71
progress, in Adorno's aesthetic theory, 118–19, 121, 123–26

Quine, Willard van Orman, 62

Rauschenberg, Robert, 36, 110
Rebentisch, Juliane, 127, 128n11, 165n20
Return to Castle Wolfenstein, 189, 190–92, 193–94, 195, 198, 199, 200, 203n17
Return to Castle Wolfenstein: Operation Resurrection, 204n33
rhizome, 89
Richter, Hans, works by: *Rhythmus,* 160
Riefenstahl, Leni, works by: *The Last of the Nuba,* 186–87; *Olympia,* 190; *Triumph of the Will,* 168, 190
Rilke, Rainer Maria, 115n15
Robinson, Walter, 202n16
Rodowick, D. N., 4–6
Rolling Stones, The, works by: "Sympathy for the Devil," 157–58
Ronell, Avital, 103, 107, 113n1, 115n14, 115n17, 116n22
Rötzer, Florian, 70, 86n2
Rubin, Ben, works by: "Listening Post," 109, 110
Ruttmann, Walter, 169–71, 172, 173, 174, 175, 177, 182n21, 184n29
Ruttmann, Walter, works by: *Berlin: Die Sinfonie der Großstadt,* 17, 169, 170, 171, 172–73, 174–75, 177; "Malerei mit Zeit," 169–70

Sarasin, Philipp, 65n25
Sassen, Saskia, 183n34
Schivelbusch, Wolfgang, 181n12
von Schlegel, Friedrich, 127n7
Schliengensief, Christoph, 17
Schliengensief, Christoph, works by: "Foreigners Out!," 144–45, 147–48, 151n40, 151n41, 152n46

Schnapp, Jeffrey T., 201n4
Schopenhauer, Arthur, 114n9
Schwitters, Kurt, 50
Seeger, Pete, 161
Seel, Martin, 122, 128n10
Seeßlen, Georg, 151n42
Sekula, Allan, 156
Seymour, Jerszy, 48–49
Shannon, Michael, 149n10
Shaw, Jeffrey, works by: *The Legible City,* 72, 76–77
Shirer, William, works by: *The Rise and Fall of the Third Reich,* 188
shock: Adorno's concept of, 139, 140–42, 143, 150n29; aesthetics of, 9, 17, 34, 131–48, 151n29; Benjamin's concept of, 139, 140–42, 143, 150n29, 151n37; Freud's concept of, 134, 135, 139–40, 141–42, 143, 144, 149n9, 151n35; McLuhan's concept of, 142–43, 144, 151n35, 151n37; as physiological or psychological response, 131, 133, 134, 138, 139–40, 141–42
Simanowski, Roberto, 98n2, 100n22
Simmel, Georg, 132, 133, 134, 139, 149n9
simulacrum, 16, 71, 72–73, 74, 75, 77, 80, 84, 86, 103
Sinatra, Nancy, 157
Singer, Debra, 110
Sloterdijk, Peter, 131, 134, 135
Slotkin, 203n25
Smith, Roberta, 115n19
Sobchack, Vivian, 19n13
Sonderegger, Ruth, 128n10
Sontag, Susan, works by: "Fascinating Fascism," 186–87, 188–89, 191, 192, 193, 200, 201
Stein, Gertrude, 122
Stella, Frank, works by: *Shaped Canvases,* 122
Strathausen, Carsten, 183n30
Struth, Thomas, 60
sufferer's songs, in Jamaican music, 160–61. *See also* Poledna, Mathias
Surowiecki, James, 185n48
surrealism, 81, 132, 140

Taylor, Mark C., 182n20
Thacker, Andrew, 181n12
Thaemlitz, Terre, 40
Thorburn, David, 54, 58
Tiravanija, Rikrit, 76, 111–13
Toffler, Alvin, 132
Tomb Raider, 190, 191, 202n12
Tomkins, Calvin, 116n25
Tuchmann, Phyllis, 65n34
Tucholsky, Kurt, 170, 182n18

Uricchio, William, 4–6

Vertov, Dziga, 170, 182n21
Vertov, Dziga, works by: *Man with a Movie Camera,* 4, 171
Virilio, Paul, 69–70
Vischer, Robert, 104

Wagner, Richard, 122
Waldenfels, Bernhard, 71

Wall, Jeff, 110
Wegenstein, Bernadette, 19n13
Weibel, Peter, 59–60, 61, 70, 71
Wellmer, Albrecht, 128n10
Wilden, Anthony, 139–40
Willeman, Paul, 63n10
Williams, Raymond, 58
Winthrop-Young, Geoffrey, 64n18, 66n40
Wolfenstein 3D, 200
Worringer, Wilhelm, 104
Wutz, Michael, 64n18

Young, Joan, 116n26

Zielinski, Siegfried, 54, 57, 58
Zielinski, Siegfried, works by: *Deep Time of Media,* 54–56, 64n15